ADOPTION POLITICS

ADOPTION POLITICS

Bastard Nation and Ballot Initiative 58

E. Wayne Carp

University Press of Kansas

Published by the University Press of Kansas (Lawrence, Kansas 66049), which was organized by the Kansas Board of Regents and is operated and funded by Emporia State University, Fort Hays State University, Kansas State University, Pittsburg State University, the University of Kansas, and Wichita State University

Library of Congress Cataloging-in-Publication Data

Carp, E. Wayne, 1946–

Adoption politics : Bastard Nation and ballot initiative 58 / E. Wayne Carp.

p.   cm.

Includes bibliographical references and index.

ISBN 0-7006-1305-6 (cloth : alk. paper)

1. Adoption—Government policy—Oregon.   2. Adoption—Law and legislation—Oregon.   3. Birth certificates—Political aspects—Oregon. 4. Referendum—Oregon.   5. Bastard Nation (Organization).   I. Title.

HV875.56.O7 O37   2004

362.734—dc22   2003020029

British Library Cataloguing in Publication Data is available.

Printed in the United States of America

10 9 8 7 6 5 4 3 2 1

The paper used in this publication meets the minimum requirements of the American National Standard for Permanence of Paper for Printed Library Materials Z39.48-1984.

For
Carl Schulkin, Robert Middlekauff,
and Clarke A. Chambers

Historians, mentors, and friends

CONTENTS

ILLUSTRATIONS

ACKNOWLEDGMENTS

I am happy for this opportunity to thank the many people and institutions who have contributed to this project. To begin with, this book could not have been written without the assistance of the Executive Committee of Bastard Nation, which allowed me to subscribe to its Internet e-mail discussion list from April 1998 to the present. To the members of the committee I owe the invaluable oral testimonies and cooperation of many people, both advocates and opponents of Measure 58. I offer special thanks to Helen Hill, who sat for two extensive interviews and provided numerous documents for this project, and to Shea Grimm, whose e-mail messages provided me with special insight into the complexities of Bastard Nation's policies and politics. Any errors of fact or interpretation are mine and should not be ascribed to Bastard Nation, whose members went out of their way to educate me on the organization's history, policies, and behavior during the Measure 58 campaign.

Also invaluable were interviews with Delores Teller, who threw much light on the Oregon Adoptive Rights Association's position on Measure 58, and Donna Harris, campaign manager of Measure 58. I am also greatly indebted to attorney Thomas McDermott, who explained the strategy that Measure 58 intervenors took in defending the initiative. I am also immensely thankful that at the early stages of this study Frederick Greenman provided me with documents and counsel about various legal issues.

Interviews with members of groups who opposed Measure 58 were just as essential to the writing of this book. I owe a special debt of gratitude to attorney I. Franklin Hunsaker, who gave me his personal perspective on the legal proceedings as Measure 58 wended its way through the courts. He also generously provided me with legal documents, including appellants' briefs and trial transcripts. I offer heartfelt thanks also to attorney Warren Deras for his patient instruction in the complex ways of Oregon's initiative law, his role as treasurer of Concerned Adoption Professionals, and his generous cooperation in providing me with many documents of the initiative campaign. I am deeply grateful to Michael H. Balter, executive director of the Boys and Girls Aid Society of Oregon, for two interviews and for providing me with helpful insights about how a large institution makes decisions as well as his own philosophy of social work. Nancy Simpson and Lauren Greenbaum, both of the Boys and Girls Aid Society, assisted me greatly by explaining their role as part of the opposition to Measure 58 and their relationship to Concerned Adoption Professionals. Through telephone conversations and her generous sharing of documents, the woman here called "Cindy" helped me better understand the perspective of birth mothers; I especially appreciate her lending me tapes of various media programs. Interviews with social workers Paula Lang and Doug Alles of Catholic Charities were invaluable in helping me untangle the relationship between Catholic Charities and Measure 58. I am extremely grateful to James R. Wheeler of Columbia Adoption Services, who explained to me the complicated negotiations behind HB 3194. I would also like to thank William L. Pierce, president of the National Council for Adoption, who allowed me to use a number of important documents relating to Measure 58 and for answering numerous questions about his role in the events described in these pages.

I am also indebted to the Honorable Judge Paul J. Lipscomb of the Oregon Circuit Court and the Honorable Judge Paul J. De Muniz, now of the Oregon Supreme Court, who granted me interviews. Their insights into the judicial process in general and Measure 58 in particular were an invaluable learning experience for me. Special thanks to Colette Burghart, program representative, Elections Division, Office of the Secretary of State, Salem, Oregon, and David Wendell, reference archivist, Oregon State Archives, Salem, who answered numerous queries, located elusive materials, and sent me many state documents with amazing quickness and efficiency.

This book would have taken far longer had it not been for the generosity of Pacific Lutheran University and its provost, Paul T. Menzel, in granting me course releases and a Regency Scholarship to support a fine transcriber, Amity Smeltzer, for the oral interviews. Thanks also to the hard-working staff at Mortvelt Library, especially Sue Golden and Francesca R. Lane-Rasmus whose enthusiasm for and persistence in hunting up arcane references using complicated databases was of great assistance at critical moments of this study.

Jennifer Browning, Naomi Cohen, and Susan A. Dwyer-Shick gave me much-needed tutoring in legal matters. Paula Shields, Steven H. Mintz, and LeRoy Ashby read the entire manuscript, offered insightful comments, and helped improve it. Barbara Melosh also read the work and offered cogent and critical advice that was of immense help. At the University Press of Kansas, I have been fortunate to have the outstanding editorial guidance of Nancy Scott Jackson, who continually kept me from getting lost in a forest of detail. She demonstrated that old-fashioned editing is not yet dead at university presses. I am also deeply indebted to Donna Bouvier for her thoughtful and meticulous copyediting of my manuscript. She is a gem. Finally, no words of thanks can do justice to my friend and PLU colleague, Mark Jensen, who read every word of this book, some of them twice, and has never failed to improve my prose or to provide wry comment. If I have not always followed the suggestions these readers gave, I hope they will understand. This book, imperfect though it still may be, is much better thanks to their comments.

PRINCIPAL PARTICIPANTS

FROM BASTARD NATION
Shea Grimm, founder and member of the Executive Committee, Washington
Marley Greiner, founder and chair of the Executive Committee, Ohio
Damsel Plum, founder and member of the Executive Committee, California
Lainie Petersen, founder and member of the Executive Committee, Illinois
Mary Anne Cohen, birth mother and member, New Jersey
Ron Morgan, member, California
Helen Hill, state director and chief petitioner, Measure 58, Oregon
Donna Harris, campaign manager, Measure 58, Oregon
Donna Martz, member, Texas
Joanne Nichols, member, Oregon
David C. Ansardi, member, Alabama
Julie M. Dennis, member, Washington
Cynthia Bertrand Holub, member, Pennsylvania
August ("Toff") Philippo, member, New York
Albert Wei, member, London, England
Curtis Endicott, member, Oregon
Linda Corbin, birth mother and member, Oregon

FROM THE AMERICAN ADOPTION CONGRESS
Jane Nast, president
Kate Burke, past president

FROM THE OREGON ADOPTIVE RIGHTS ASSOCIATION (OARA)
Delores Teller, president
Darlene Wilson, member of board of directors and state
confidential-intermediary searcher

FROM THE OPPOSITION TO MEASURE 58
Warren C. Deras, attorney, treasurer of
Concerned Adoption Professionals, Oregon
John Chally, adoption attorney, Portland, Oregon
William L. Pierce, president, National Council for Adoption, Washington, D.C.
Michael H. Balter, executive director, Boys and Girls Aid Society of Oregon
Nancy P. Simpson, manager of the adoption unit,
Boys and Girls Aid Society of Oregon

Lauren Greenbaum, lead adoption counselor,
Boys and Girls Aid Society of Oregon
James Wheeler, director, Columbia Adoption Services
"Cindy," birth mother, Oregon

FROM CATHOLIC CHARITIES
Paula Lang, pregnancy support and adoption services program manager
Douglas S. Alles, director of social services and executive director
Dennis Kennan, executive director
Robert J. Castagna, director of the Oregon Catholic Conference

FROM THE MEDIA
Patty Wentz, reporter, *Willamette Week*
Bill Graves, reporter, *Oregonian*
Spencer Heinz, reporter, *Oregonian*
Margie Boulé, columnist, *Oregonian*

LAWYERS
Fredrick F. Greenman, Jr., attorney, New York City, for Measure 58
Thomas McDermott, attorney, Portland, Oregon, for Measure 58
I. Franklin Hunsaker, attorney, Portland, Oregon, against Measure 58
Katherine Georges, assistant attorney general, Portland, Oregon, for Measure 58
Loren D. Podwill, attorney, Portland, Oregon, against Measure 58
Roy Pulvers, attorney, Portland, Oregon, for Measure 58
David Schuman, deputy attorney general, Portland, Oregon, for Measure 58

JUDGES
Albin W. Norblad, judge, circuit court, Marion County, Salem, Oregon
Paul J. Lipscomb, presiding judge, circuit court, Marion County, Salem, Oregon
Mary J. Deits, chief judge, Oregon Court of Appeals
Paul J. De Muniz, presiding judge, Oregon Court of Appeals
David V. Brewer, judge, Oregon Court of Appeals
Robert D. Durham, associate justice, Oregon Supreme Court
Virginia Linder, associate judge, Oregon Court of Appeals
Sandra Day O'Connor, associate justice, U.S. Supreme Court
Clarence Thomas, associate justice, U.S. Supreme Court

OTHER IMPORTANT PEOPLE
Betty Jean Lifton, author, New York
Kitty Piercy, Democrat, house minority leader, Oregon legislature
Edward Johnson, Oregon state registrar
Phil Keisling, Oregon secretary of state
Hardy Myers, Oregon attorney general

INTRODUCTION

Adoption touches upon almost every conceivable aspect of American society and culture and commands our attention by the enormous number of people who have a direct, intimate connection to it. Some experts put this number as high as six out of every ten Americans.[1] The 2000 U.S. Census estimates that 1.6 million children under eighteen live with adoptive parents, and that 2.5 percent of American families include an adopted child.[2] In 1996, it is estimated there were a total of 108,463 domestic adoptions, of which 54,493 (50 percent) were unrelated domestic adoptions.[3] Because of the dearth of healthy white infants for adoption, 19,458 of adoptions in 2002 were intercountry adoptions, slightly less than half of them from Russia and China.[4] In short, adoption is a ubiquitous social institution in American society that touches far more people than most of us imagine.

For the past thirty-five years, however, the traditional system of adoption has been under challenge by adopted adults. Separated at birth from their birth mothers, these adopted adults have been thwarted in their search for members of their original family by a system of state laws that seal adoption records, making them inaccessible without a court order. These adoption records—court records, adoption agency records, and birth certificates—contain crucial information that would permit adopted adults to locate their birth parents. In the case of birth certificates, for example, one would find the name of the adopted child's birth mother, the hospital where the birth took place, the date of birth, and (in rare cases) the name of the birth father. By 1998, only two states, Alaska and Kansas, which had never sealed their records, permitted adopted adults unconditional access to their birth certificates. In that year, however, Bastard Nation, a radical adoptee rights organization, made history by victoriously running the first citizen-enacted adoption initiative, Oregon's Measure 58, which gave adult adoptees the right to access their original birth certificates. A milestone in the history of the adoption reform movement, Measure 58 has the potential to revolutionize adoption practices in the United States by serving as a model for other states.

Adoption Politics tells the story of Measure 58. It begins with an overview of the history of adoption records and the adoption search movement in the United States. The story of adopted adults' efforts to secure recognition of their constitutional and legal rights is one filled mostly with failure. Since the mid-

1970s, individual adoptees have brought lawsuits in lower state courts attempting to gain access to their adoption records for "good cause." Generally, state and federal judges have refused adopted adults access to their records. In response, movement leaders turned to state legislatures, which have in some cases enacted reform legislation to establish voluntary adoption registries and confidential intermediaries. Chapter 2 outlines the birth and development of Bastard Nation, a radical adoptee organization founded on frustration with the reform legislation of an older generation of movement leaders. Chapter 3 provides biographical sketches of Measure 58 leaders Helen Hill and Shea Grimm. Chapters 4 and 5 trace the politics of this initiative, which was filled with unforeseen difficulties for both Helen Hill, an amateur politician, and her opponents, more experienced campaigners. Understanding the numerous intricate steps necessary to meet deadlines and file documents, winning the inevitable court challenges, and collecting tens of thousands of signatures were crucial just to get the initiative on the ballot. In these often detailed processes lay one of the keys to Measure 58's victory. For the opposition, underestimating their opponent, losing court battles, and failing to anticipate the future resulted in ultimately losing the election. There are several important themes running through both these chapters, including the importance of grassroots politics; ways in which the advocates and opponents of Measure 58 organized themselves; their strategies, ideologies, emotions, and compromises; and the nature of power, authority, and charismatic leadership.

Chapter 6 describes the ultimately victorious Measure 58 campaign run by Bastard Nation. My original thesis—that a small, unknown, underfinanced adoption rights organization, Bastard Nation, acted as David against a well-financed, conservative, and well-organized Goliath that included adoption agencies, the news media, the ACLU, religious organizations, and ad hoc citizen political groups—proved to be wrong. Instead, David defeated Goliath by being better staffed, organized, motivated, and financed. Chapter 7 explores the intricate political wrangling behind the Oregon legislature's successful effort to amend Measure 58, adding a contact preference form that allowed birth mothers to place a letter with the original birth certificate indicating whether or not they wanted contact with the person they had relinquished for adoption.

Chapters 8 and 9 detail the opposition's legal challenge to the constitutionality of Measure 58. The opposition's legal argument relied heavily on the retroactive nature of Measure 58 and a birth mother's right to privacy, which, opponents argued, was to be found in the U.S. and Oregon Constitutions. They supported their legal arguments with the history of Oregon's sealed adoption statutes, state laws governing sealed adoption records, and depositions from unidentified birth mothers, adoption lawyers, and ex-judges. Defense counsel countered by denying that birth mothers had constitutional privacy rights or that the state of Oregon had entered into a contract with birth mothers promising never to reveal their identities. The legal arguments used by both the opponents and the supporters of Measure 58 were never publicized by the Oregon media and are disclosed in detail for the first time in this book. Yet they are crucial to understanding the hazards of initiative politics, the emotion and logic of both sides of the sealed adoption records controversy, and the intricacies of the American legal process.

My methodology is interdisciplinary, drawing on oral history, demography, psychology, psychiatry, social work, political science, history, and the law. My judgments on the nature and relationships of the adoption triad— adoptees, birth parents, and adoptive parents—are based not only on primary sources but also on biographies, novels, and works of nonfiction written by authors who do not play a role in this book. Still, I am not a member of the adoption triad, and I am male. The adoptee search movement has been predominately female, as was the leadership of Bastard Nation and Measure 58. Although being personally removed from both the adoption triad and the Measure 58 experience may not make me more objective, it does, to borrow Alan Gallay's phrase, "allow me to be differently subjective."[5] Not being a member of the triad is thus both an advantage, in that I can view both sides dispassionately, and a handicap, as there are certain emotional and mental states important to the participants in this story that I can never experience. In order to minimize this handicap, and to attain my goal of presenting each side of the adoption records debate clearly, I allow adult adoptees and birth mothers to speak for themselves and at length in these pages.

While writing this book, I harbored hopes of affecting public policy and the hearts and minds of adoption triad members, social workers, and legislators. Though I offer these observations with humility, I am of the conviction that all members of the adoption triad have rights that should be protected. For the past thirty-five years, members of the adoption triad, social workers, and legislators have battled with each other over who should have access to adoption records. Over that same period of time, a social and legal revolution had occurred in America, strengthening the rights of individuals and increasing openness in government. These changes have deeply affected adoption practices, which have undergone a similar revolution, resulting in such developments as the adoptee search movement and open adoption. The passage of Measure 58, amended by the Oregon legislature's HB 3194, exemplified these revolutionary changes. In blending adopted adults' access to their original birth certificate with a protection for birth mothers' right to privacy through a contact preference form (without legal penalties for violation), Measure 58 should be viewed as a model piece of legislation for other states to emulate.

My research for this book led me to a startling revelation: the ideological distance between advocates and opponents of Measure 58 was not that great. Even the measure's opponents, including adoption agencies, favored giving adoptees some access to birth records. Recognizing this fact may be the starting point for cutting the Gordian knot of this agonizing social problem that has affected millions of Americans for decades.

1

The Problem

Annetta Louise Maples was less than a year old in 1946 when Missouri's Jackson County Family Children's Services Social Agency placed her with adoptive parents. She was not quite two when a decree was entered finalizing her adoption as the lawful child of her new parents. While growing up, Maples learned of her adoption and was troubled by it. Like many adopted persons, she was respectful of her adoptive parents' feelings and never asked to see her adoption papers because, she feared, "they would be hurt." Like many adopted adults, however, Maples decided to risk that hurt and even the possibility of jeopardizing her relationship with her adoptive parents by beginning a search for her biological parents. In 1973, at age twenty-eight and financially independent, she contacted the Family Children's Services Social Agency to request her "birth specifics." A social worker referred Maples to the supervisor of adoption services of the Jackson County Juvenile Court, who provided her with information on her birth parents' health, a copy of her adoption decree, and other nonidentifying information.[1] Unsuccessful in discovering the identity of her biological parents, Maples then petitioned the Juvenile Division of the Circuit Court of Jackson County for an order to allow her to inspect her adoption records. Maples' lawsuit eventually wound its way to the Supreme Court of Missouri, where the Court ruled against her and upheld the state's sealed adoption records statute.[2]

The Maples case was one of the first of many failed attempts by adopted adults during the ensuing twenty years to use state and federal courts in order to gain access to their adoption records.[3] They also organized themselves into adoptee search groups, which evolved into lobbying organizations working to change the laws governing sealed adoption statutes. To understand what motivated these adopted adults we must examine the historical forces that created sealed adoption records in the first place.

First, however, it is important to clarify just what "adoption records" are. Although it is commonly imagined that they are a single, tangible, entity—a thick file folder crammed with data and located at an adoption agency—the reality is much more complicated. There are, in fact, three sources of family information about an adopted person: the records of the court that approved the final adoption (including preliminary proceedings, if any); the state repository for birth certificates; and the case files of the adoption agency, which would contain social, family, and medical information on the birth and adoptive parents as well as the adopted child. Depending on when one lived, a particular adoption record might not even exist. There were, for example, few birth certificates issued in the United States before 1916, and state birth registration areas were not completed until 1933. This meant that there were children born as late as 1930 (though by then usually in rural areas) whose births were recorded only in family bibles, baptismal or church records, midwife reports, or personal papers. Private adoption agencies did not come into existence until the 1910s, and their recordkeeping was minimal until the 1920s. The paucity of information in all adoption records, especially in the earliest ones, is both surprising and unnerving.[4]

What is perhaps the biggest surprise for anyone who studies this subject is that for nearly a century after the enactment of the earliest adoption law in America, the Massachusetts Adoption Act of 1851, adoption records, with few exceptions, were open to inspection by members of the adoption triad (birth parents, adoptees, and adoptive parents). The story of how they were sealed is a complicated one. In fact, adoption records have been sealed *twice* during the twentieth century. The first time, adoption triad members were not excluded from viewing their records. In 1917, lawmakers enacted the Minnesota Children's Code, which was the first law containing a clause making adoption court records confidential. The law was not intended to, and did not, prevent adoptees from viewing their records. Rather, lawmakers stated explicitly that the goal of Minnesota's sealed adoption law was to keep the *public* from viewing the records. Because of the stigma of shame and scandal that surrounded adoption and illegitimacy during the first quarter of the twentieth century, Minnesota lawmakers wished to prevent access to adoption records by potential blackmailers, who might threaten adoptive parents with telling the public about the child's adoption, or nosy neighbors, who might discover the child's illegitimacy. Sealing court and adoption agency records was never meant to exclude members of the adoption triad from examining their adoption records. In fact, with a few exceptions, the confidentiality clauses in the twenty-four states that had enacted them by 1941 specifically exempted from the law "parties in interest" (birth parents) and "parties of record" (adoptive parents and adopted persons). Thus, on the whole, during this time adopted adults had no difficulty accessing their records.[5]

In addition, there were twenty-four other states that had not enacted adoption laws with confidentiality clauses. In those states, court records were easily available to the public. Oregon's adoption records are a case in point. In 1864, five years after statehood, the legislature enacted Oregon's first adoption law. Under the 1864 act, the county court could decree a name change if the adoptive parents requested so in a petition. The law mandated that the court should report all adoptions and name changes to the secretary of state, who then would have them "published in tabular form with the statutes of the following year."[6] Columns in the tables showed the date of adoption, present and former names of the child, name of the adoptive parents, and the county of adoption. From 1864 to 1921, until the legislature repealed that section of the act, the state published this information annually.[7] Nevertheless, a 1919 statute gave county judges authority to seal the adoption records of "any foundling, abandoned, or illegitimate child at his discretion" in the county archives "to be unsealed only on judicial order."[8] Although not explicit on providing access to adopted adults, the intent of Oregon's 1919 law was probably like that of Minnesota's Children's Code of 1917 and others whose motive was to prevent the public, especially those with a criminal intent, from having access to this information, and to protect children whose lives could be ruined by the social stigma of illegitimacy and adoption. In 1921, the state closed another loophole that would have exposed adopted children's identities to the public and stopped publishing name changes.[9]

Before the 1950s, adopted adults also had little difficulty in accessing their records from adoption agencies. State statutes remained silent on the regulation of adoption agency records, leaving it by default to the discretion of the agencies' directors. In the early twentieth century, social workers began keeping detailed records of adopted children for the sole reason that these adopted persons might return one day to the agency to recover their social history and make contact with their family of origin. For the next half-century, social workers cooperated with birth parents and adopted adults who returned to agencies requesting both nonidentifying and identifying information. The Children's Home Society of Washington even conducted searches for adoptees who were looking for original family members. Social workers also provided adoptive parents with information about their child.[10]

Good intentions led to amending and sealing the birth certificates of adopted persons. Progressive-era child welfare reformers vigorously lobbied state legislatures to remove the stigma of illegitimacy from both the unwed mother and the child. But making birth records confidential and eliminating the word "illegitimate" from birth certificates did not obviate the stigma of adoption from these documents. For reformers and adopted children, there still remained the problem of birth certificates. Minnesota's 1917 Children's Code was the first law to stipulate that when the court approved an adoption, the decree could reflect a change in the child's name, but birth certificates still carried the names of the adopted child's biological parents.[11] How then could the public—in the guise of school officials and employers—be prevented from discovering the child's adoptive and possibly illegitimate status?

It was left to two enterprising registrars of vital statistics—not state lawmakers, social workers, or adoptive parents—to come up with the idea of issuing new birth certificates to adopted children. The topic was first broached in an important public forum at the 1930 annual meeting of the vital-statistics section of the American Public Health Association. At that meeting Sheldon L. Howard, Illinois State Registrar of Vital Statistics, and Henry B. Hemenway, Medical Assistant Registrar at the Vital Statistics Division of the Illinois Department of Public Health, presented a paper advocating several amendments to the Model Law for Birth Reporting. In support of the changes, Howard and Hemenway articulated a need to increase the statistical accuracy of birth records, widen the professional influence of registrars, and promote the welfare of illegitimate and adopted children. No longer seeing themselves as mere statisticians, Howard and Hemenway described registrars of vital statistics as "guardians and trustees of the interests of the people," especially in relation to birth records.[12] The two characterized their professional brethren as "missionaries, who should bring about the rectification of the existing evils" in the birth registration of children born out of wedlock. By "evils" they meant the disclosure of illegitimacy on birth certificates. They agonized over the psychological damage such information might inflict on the child. Reflecting the increasing incorporation of psychological concepts by social workers and mental health officials into professional discourse, Howard and Hemenway worried that the revelation of illegitimate status to public officials was "likely to permanently impair otherwise peaceful mental conditions and happy lives." They called on registrars to reform the Model Law for birth registration in order to "insure for these children immunity from unnecessary embarrassment, pain, or disgrace, from the time of the launching of their individual careers—their advent into school or employment."[13]

Hemenway and Howard were referring specifically to the section of the Model Law covering adopted children, which stopped short of offering sufficient protection from the stigma of illegitimacy or adoption. As written, it merely stated that after the court had issued the adoption decree, it might also order that "the name of the child be changed according to the prayer of the petition." Hemenway and Howard proposed that the Model Law be amended so that when the name of the child was changed the clerk of the court would forward the adoption decree to the state registrar of vital statistics. Upon receiving the decree, the registrar would "make a new record of the birth in the new name, and with the name or names of the adopting parent or parents." The registrar would then "cause to be sealed and filed the original certificate of birth with the decree of the court." The birth records were to be sealed from the prying eyes of the public, not from those directly involved in the adoption, who were to be permitted to view them. Hemenway and Howard specifically recommended that the "sealed package shall only be opened upon the demand of said child, or his natural or adopting parents, or by order of a court of record."[14] Vital statisticians shared the basic assumptions of Progressive-era child welfare reformers that the birth records would be sealed to preserve family information for those connected to the adoption, not to prevent them from viewing such data.

With adopted adults increasingly requesting birth certificates in order to verify their age for employment, Social Security benefits, and draft registration, state legislatures responded positively to the registrars' recommendations. By 1941, thirty-five states had enacted legislation instructing the registrar of vital statistics to issue a new birth certificate using the new name of the child and those of the adopting parents in place of the original one.[15] Oregon did the same. In that year, the legislature passed a law ordering the state registrar, upon receipt of an adoption decree, to prepare a supplementary birth certificate in the new name of the adopted person. The state registrar was then to seal and file the original certificate of birth with the certified copy of the adoption decree. The legislators had no intention to keep adult adopted persons from gaining access to their birth certificates. The law stated that the original birth certificate, though sealed, could be opened by the state registrar "upon the demand of the adopted person if of legal age or by order of a court of competent jurisdiction."[16] By 1948, nearly every state had embraced Hemenway and Howard's recommendation of issuing a new birth certificate upon receiving a court-ordered decree of adoption, the records being open to adopted adults.[17]

But in the 1950s a second movement to seal the records *from* adoption triad members slowly gained momentum. As early as 1919 the Oregon legislature gave county judges the discretion to seal the records of "any foundling, abandoned or illegitimate child" and store them in the county archives to be unsealed "only on judicial order."[18] By the end of the 1930s, states such as California (1935), New York (1935), Oregon (1939), and Maryland (1939) had sealed their adoption court records.[19] With the tremendous increase in illegitimate births during World War II and the pronatalism and baby boom of the postwar years, adoptions soared, and so did the number of states passing laws sealing adoption court records. By 1948 a majority of states had sealed their court records.[20] In 1957, Oregon amended a conflict in the law that specified that adoption records be sealed but continued to allow adopted adults to access them "upon order of a court of competent jurisdiction."[21] Why state legislators were moved to act at this time is difficult to say. One legal historian has suggested that the sole reason lawmakers sealed adoption court records was to protect "adoptive parents and their adoptive children from being interfered with or harassed by birth parents."[22] While this may have been an important reason, it was certainly not the only one. Preventing gossips and blackmailers from gaining access to the records was another.[23]

Adoption agencies followed a similar path of preventing members of the adoption triad from gaining access to the information in their adoption records, but their pattern of closure was more complex. Adoption records had never been completely open. The relationship between birth mothers and adoptive parents had always been suspect. Progressive-era social workers incorporated secrecy between birth and adoptive parents into the adoption case records they created. The relinquishment form of the Children's Home Society of Washington (CHSW), for example, contained a section prohibiting birth parents from searching for their children. Unwed mothers who wished to relinquish their infants for adoption also played a role in making adoption agency records confidential. In their almost obsessive investigation of the unwed mother's background, social workers revealed to family members, employers, and friends the single woman's pregnancy. To escape the possibility of shame and scandal, these women turned from nonprofit adoption agencies to commercial ones, like the Cradle Society in Chicago, Illinois, or the Willows in Kansas City, Missouri. In these agencies, workers asked few questions and kept no written records.[24] In 1937, the Child Welfare League of America (CWLA), the leading private adoption organization in the nation, concerned about the practices of these commercial agencies, undertook an investigation. A supervisor of one of the CWLA's member agencies reported:

> If children's agencies, members of the League, would be more flexible in their treatment of the problems of illegitimacy there might be less hesitance on the part of the mother about a regular agency. More mothers of the middle class families and those of higher educational and cultural advantages would turn to the accredited children's agencies for placement of their children if they could feel certain that their confidences would be respected and no publicity of any sort attached to the proceedings. . . . Privacy and an appreciation of their own inner feeling of suffering is what these mothers are looking for.[25]

As a result of statements such as these, in November 1938 the CWLA's board of directors issued for its member agencies' guidance ten safeguards, or "Minimum Standards in Adoption," two of which stressed secrecy for adoptive parents. One standard stated that "the identity of the adopting parents should be kept from the natural parents." The second specified "that the adoption proceedings be completed without unnecessary publicity."[26] Although this standard would benefit adoptive parents, it was exactly what many birth mothers were looking for and why they had been bypassing CWLA member agencies for commercial ones.

Two other factors were crucial to the decision by adoption agencies to close their records to birth mothers. One was the changing demographics of adoption agencies' clientele: postwar unwed mothers were younger (a median age of eighteen years instead of twenty-two) as were the children they were relinquishing (four days old rather than four years). Secrecy was much easier to impose. The other factor was the uncritical acceptance by the social work profession of psychoanalytic theory, tenets of which by 1958 had been incorporated into the CWLA's influential *Standards for Adoption Service*. It stated that unwed mothers "have serious personality disturbances [and] need help with their emotional problems."[27] The solution to this supposed problem was to separate the unwed mother from her child, place the child for adoption, and make sure that if the mother ever returned to the agency for information, she be denied access.[28] By the end of the 1950s, birth mothers were shut out from accessing information from adoption agencies.

Between the 1950s and the 1970s, adopted adults also found access to their adoption agency records barred. Whereas before World War II adoption agency workers willingly shared nonidentifying and identifying information with their clients, after the war they punctiliously refused. The process was uneven, the reasons not always clear. And there were exceptions: Alabama did not seal its adoption records until 1991. Records, however, had never been totally accessible, even to adult adopted persons. Social workers, acting in what they felt to be the best interests of the child, had always selectively withheld certain facts about the child's background. If a child was light-skinned, social workers would deliberately not tell an adopted adult that one of his or her parents were African American or Native American. They also withheld information about a child's birth status (for example, if he or she was illegitimate) and the parents' social and medical background (for example, if the father had been imprisoned or the mother had a history of venereal disease). They believed such information to be "useless" and potentially damaging to the child. A sincere wish to spare the individual painful emotions or, as they saw it, social stigma, motivated these omissions.[29]

But beginning in the 1950s social workers began to stonewall adopted adults when they returned to the agency. Freudian psychology was popularized by Florence Clothier, a prolific and influential psychiatric social worker at the New England Home for Little Wanderers, among others.[30] By the late 1950s adopted adults who returned to an adoption agency searching for original family members were perceived as pathological and, by extension, represented a failure of the adoptive process. In 1958, one CHSW adoption worker described an adult adoptee searching for his birth parents thus: "the troubled adult was a pretty unhappy, disturbed person."[31] Alongside psychoanalytic theory, adopted adults found that they had to overcome an increasing stress on social work professionalism, an unintended consequence of state lawmakers' desire to crack down on "welfare cheats" by publishing the public assistance rolls. Social workers resisted these efforts by legislatures to harass their clients, but in the process they often broadened the principle of confidentiality to include adopted adults as well as those on public assistance.[32]

Birth records were sealed too. After World War II, enjoying prosperity and a baby boom, Americans moved to suburbia and created a family-centered culture that stressed early marriage, large families, and domesticity. Responding to the pronatalism of the age, Children's Bureau officials began to justify keeping birth records secret by invoking the need to protect adoptive parents from the possible interference of the birth parents. In 1949 they recommended that both sets of parents should remain unknown to each other. Such a concern reflected a long-standing fear of social workers. But in the context of birth certificates, this was the first time that Children's Bureau or public health officials acted on this fear, the first time they had justified confidentiality for reasons other than the welfare of the adopted child.[33] State legislatures began following the Children's Bureau's advice. In 1957, for example, the Oregon legislature proposed repeal of its 1941 statute granting adopted adults access to their original birth certificates; instead, these documents could now be opened by the state registrar "only upon an order of a court of competent jurisdiction."[34] In committee, state senator Warren Gill, joined by two other senators, opposed the bill on the grounds that "you shouldn't take away the right of an adopted child to find out anything he wants to about his parentage."[35] However, as Kathleen O'Brien put it, the "committee decided ultimately that potential 'heartbreak' to adoptive parents outweighed the adopted person's 'curiosity,' and approved the change unanimously."[36] By 1960, in twenty-nine states, adoptees could access their original birth certificates only by petitioning a court. But in twenty others, adopted adults were still free to inspect their records. Four more states closed their birth records in the 1960s, six more did so in the 1970s, and seven more after 1979. Only two states, Alaska and Kansas, never closed their birth records to adopted adults.[37]

In response to these developments, Jean M. Paton, a middle-aged, twice-adopted ex–social worker, single-handedly pioneered the adoptee search movement.[38] In 1953, Paton founded the Life History Study Center as well as the first adoptee search organization, Orphan Voyage. The center's initial goals were to make adoptees visible, give them a social identity, and overturn the belief that "the adult adopted [person] had nothing to say."[39] In 1954 Paton published *The Adopted Break Silence*. For the first time, a book recorded verbatim the thoughts of adopted adults on a multitude of subjects ranging from their attitudes toward being adopted to their attempts to locate their original family members. Through her research, Paton reached a number of conclusions, one of which was that adoptees had a psychological need to search for their birth parents.[40]

Paton's plea for rethinking adoptees' experience and for creating a national adoption registry was greeted by silence. Her one-woman crusade garnered no national media attention, caused no adoption agencies to liberalize their records disclosure policy, and impelled no state legislatures to repeal their sealed adoption records statutes. The reasons for Paton's lack of influence are not hard to identify. By not politicizing the closure of adoption records—a public issue—but instead focusing steadfastly on search and reunion—a private issue—Paton had inadvertently isolated the movement from public opinion and the political process. She had turned the movement, such as it was between 1953 and 1971, into a one-woman show, ensuring that by almost any standard, it would have little effect outside a small circle of supporters. Moreover, the conservative, conformist 1950s were hardly a time for challenging conventional notions, whether in politics, social work institutions, or family relations. As Paton herself later admitted, "I realized that I was going one way and the culture the other—toward sealed records."[41]

By the early 1970s, demographics, attitudes, and leadership had changed. Three developments were responsible for the new adoptee search movement to emerge. First was the long-term precondition: the buildup of a critical mass of adopted adults in the twenty-five years following World War II who had grown up in a world of sealed adoption records. Unlike their pre–World War II counterparts, this group had been denied easy access to their adoption records.[42] Their thwarted desire to view their records provided the tinder from which the new search movement ignited.

Another precipitant of the new search movement was the Sixties, characterized by grassroots protest movements, sexual experimentation and freedom, and the rise of rights consciousness. The era began with the civil rights movement, the campaign against poverty, the Vietnam War, campus unrest and New Left student protesters, and the growth of a "counterculture" during the

Kennedy and Johnson administrations. By the late 1960s and early 1970s "identity politics" overshadowed earlier liberal movements as ethnic and racial self-interest groups organized to gain political legitimacy, economic power, and cultural authority in the Black Power, feminist, Native American rights, and gay liberation movements. These movements were grounded in a vision of egalitarian, participatory democracy that questioned existing systems of authority based on hierarchy, expertise, or wealth. The movements' democratic ethos sought to include all people in society, empower individuals through social participation, and create a loving community from atomistic and alienated youth. Outrageous, exasperating, and heroic, they fundamentally challenged and transformed the nation's political and social institutions, and racial and sexual mores.[43]

Of particular importance to the origins of the new adoptee search movement was the sexual revolution, which successfully challenged many of the sexual taboos of the 1950s, including the stigma of illegitimacy. By the late 1960s, the stigma of having a child out of wedlock or being born out of wedlock had greatly lessened. Indeed, in the youth counterculture's philosophy, unrepressed sexuality "represented both a personal act of liberation and a form of radical politics." Social protest and landmark decisions on voting, school prayer, criminal rights, libel law, pornography, and school and housing segregation signaled that "a Rights Revolution was at hand." By the beginning of the 1970s, many adopted adults viewed their adoptive status in terms of liberation and rights, not shame and fear.[44]

Finally, there was a specific trigger. In 1971 the new adoption search movement's most vocal and visible leader emerged: Florence Ladden Fisher, a New York City homemaker. Fisher had been adopted as an infant, but that fact was kept from her until she became a young adult. During a long and frustrating search for her birth parents, Fisher was denied knowledge about the identity of her family by lawyers, doctors, the clerk of New York's Surrogate Court, and the nuns of St. Anthony's Hospital. She finally located her mother after twenty years of searching.[45] Fisher's traumatic odyssey led her to found the Adoptees Liberty Movement Association (ALMA). Along with aiding adopted adults searching for their birth parents, ALMA's principal goals were "to abolish the existing practice of 'sealed records'" and to secure the "opening of records to any adopted person *over eighteen* who wants, for any reason, to see them."[46] Fisher added a completely different tone and emphasis to the movement, which clearly differentiated it from earlier search groups, such as Paton's Orphan Voyage. She was unabashedly militant. Her rhetoric was angry and inflexible, and she refused to compromise when advancing the movement's goals. Typically, she was quoted in the press as declaring: "We demand free access to our original birth certificates and the records of our adoption."[47] The emphasis on adopted adults' rights and the demand to repeal sealed adoption records statutes were unprecedented.

From her headquarters in New York City, Fisher organized local branches of ALMA beginning in Chicago, Los Angeles, and Fort Lauderdale. In 1973 Fisher published a book recounting the dramatic story of her success in reuniting with her birth family entitled *The Search for Anna Fisher*. By 1974, Fisher had become the undisputed leader of the adoption search movement and the head of the nation's largest and most influential adoption activist group.[48] ALMA's example started a movement that spread like wildfire, leading to the creation of hundreds of other adoptee search groups across the United States, Canada, and the United Kingdom with names like Yesterday's Children (Illinois), Adoptees' Identity Movement (Michigan), and Reunite (Ohio). By 1975, over 3,000 adopted adults and 1,500 mothers had returned to 155 adoption agencies searching for information about their families and children. The first generation of the adoption rights movement was thus characterized by small isolated groups involved in personal search and reunion activities with charismatic leaders like Jean Paton and Florence Fisher, whose ideology revolved around adoptee rights.

Initially, adoption search organizations neither lobbied state legislatures nor filed rights-based lawsuits to repeal sealed adoption records statutes. Adoption activist leaders concentrated on organizing at the grassroots level and aiding adoptees in their search for their birth parents. Indeed, before May 1977, as Florence Fisher noted, ALMA had "*never* advocated any legislative change" to state laws because if they tried "to change the law State by State the adoptees who are being hurt by the present laws would all be dead and buried before the States would open up unconditionally."[49]

Instead ALMA favored challenging the constitutionality of the sealed adoption law in the U.S. Supreme Court and having the Justices declare all state laws sealing adoption records unconstitutional. By late 1975, Fisher was contemplating such a lawsuit in anticipation of an appeal to the U.S. Supreme Court. It was not until May 1978, however, that ALMA filed a class-action federal lawsuit in the U.S. District Court against New York's sealed adoption records law. The District Court dismissed ALMA's suit on the merits. On appeal, in *ALMA Soc'y, Inc. v. Mellon* (1979), the United States Court of Appeals for the Second Circuit considered for the first time the constitutional arguments of adopted adults and dismissed the case on its merits.[50] Thus, ALMA pioneered the search movement's wide-ranging and creative legal arguments based on rights and prompted the court's reasoning for rejecting those arguments and upholding the state's interest in keeping the records sealed.

ALMA challenged the validity of New York's sealed adoption records law on the basis that adoptees were constitutionally entitled to the information contained in the adoption records without showing "good cause." This constitutional right to know one's origins, ALMA claimed, was to be found in the First, Thirteenth, and Fourteenth Amendments. Sealing adoption records, ALMA argued, prevented adoptees from acquiring useful information and ideas (such as knowledge of their birth parents), a penumbral right the Supreme Court had recognized as being within the protection of the First Amendment.[51]

A second constitutional argument gave a novel twist to the Thirteenth Amendment, which prohibited not only slavery and involuntary servitude, but also badges or incidents of slavery. According to ALMA's brief, one of the five badges or incidents of slavery the amendment's framers had in mind was the severing of the parental relationship, depriving the children of slaves of the care and attention of their parents. ALMA drew the analogy that the state's preventing adopted adults from communicating with their birth parents was akin to antebellum slave children's being sold before they were old enough to remember their parents. ALMA argued that because New York's sealed adoption records law prevented them from ever knowing their "natural origins," it had abolished their relation with their birth parents. Like slave children, adopted adults were prohibited from communicating with their birth parents and were thus forced to wear a badge of slavery.[52]

A third constitutional argument alleged that sealed adoption laws violated the Fourteenth Amendment in two ways: It infringed on the fundamental right of privacy, which included the right to know one's origins, and it violated the Fourteenth Amendment's equal protection clause by creating a suspect class, which deprived adopted adults of an information right that nonadopted persons possess. ALMA's claim that adoptees were treated as a suspect class rested on earlier Supreme Court decisions recognizing persons born out of wedlock as a quasi-suspect class. Any legislation affecting them was entitled to strict judicial scrutiny, which meant that any state legislation interfering with their rights had to be narrowly constructed and justified by a compelling state interest.[53]

In denying ALMA's First Amendment argument, the Appeals Court for the Second Circuit held that adopted adults had no "fundamental" right to learn the identity of their birth parents. Instead, the adoptees' right to that knowledge had to be balanced against the birth parents' right of privacy, the right to be left alone. To maintain this balance, the Court sided with the adoptive parents, the "family unit already in existence."[54]

The court also found no merit in ALMA's invocation of the Thirteenth Amendment "badges," or incidents of slavery, position. It reasoned that if it allowed ALMA's "absolutist view," it would render the Fourteenth Amendment's due process and equal protection clauses superfluous, which it could not permit. As the Second Circuit dryly put it, "We are appropriately reluctant to reach such a result." Moreover, the Court pointed out that it was not New York State's sealed adoption statute that deprived adopted adults of their birth parents, but the adoption statute itself, which ALMA's brief did not challenge. The Second Circuit ruled that ALMA's Thirteenth Amendment argument was "misdirected."[55]

Finally, the Court rejected ALMA's Fourteenth Amendment claim that adoptees were denied equal protection because adoptees were like persons born out of wedlock. It stated that the analogy was false: sealed adoption statutes bore no relationship to illegitimacy. Adoptees shared none of the social stigma or legal liabilities that rendered illegitimacy a quasi-suspect classification and thus were not entitled to strict scrutiny.[56] Although the Appeals Court for the Second Circuit rejected ALMA's claim, it subjected the New York adoption records statute to a closer inspection and found that the records served compelling state interests. In particular, the law sealing the records was directly related to the important state policy of encouraging the adoption of abandoned and neglected children. The Court reasoned that because secrecy protected the privacy of both adoptive and birth parents, it encouraged the use of regulated adoption institutions without fear of interference or disclosure, thus promoting the best interests of the children, the principle underlying the adoption laws. The Court concluded that the encouragement of adoption and the protection of birth parents' privacy were compelling state reasons justifying sealed adoption records and overrode adult adoptees' right to know.[57] The decision in ALMA would stand unchallenged by other federal appeals courts and the U.S. Supreme Court for the next twenty years.

A second generation of the movement may be said to have begun in 1978, when Jean Paton founded a national umbrella organization, the American Adoption Congress (AAC). Paton, despairing over the multiplicity of adoptee search groups and the ineffectiveness of the movement in changing adoptee records laws, hoped that a large, centralized organization composed of adopted adults would be more effective. She was wrong. Within three years, Paton was denouncing the AAC for commercialism and for admitting professional social workers into what she had envisioned as an all-adopted-adult organization. Paton fumed that having an MSW or a Ph.D. was more important to the AAC's leadership than being an adopted adult. She contended that individual egos and jockeying for place in the hierarchy were taking precedence over developing strategies for opening adoption records. The result,

Paton said, was that AAC leaders failed to set priorities or standards for its board of directors and had not even formulated a budget or set forward a statement of purpose for regional field workers. The AAC ignored its founder's harsh complaints. Paton forecast the organization's death if it did not change its ways.[58]

In fact, the AAC differed from the first generation of adoptee search movement groups in its form of organization, the composition of its membership, its mission, its style, and its ideology. Rather than being led by a charismatic leader, the AAC was a democratic, bureaucratic, hierarchical organization with an elected president at the top and a large board of directors. In addition to adopted adults, the AAC admitted to membership social workers, educators, birth mothers, and adoptive parents. It was dedicated to educating the public about sealed adoption records and lobbying legislators to repeal sealed records laws. Leaders of the AAC, whether out of tactical advantage or sincerity, began calling the movement the "adoption reform movement."[59]

During the late 1970s, the inability to gain access to adoption records by claiming constitutional rights led AAC leaders to emphasize arguments based on psychological needs rather than rights. As adoptee rights rhetoric declined, a second ideology arose that soon dominated and legitimized the movement in the public's eyes: the psychological argument that knowledge of one's birth parents was crucial to the adopted person's self-identity. In contrast to the red-hot rhetoric of "adoptee *rights*" that militant activists like Florence Fisher used, the public was presented with the cool, objective, pseudoscientific discourse of social-science research supporting the thesis that searching for one's biological family was of great therapeutic value and of little risk or harm to the participants. These ideas were widely disseminated in the mid- and late 1970s by three Los Angeles professionals: a child psychiatrist, Arthur D. Sorosky, and two social workers, Annette Baran and Reuben Pannor. They quickly became the intellectual leaders of the search movement, demonstrating an uncanny knack for using the mass media as a research database as well as for advocacy and self-promotion. No other body of work would be so universally cited as representing an accurate portrait of the psychological dynamics of adopted adults and birth parents searching for their biological relations as that of these three.[60]

Between 1974 and 1978, Sorosky, Baran, and Pannor published eleven articles and a book. In one year alone, January 1974 to January 1975, they published four articles, three of which appeared in the social work journals *Social Casework*, the *Journal of Youth and Adolescence*, and the *Journal of Jewish Communal Service*. The fourth appeared in the mass-circulation magazine *Psychology Today*, insuring wide dissemination of their findings. All of the articles contained virtually the same information, often with identical wording. All advocated opening adoption records, either by refuting the unfounded fears of birth parents, adopted adults, and adoptive parents or by trumpeting the positive results of a policy of searching and open records. Single-handedly, these researchers provided proponents of open adoption records with language and arguments that bore the incontestable cachet of social science and medical authority.[61]

Addressing the motivation of adopted adults who searched for their birth parents, Sorosky, Baran, and Pannor removed the stigma from searching. They discovered that a mere 4 percent of searchers in their sample of 50 adoptees conformed to the "standard psychiatric assumption that the search for the natural parent was a search for love and affection."[62] Instead, their evidence demonstrated that for most adopted persons searching for one's birth parents stemmed from "an innate curiosity about their genealogical past."[63] The desire for background information was "ubiquitous to all adoptees" because adoptive parents either withheld genealogical information from them or revealed the adoption late in the child's life, thereby shocking and confusing them.[64] Those who searched did so "simply because they have bright, curious minds and approach all of life's mysteries in the same manner."[65] Searching was also triggered by life-cycle events, such as marriage, the birth of the adopted adult's first child, or the death of an adoptive parent, that produced a feeling of "genealogical bewilderment"—a psychological disturbance afflicting adopted adults.[66]

Sorosky and his associates qualified their argument by noting two exceptions to their benign theory of universal adoptee search motivation. They admitted the existence of obsessive and neurotic adoptee searchers and identified what they labeled "quasi-searching," the practice by adolescent adoptees who were merely acting out. But they left the distinct impression that these searchers were a small minority who could be safely ignored. According to the researchers, what most concerned adopted persons who searched for biological family members—their "uppermost consideration"—was "the need to establish a clearer self-identity."[67] Not only was searching not a sign of mental instability, the adoption researchers reported, but the overwhelming majority of adult adopted persons in their study "personally benefited from the reunion" and felt more "whole and integrated as individuals.[68]

In their articles in professional psychiatric journals, however, Sorosky and his team painted adopted persons as psychologically damaged by the very fact of being adopted. Completing a review of the psychoanalytic literature on the incidence of identity conflicts in adopted persons, Sorosky, Baran, and Pannor found that they fell into four categories: "(a) disturbances in early object relations; (b) complications in the resolution of the oedipal complex; (c) prolongation of the 'family romance' fantasy; and (d) 'genealogical bewilderment.' "[69] Two years later, the researchers expanded on their findings. Adopted adolescents were now held to be more prone than nonadopted adolescents to aggressive, sexual, identity, dependency-independency, social, and future conflicts. They also were said to be uniquely prone to develop symptoms of an "adoption syndrome," which included genealogical bewilderment, compulsive pregnancy, the "roaming phenomenon," and the search for biological relatives.[70] In these articles, Sorosky, Baran, and Pannor were responsible for providing the search movement with its most prominent psychological rationale: adopted persons searched because adoption itself had damaged them. With the publication *The Adoption Triangle* (1978), their numerous and scattered articles were brought together, and their position on adoptees' need to search became tremendously influential in the search movement, as well as with the public, social workers, and lawmakers.[71]

Sorosky, Pannor, and Baran's studies were rife with methodological problems. Since no national databank of adoption existed and they were not allowed to examine sealed adoption records, it was impossible for them to draw a random, representative sample. As a result, their research design and methodology were deeply flawed. Their sample was so small, self-selected, and unrepresentative of the adoption triad community at large that, statistically speaking, their conclusions were meaningless. They based their initial articles on interviews with and letters from a total of 22 adoptees, 47 birth mothers, 170 adoptive parents, and 11 cases of reunion between adoptees and birth mothers.[72] Their appeal in the *Los Angeles Times* for adoption triad members to write them produced "thousands of letters," yet this sample too remained vague or self-selected and unrepresentatively small.[73]

Not only was the methodology employed by Sorosky, Baran, and Pannor deeply flawed, but their research skills, too, left much to be desired. They failed to uncover a significant body of research that contradicted their sweeping assertion that adolescent adoptees suffer from genealogical bewilderment or identity conflicts. In particular, they ignored a mountain of data indicating that 95 percent of adopted children were never referred to professionals for therapeutic help of any sort. Moreover, in the nearly fifty years since Sophie van Senden Theis's 1924 follow-up study of adoption outcomes, researchers had conducted fourteen additional studies evaluating 2,616 adoption placements. They found that approximately three out of four were "successful." But Sorosky, Baran, and Pannor cited none of these studies.[74]

In the 1980s and 1990s, the psychological approach of the adoption reform movement became dominant. The three researchers' work was repeatedly cited uncritically by experts in professional journals of education, pediatrics, psychiatry, social work, child welfare, and law and was widely disseminated by the news media.[75] Prominent in spreading these ideas to the public was Betty Jean Lifton, raised in New York City, a graduate of Barnard College, and a professional writer who was well connected to the East Coast intelligentsia through her husband, author and psychiatrist Robert Jay Lifton.[76] Lifton became a leader in the adoptee search movement in 1975 with the publication of her book *Twice Born: Memoirs of an Adopted Daughter,* which became a best seller. Lifton was quoted extensively in the *New York Times* in the next two years as an adoption rights authority. The paper opened its magazine section to Lifton, who contributed an article that encouraged adoptees to search for their biological parents, denounced adoption agency secrecy, and advocated opening sealed adoption records. Lifton cited the work of several psychiatrists, including the research of Sorosky and associates, and repeated their claims that "virtually all adoptees feel a sense of 'genealogical bewilderment' which expresses itself in a need to search" and that "the majority of adoptees felt that they had personally benefited from the reunion" whether it was successful or not.[77]

Lifton's writings, however, profoundly stigmatized adoptees and contributed ammunition to a growing faction within the adoptee search movement that was anti-adoption. Whereas Sorosky, Baran, and Pannor—in the popular media, at least—downplayed the psychological difficulties caused by adopted persons' inability to access their adoption records, Lifton made them central to her argument. In a letter to the editor of the *Times,* Lifton pointed out that serial killer David Berkowitz was adopted and claimed that that fact played an important role in explaining his behavior. Repeating the inaccurate generalization that adoptees were disproportionately represented in psychiatric clinics and residential treatment centers around the country, Lifton declared it was no coincidence "that a man who was not permitted to know whose son he was, signed himself 'Son of Sam.'" Lifton called for adoption records to be opened "so that future generations of adoptees do not have to vent their rage and frustration inward on themselves, like those in our clinics, or outward, like David Berkowitz on society."[78]

Lifton also gave credence to the idea of "adopted child syndrome," a "disorder" not found in the standard reference of psychiatry, the *Diagnostic and Statistic Manual of Mental Disorders* (DSM-IV). David Kirschner, a clinical psychiatrist who coined the term in 1978, claimed that adopted child syndrome was marked by a cluster of behaviors such as theft, pathological lying, learning disabilities, fire setting, promiscuity, defiance of authority, preoccupation with excessive fantasy, lack of impulse control, and running away from home. As late as 1990 Kirschner qualified his findings as atypical of adoptees in general and noted that "there were millions of adopted children who grow up normally and do not become mass murderers."[79] But it was Lifton who popularized the concept by asserting that "most adoptees exhibit" some of the traits of the adopted child syndrome "as a result of their confusion of their heritage." Drawing on Kirschner's work, Lifton publicly linked closed adoption records with the most infamous serial killers in American history (all of whom had been adopted), citing the likes of "David Berkowitz ('Son of Sam'), Kenneth Bianci ('the Hillside Strangler'), Joseph Kalinger ('the Philadelphia Shoemaker'), and Gerald Eugene Stano (who killed 32 people in Florida)."[80] Her effort to gain access for adoptees to sealed adoption records by suggesting the harmful psychological effects of sealing them inadvertently stigmatized all adoptees as serial killers.

The dominance of this psychological ideology culminated in the early 1990s in therapeutic advice and self-help adoption publications that were profoundly anti-adoption. One of the most popular, Nancy Newton Verrier's *The Primal Wound: Understanding the Adopted Child,* also rested on pseudo-scientific psychoanalytic theories, claiming that adoption was a traumatic experience for the adoptee. According to Verrier, the trauma began with the child's separation from the birth mother and ended "with his living with strangers."[81] As a result, "the primal experience for the adopted child [is] abandonment," a form of post-traumatic stress disorder characterized by depression, anxiety, helplessness, numbness, and loss of control. Although Verrier suggested some ways of healing this "wound," she pessimistically concluded that adoptees would live out the rest of their lives with "a perpetual feeling of being a victim, of being powerless, of being helpless to help oneself."[82] The idea that traditional adoption was by definition dysfunctional was also the basic assumption behind the launching in 1990 of the journal *Adoption Therapist,* which contained such articles as "The Adult Adoptee: The Biological Alien" and "The Orphaned Element of the Adoptive Experience."[83]

As a result of the adoption reform movement's reliance on an ideology that labeled adoptees psychologically damaged as a result of secrecy in adoption (and birth mothers experiencing relinquishment of their infants as a profound loss), a growing faction within the adoptive reform movement, led by AAC members Annette Baran and Reuben Pannor, called for the end of adoption as it had been practiced for a century and half. Baran and Pannor would make open adoption (or, as they called it, "guardian adoption")—a process where birth parents and adoptive parents meet, exchange identifying information, and continue contact, sharing information about the child along a spectrum ranging from a letter once a year to co-equal parenting responsibilities—the law of the land and prohibit couples who were contemplating adoption from pursuing any other alternative.[84]

Armed with the psychological need arguments of Sorosky and his associates, Lifton, Verrier, and a host of others, adopted adults began individually to challenge laws that sealed adoption records in state courts. Almost without exception, access to these records may be obtained only by court order that requires a showing of "good cause" or a "compelling reason." However, what constitutes "good cause" is nowhere defined by statute and thus is largely a matter of judicial discretion. At one extreme, in 1980, a Missouri appellate judge ruled against opening the adoption records of James George, a thirty-three-year-old adopted adult who was dying of leukemia. George's one chance of survival was to find a suitable bone marrow donor, which meant a donor from his immediate biological family. The judge contacted the alleged natural father, who denied paternity and refused to be tested for compatibility. There the matter ended. The Missouri appellate court rejected the sick man's application to see his records, holding that the increase in his chances of survival, even if he could find his birth parents, was too slight to justify opening the records.[85] At the other extreme, a claim of psychological health,[86] a need for medical records or information,[87] or the necessity to ascertain an adoptee's right to an inheritance[88] triggered the good-cause standard in judicial decisions in New York, Washington, D.C., and Louisiana. Thus, adopted adults were slightly more successful in gaining access to their adoption records by broadening the definition of "good cause" than by challenging the constitutionality of sealed records laws.[89] But the larger point is that in the thirty-year history of the adoptee search movement, constitutional arguments have generally been rejected in state and federal courts and few state courts have been persuaded to authorize access to birth or adoption records for good cause.[90] The fact is, if judges granted adoptees easy access to their adoption records for good cause there would hardly be a reason for a social movement demanding that the records be unsealed.

Thwarted in both state and federal courts in their effort to gain adoptee rights, second-generation search leaders began converting social workers to their point of view and lobbying state lawmakers to pass legislation to unseal adoption records based on the idea that all adoptees were psychologically damaged and needed to find their roots. Consequently, during the 1980s and 1990s, a small revolution occurred among social workers, adoption agencies, and state legislatures. Adopted adults increasingly encountered sympathetic attitudes from these institutional representatives. Individual adoption agencies as well as the Child Welfare League of America established more liberal disclosure policies and standards.[91] State lawmakers also began to pass statutes that both facilitated searches and preserved the privacy of triad members. By far the most common legislative reform lawmakers embraced in order to satisfy the privacy rights of adoptees and birth mothers was the voluntary adoption registry, where both parties register their names with the state, consent to a meeting, and are informed of a match. In 1983, the Oregon legislature created a voluntary adoption registry program whereby birth parents and adopted adults could register their willingness to the release of identifying information to each other. In addition, it provided for the disclosure of identifying information to birth parents and adopted children through a licensed social worker, if both were registered and a match made. Finally, it provided for the direct transmission of nonidentifying health, social, and genetic information to adopted adults and birth parents.[92] Oregon's voluntary adoption registry aimed to protect the rights of all triad members, as the state's lawmakers articulated in the statute's preamble:

> The state recognizes that some adults who were adopted as children have a strong desire to obtain identifying information about their birth parents while other such adult adoptees have no such desire. The state further recognizes that some birth parents have a strong desire to obtain identifying information about their biological children who were adopted, while other biological parents have no such desire. The state fully recognizes the right to privacy and confidentiality of birth parents whose children were adopted, the adoptees and the adoptive parents.[93]

Less common was the confidential-intermediary system, in which a court-appointed intermediary acted as a neutral go-between for the adult and the birth parents. This person was permitted to read the adoption file, locate the birth parents, and inquire whether they were interested in meeting the now-grown child they had relinquished for adoption. In 1993, the Oregon legislature enacted a "search and consent" confidential-intermediary system, through which the requestor paid the intermediary a $400 fee. By 1998, twenty-five states had established formal or informal voluntary adoption registries and an additional seventeen states had confidential-intermediary systems in place.[94] On paper, these laws seemed to be the perfect solution to the problem of privacy for birth mothers and justice for adoptees. In practice, however, adoption registries and confidential intermediary systems have proven to be cumbersome, expensive, and ineffective.[95] Furthermore, many adopted adults remained frustrated by what they considered "conditional access" or "compromise" legislation—voluntary adoption registries and confidential intermediary systems—and by the ineffectiveness of adoption activism. Thus was the third generation of the adoption reform movement—and Bastard Nation—born.

2

New Kid on the Block

B astard Nation (BN) took its name from the e-mail signature line of one of its founders: "Marley Elizabeth Greiner, Citizen, Bastard Nation."[1] The message had appeared on the Internet Usenet newsgroup <alt.adoption>, the largest adoption-related discussion group on the Web, with thousands of subscribers.[2] Greiner, an Ohio adoptee with a master's degree in history from Ohio State University, had a long history of political activism. During the 1960s, she participated in anti–Vietnam War protests and supported the United Farm Workers' grape boycott. She also cofounded the (Ohio) Stark County Women's Political Caucus and later the Stark County chapter of the National Organization for Women. She was well read in the history of labor and radicalism and influenced by the gay rights activist organization Act Up.[3] Greiner believed that adoptees had been bastardized by a society and an adoption system that "refused to recognize our full humanity and citizenship simply because of the dirty little secret of our birth. Our invisible, yet very real community, was bonded by the legal denial of identities, our birth records, our heritage, and our genetic histories. Bastard Nation was our native land."[4] Sometime later, BN's mission statement elaborated on the meaning of its name. It stated that Bastard Nation had "reclaimed the badge of bastardy" from those who had attempted "to shame us for our parents' marital status at the time of our births." Defiantly it continued: "We see nothing shameful in being adopted, nor in being born out of wedlock, and thus we see no reason for adoption to continue to be veiled in secrecy through the use of the sealed record system and the pejorative use of the term *bastard*."[5]

Enthusiasm for, and denunciation of, this virtual community was immediate and startling: over the next couple of months complete strangers began referring to themselves as citizens of Bastard Nation and assuming mock titles in their virtual country. There was Michelle, the "Talk Show Tart," Lori, the "Canadian Regional Bastard Queen," Gavi, the "Secretary of Vagina Defense," and Beth, "Head of the RedHaired Bastards," just a few of the original thirty-five members of Bastard Nation.[6] A few adoptive parents denied that their children were bastards and denounced BN as a dangerous political organization.[7] Enthusiasm for creating a virtual Bastard Nation online, however, far outweighed criticism. In the spring of 1996, the second of the four original BN founders, Damsel Plum (née Alfia Wallace), a thirty-two-year-old New York City adoptee, mother of two, and a Yale-educated linguist living in Marin County, California, contacted Greiner and told her she wanted to put up a BN Web page.[8] It went up on June 16, 1996, and immediately began to receive more than a thousand hits a month.[9] Shortly thereafter, the two other founders of BN, Shea Grimm, an adopted adult of mixed Native American ancestry with a law degree from the University of Washington, and twenty-seven-year-old Lainie Petersen, an adoptee and birth mother and a third-year student at Garrett-Evangelical Theological Seminary in Evanston, Illinois, approached Greiner on alt.adoption with the idea of starting a more elaborate adoption rights organization, to which Greiner readily agreed.[10] It was then that Grimm came up with the idea that BN should be incorporated as a nonprofit organization and Petersen with the notion that BN ought to sponsor a conference like other adoption organizations. According to Plum, she and Grimm did most of the organizational work to create BN, but neither wanted to be Executive Chair. They asked Greiner, who was twenty years older and had much more experience as a political activist, to assume the chief leadership position.[11]

Bastard Nation self-consciously differentiated itself from mainstream adoption groups by its style, radicalism, and refusal to compromise. BN's leadership was technologically savvy, light years ahead of other adoption reform groups. Its members were comfortable using e-mail and deployed a sophisticated Website that would be central to the campaign for Measure 58. BN was also young at heart. Its members had a dark sense of humor, which embraced the ribald or scandalous with a verve absent from other movement groups. For mainstream activist groups there was nothing funny about being an adopted adult and searching for biological kin or trying to gain access to adoption records. Most personal search narratives are emotional roller coasters of disappointment, sadness, anger, and rage, punctuated by endless hope and ending with the frenzied happiness of a reunion. Similarly, if one peruses any issue of the *Decree,* the American Adoption Congress (AAC) newsletter, there is not a hint of humor, only articles dedicated to the cause of opening adoption records, AAC activities, and state legal developments.

In contrast, for members of Bastard Nation, every aspect of adult adoptee life, including the very fact of being adopted, was fair game for black humor, satire, or irony. For example, there were "Knock, Knock" jokes, which satirized the short shrift society gave adoptees:

> Knock, Knock.
> Who's there?
> An Adoptee.
> SLAM![12]

There were "Bastard Recipes," which used black humor to confront abandonment and condemn sealed adoption records:

> Who's My Papa Pot Pie
> Bunch-a-Bologna Sandwich
> Cajun Style Blackened Records
> Chopped Files on Toast (clean your plate, ungrateful child)
> Clam-up Chowder
> Strawberry Short-a-Mother Cake
> Don't Ask Why Stir Fry[13]

There were even "Bastard Cheers," which members used to remind themselves of their unknown birth parents, as a spur to continue to fight for open adoption records:

> Pricetag, Pricetag,
> On My Ass,
> I Live Under A
> Looking Glass.
> I See Mama,
> I See Pop,
> Two More Somewhere,
> I Won't Stop!
> Bastard Gonna
> Reach the Top!
> Goooooooooo Bastards[14]

In addition to employing a different style from mainstream adoption activist groups, Bastard Nation held more radical goals. BN's leaders envisioned themselves as successors to the militant tradition of William Lloyd Garrison, John Brown, and Malcolm X. In their rhetoric they claimed they would never back down, they would never compromise, and they would be heard. BN's primary goal was "the opening of all adoption records, uncensored and unaltered, to an adoptee upon request, at age of majority." Disgusted with decades of the movement's tactical pragmatism, BN's mission statement declared that it did not support "mandated mutual consent registries or intermediary systems in place of fully open records, nor any other system that is less than access on demand to the adult adoptee, without compromise, and without qualification."[15] For BN, "conditional access" systems enacted by state legislatures, such as adoption registries and confidential intermediary systems, contributed to "the psychology of self-defeatism in adoption reform." These mechanisms had forfeited adoptees' rights in favor of systems that were understaffed, ineffective, and costly to adoptees.[16]

BN's radicalism extended to attacking the theoretical underpinning of the adoption reform movement. In marked contrast to mainstream adoption activist organizations such as the AAC, leaders of Bastard Nation emphatically denied the ideology of adoptee psychopathology. They were openly skeptical of Nancy Verrier's claims in *The Primal Wound*. And from their own personal experience, they pointed out that many adoptees were happy to have been adopted; some did not desire to search. Some BN members were birth mothers. Still, BN members blamed the various systems of "conditional access" legislation and its supporting ideology on some birth mothers and adoptive parents, who supported adoption registries and confidential intermediary systems. "Open records," Plum declared, "is about rights, not about wounds, nor about facilitating reunions, which the government has no business doing anyhow."[17]

As a third-generation adoption activist group, Bastard Nation had an organizational structure totally new to the adoption reform movement: it was neither charismatic, bureaucratic, nor democratic. In October 1996, the Executive Committee was formed, with Marley Greiner assuming the position of Executive Chair. Greiner, who did not wield any real power, was joined by Damsel Plum, Shea Grimm, and Lainie Petersen. It was a self-perpetuating oligarchy: its members replaced themselves and never held elections, nor did they ever consult the membership on decisions. Also unlike the leadership of mainstream activist groups, BN's female leadership was, with the exception of Greiner, young (a median age of twenty-eight), and all were college-educated and computer-savvy.

The Internet was the glue that held Bastard Nation together. In fact, it cannot be overemphasized that BN was first and foremost an electronic *virtual* adoption activist community.[18] Except for small annual meetings, leaders and members never met face to face. BN's Website was the first step in electronically connecting Bastard Nation's leaders and members. Under Plum's leadership, the Website was artistic, sophisticated, and substantive, filled with testimonials from adoptees about the problems of searching under the closed-records system and information about where to send letters of protest or where to picket. Although it provided information, BN leaders viewed the Website mainly as a vehicle for recruiting activists to the cause of adoptee rights.[19] Complementing its Website was BEST (Bastards E-mail Special Training), a members-only e-mail list established in March 1997, where leaders and members could discuss issues and disseminate news. Through the Internet, the Executive Committee was quickly able to reach other like-minded members. Soon, local affiliates sprang up in Seattle, Oregon, the San Francisco Bay area, Texas, Philadelphia, and Ohio. State directors were appointed whose jobs were to recruit new members, organize protests, and lobby state legislatures on adoption records.

Bastard Nation leaders chose protest as one primary strategy to mobilize public opinion in support of adoptee rights. Although mainstream adoption reform groups still used protests, like therapist and adoption activist Joe Soll's original Adoption Circle annual marches on Washington, D.C., in the late 1980s, they had taken on a ritualistic quality that no longer shocked the public or converted legislators to the cause of opening adoption records. In contrast, BN protests were intense, unpredictable, and central to its identity as a "by any means necessary" radical adoption organization. For example, BN leaders immediately saw the media value of connecting protest to Hollywood. Lifetime BN member and social worker Bill Betzen suggested educationally picketing the prizewinning film *Secrets and Lies* to gain attention to the cause of adoptee rights.[20] On February 2, 1997, Bastard Nation set up "positive pickets" in seven cities across the nation, in front of movie theaters that were showing *Secrets and Lies*. The movie is the story of a black British adult adoptee who, after legally accessing her original birth records from the British government agency holding them, searches for and is reunited with her white birth mother. From that basic premise, the rest of the film plays out the complicated and unsentimental consequences that arise when an adopted adult makes "first contact" with his or her birth family. According to the 2,500 flyers BN handed out, the purpose of the "positive pickets" was to inform the public that birth records in the United Kingdom were open. In contrast, adoption birth records in the United States were sealed in all but two states, Kansas and Alaska. In the other forty-eight states, adult adoptees were forbidden access to their original birth certificates unless they could show judges "good cause," and even then access was rarely granted.[21]

BN leaders considered their first foray into the streets quite successful. The protest gained widespread publicity in the newspapers and local TV markets where the protests took place. BN also announced its presence in the adoption reform movement in an explosive way. BN leaders gleefully noted that even rivals such as AAC interim president Jane Nast and adoption author Betty Jean Lifton "jumped on the Bastard Nation bandwagon and contributed to the success of the event," as did a number of other moderate adoption reform groups.[22]

In the symbiotic culture of Hollywood and liberal politics, one hand washes the other. Hearing about Bastard Nation, Mike Leigh, director of *Secrets and Lies,* said, "It isn't for us to do anything other than support them, because obviously it is a human right, which needs to be respected." Putting his conviction into action, Leigh and Brenda Blethyn, the film's Oscar-nominated star, appeared on March 10 with BN members at an open-records rally in front of a Beverly Hills theater where *Secrets and Lies* was playing. When the film received five Oscar nominations, including one for best picture, BN shrewdly capitalized on the media's interest in glamorous events and held a black-tie rally and picket at the Academy Awards in Beverly Hills on March 24, 1997. BN member Ron Morgan, a writer, Web designer, and contractor attended the event, which resulted in a live interview with CNN. In addition, BN members were interviewed by more than sixty other media outlets.[23]

Along with marches and pickets in 1997, BN members debated open records on radio and TV, wrote letters to the editor published in newspapers across the nation, and engaged in campaigns to influence legislatures in Illinois, Texas, and Pennsylvania. Though ideologically opposed to using search and reunion arguments for opening adoption records, BN leaders had all reunited with their birth families and sympathized with triad members who still had not found theirs. Thus, although they ridiculed the "woundies"—BN's derisive term for those who believed that adoption had psychologically wounded them and that reunions would heal the wound—Shea Grimm constructed a sophisticated Website filled with information for adopted adults who were beginning searches.[24] BN also supported Tony Vilardi's International Soundex Reunion Registry, a free, nonprofit, mutual consent adoption registry dedicated to reuniting adult family members separated by adoption or divorce. However, BN's primary goal remained lobbying legislatures to change adoption laws. Thus, as early as December 1996, BN incorporated and received 501(c)(4) nonprofit status, which enabled it to lobby state and federal legislatures.[25]

Except for its protests, BN's various activities—appearing on radio and TV shows, writing letters to the editor, and selectively lobbying state legislatures—hardly differed in kind from the activities of other adoption reform groups. Even ideologically, BN differed little from the AAC. In spring 1996, ex-AAC president Kate Burke declared on the front page of the *Decree* that "open records is a civil rights issue" though, as the "umbrella" organization of the movement, the AAC annual convention featured speakers from across the ideological spectrum[26]. Though BN's leadership caricatured the AAC's ideological stance based on the national organization's pragmatic political behavior—the AAC frequently supported legislation that did not give unconditional access to adoption records—BN's own radicalism was never as revolutionary as its rhetoric. At the tactical level its modus operandi was educational, lawful, peaceful protest.

But for all its similarity under its rhetorical excess, BN *did* differ from the AAC and other mainstream adoption reform groups. Most movement groups tried to cooperate with each other. BN appeared to, but it would never depart from the principle of supporting only legislative bills that called for unconditional open records. Bastard Nation was happy to work with any adoption reform group, but only on its own terms. More important, BN agitated for direct, specific, and immediate action. In contrast, the AAC's board of directors announced that its number one objective in 1996 would be to begin "strategic planning" to "help us achieve our goal to 'come of age' in our 18th year of operation." This was followed by the announcement of membership elections, a revision of AAC bylaws, distribution of training literature to regional and state branches, and a promise to develop policies of financial support for educational programs in these same branches.[27] Nowhere did the AAC leadership mention plans for agitating and lobbying the issue of sealed adoption records.

Shea Grimm, Damsel Plum, and Marley Elizabeth Greiner, three of the four original Bastard Nation Executive Committee members, being awarded "Queen B" certificates at the first Bastard Nation conference, Chicago, 1997.

The focus of BN's conferences also differed from those of other groups. In July 1997, BN held its first conference in Chicago, where members finally met each other in person and made formal presentations on adoptee rights. While the AAC conference in 1996 was a sprawling affair, with "something for everyone" in the more than fifty workshop presentations,[28] BN's much smaller conference concentrated on political matters. Among its thirteen workshops were sessions entitled "Know Thine Enemy," an examination of the political and ideological forces behind the anti-adoption movement; "Cops Are Our Friends," a training session for anticipated confrontations with the urban constabulary; and "The Right to Privacy and Open Records," an exploration of the legal concept of the right to privacy in light of the recently passed Tennessee open records decision.[29] The political nature of the conference was highlighted by the choice of the keynote speaker: attorney Randy Shaw, head of San Francisco's Tenderloin Housing Clinic and author of *The Activist's Handbook: A Primer for the 1990s and Beyond*,[30] a step-by-step guide for political activists on running grassroots election campaigns to achieve social change. Chapters discussed the intersection of legislative strategy, ballot initiatives, direct action, and the media. Many members of the BN Executive Committee had already read the book.

An anomaly in this highly politicized conference was the workshop "Art for Adoptees," described in the program as "a hands-on workshop in artistic expression for adoptees" presented by "Adoptee/Art Therapist Helen Hill."[31] Little did anyone anticipate that BN's singular contribution, Measure 58, would spring from the head of Helen Hill, who, with the aid of Shea Grimm, a long-time adoption activist, would pull off the electoral upset of the November 1998 election.

3

A Tale of Two Bastards

Helen Hill was born in 1955 in the Fairmont Maternity Home in Missouri and was adopted as an infant by a wealthy Kansas City family. Loving parents made sure she lacked for nothing. Her father, Salvador Sebastian Hill, a large man with high moral standards, was a prominent general contractor responsible for such notable buildings as the Truman Library and the Lyric Theater in downtown Kansas City. Betty Hill, her tall, beautiful, blonde-haired mother, was a quiet, impeccable housewife. Hill had a close relationship with her older adopted brother, Sebastian. Her parents sent Hill off to Notre Dame Our Lady of Scion, a Catholic boarding school run by Franciscan nuns, which she attended for eight years, and then to Barstow, a private preparatory school in Kansas City. On the surface, the Hills appeared to be the perfect adoptive family.[1]

But appearances were deceiving. Inwardly, Hill was a tormented child obsessed by her own appearance. "My mother was a devastatingly beautiful woman and I was this little dark-haired kid with stick legs who looked fairly hideous."[2] At the age of ten Hill discovered high on a bookshelf *The Chosen Child*, a classic storybook to help adoptive parents inform children of their adoption. Hill recalls, "I began to shake, because I knew at that instant. I knew that I was adopted and that I had been lied to. Even before that, I knew, but it was more on a cellular level. I always knew there was a secret. When there's a family secret everyone knows about it, even if you don't talk about it; it oozes out of the walls. It's like an elephant is there, but everyone says there's no elephant, but everyday you're shoveling up this elephant dung."[3]

Still, Hill needed confirmation. Her heart pounding, she asked her mother whether she was adopted. "Yes," her mother replied, "you're adopted." She went on to say that Hill had been told of her adoption long ago, and then made Hill swear never to speak of it again. With no outlet for further questions, Hill stopped talking completely. She felt overwhelmed with shame. The toxicity of other secrets in the house—secrets that would not be revealed for another twenty years—nurtured her silence. (Unknown to Salvador Hill, who thought of himself as Italian, he too was adopted, and was of Native American heritage; his wife had learned of this fact at the time of their marriage but had withheld her knowledge of it for the rest of her life; Salvador discovered it for himself late in life while going through the belongings of his deceased wife.)[4]

For the next several months, Hill did not speak a word. Her parents sent her to a psychiatrist, and gradually she returned to the land of speech.[5] Hill's life went "careening and reeling, and spinning out in all directions except the one I most needed to go in." The result was "a bit of chaos" as Hill "acted out" in other ways typical of teenagers. Her parents persevered, but they were not happy, nor was Hill. Adoption remained a taboo subject at home throughout Hill's adolescent years.

In early July 1973, a month after her high school graduation at age eighteen, Hill left home. That summer she immersed herself in the East Coast counterculture. Deciding that she needed further education, Hill enrolled that fall at Hollins College in Roanoke, Virginia, a women's liberal arts college founded in 1842 with an emphasis on the arts. In her rebellious state, she refused to accept any money from her wealthy parents. Working three or four jobs at a time to pay tuition, Hill continued to daydream about her origins. Hill's curiosity would not abate, extending to her college studies, where she took classes in ancient Greece and Rome, fruitlessly hoping that studying the origins of Western civilization might make the origins of her own life clearer. In college she fell in love with a fellow art student, married him, then became pregnant. The marriage did not work out.[6] By her senior year, the pressure of work, school, marriage, and pregnancy led to a nervous breakdown. Hill ran away again, fleeing this time from both college and husband. She hitchhiked to Oregon, she said later, because someone had told her that it was a place "where the trees were so tall you couldn't see the tops of them and the ocean was so blue it made you cry."[7]

The birth of her daughter Raine, when Hill was twenty-three, marked a watershed in Hill's life. Seeing her first blood relative was a transforming experience. It inspired a period of artistic creativity for Hill and, more important, a strong desire to turn her life around. Hill decided she would become a useful, stable person in society for the benefit of her newborn daughter. To support herself and her child, Hill worked as a waitress and sold an occasional painting or piece of sculpture. In the following decade, although she led a responsible and respectable life, Hill lived through several difficult relationships. She married and divorced twice more and bore two more children, Henry Sebastian and Seneca. Hill continued to puzzle over her origins. She made a few calls and even hired a private investigator for a short time. The calls led nowhere, and the investigator began to ask for money. He said the search could cost anywhere from $100 to $30,000. Hill was practically a pauper. She believed there was nothing she could do without a lot of money and connections. "The injustice of it was just appalling to me," she later recalled. Hill gave up the search for her birth parents and began to work on other parts of her life. She became an accomplished artist and a public school teacher.

As her children were growing up, Hill volunteered to teach art at Nehalem Elementary School, located in the small coastal town of Nehalem, Oregon, where the teachers welcomed her. Hill's life and her philosophy about art and teaching were intertwined. She believed in the power of art. A bumper sticker hanging on the wall in her art room proclaimed: "Art saves lives." Hill said she used art "as a survival mechanism" and "as a way of working through difficult and traumatic periods" of her life. During the time when Hill was searching for her birth parents, she was drawn to sketch and sculpt the shape of eggs and the path of roots. Much of her art reflects the searching process.[8] Hill was a terrific teacher. Surprisingly modest about her accomplishments in the adoption reform movement, Hill has no compunction about declaring her talents as a teacher. "When I get around children I'm gold," she says. "I'm just sort of a born teacher. I love them and I love empowering them with art." She was especially attracted to neglected children, "the ones slipping through the cracks, the ones that are kind of thin and sick and dirty all the time: those are my kids." Recognizing her abilities, teachers began to compete for Hill to visit their classroom. After four years, the school administrators offered Hill her own classroom. Despite her lack of any college degree or state certification, Helen Hill became a full-time Oregon public school teacher.

The Oregon coast in the mid-1970s and 1980s was a haven for ex-hippies, artists, environmentalists, liberals, and left-wing activists. As Hill reared her children, taught school, and pursued her art, she became a member of these circles. Her activist mindset was born of her many years of sporadic and frustrating search for her birth parents, which had convinced her of "how fucking unfair and unjust" the system was, "what a brick wall a human being comes up against just because they are adopted." According to Hill, it wasn't until she reached her mid-twenties that she began to manifest a radical consciousness in social acts. In 1982, when the Oregon State authorities began spraying herbicides on the coast, Hill took action. Along with other coastal environmental activists, she uncovered a serious, hitherto unknown physiological danger from the indiscriminate spraying of herbicides by the state. She then wrote articles for a local alternative newspaper exposing the danger to the community.

Another life-changing event occurred in 1985, when Hill was thirty. Her wealthy adoptive father died of a heart attack, leaving her a substantial amount of money. Although her steady employment as an art teacher plus a little money from art sales had kept her family afloat, times had been hard and her income had always hovered just above the poverty level. Those days were over. She purchased a fifteen-acre farm on Neahkahnie Mountain, two miles outside the town of Manzanita, one of the Oregon coast's most magnificent locations.[9] With the help of a financial adviser, Hill invested wisely. For the next several years, she devoted more of her time to her art and spent her summers traveling. But neither her financial security nor her success as a parent, teacher, and artist could blunt her inner need to ask the fundamental questions about her origins.

In the early 1990s Hill's life entered a period of crisis. She found that she could not concentrate, that nothing in her life made sense. She sank into a deep depression. She had to know who her birth parents were and who she was. She began a search. Missouri's adoption records were sealed. Hill phoned the Fairmont Maternity Home clerk, but the experience made her feel humiliated and demeaned.

> They would have my information spread out in front of them, and you could hear the pages turning. This total stranger who knows more about your background than you do is saying things like, "Oh, I see your father has a very unusual name." It's this horrible tease. And the hatred and bile that rises up in you—here I am, over forty years old, and I'm wondering what law says I can't know where I came from. My voice is cracking and I can hardly contain myself. Meanwhile, she's just sort of humming along.[10]

When the clerk refused to give Hill any information, she plunged back into depression and all but gave up her search efforts.

Hill's eventual breakthrough in her search for her birth parents came about as a result of her reading Betty Jean Lifton's *Journey of the Adopted Self*.[11] In this book Lifton asserts that the secrecy surrounding traditional adoption practice was psychologically toxic. According to her, it gave rise to "the Ghost Kingdom," a psychological space where ghosts "haunt the dark crevices of the unconscious and trail each member of the adopted triangle (parents and child alike) wherever they go." In effect, Lifton claims, "the adopted child is always accompanied by the ghost of the child he might have been had he stayed with his birth mother and by the ghost of the fantasy child his adoptive parents might have had. He is also accompanied by the ghost of the birth mother, from whom he has never completely disconnected, and the ghost of the birth father, hidden behind her."[12] Lifton believes that as a consequence of their having two selves, two mothers, and two families, adoptees feel a split in their identity, a dual sense of reality; and because of the conspiracy of secrecy about their adoption they feel a deep sense of shame, ambiguity, and alienation. Lifton asserts that the issue of identity becomes particularly important for adoptees at the age of adolescence: their difficulty in coming to terms with their adoption during these years results in many cases of identity confusion, prolonged adolescence, "eating disorders, phobias, and an underlying depression, which rises out of unresolved grief and loss"; some are moved to outright defiance, rebellion, and running away.[13] Although searching for one's birth parents is difficult—at the core of searching is the fear of the unknown—Lifton writes that the adoptee must begin the healing process by heroically setting off on this quest. Only by searching and reuniting with one's birth parents can one experience the empowerment that comes from reconnecting with one's true self.[14]

Although Lifton's discussion of ghosts has no basis in reality and her generalizations about adopted persons' identity problems were based on unrepresentative studies, Hill recognized herself on almost every page. She felt herself to be one of those people accompanied by ghosts, and she was sick and tired of it. Hill was moved to call Lifton and left a message, thanking her for writing such a great book. She also sent Lifton two of her paintings. She did not really expect an answer. Her image of Lifton was that of a best-selling New York author who would be too busy to have any time for the likes of Hill. She was amazed when Lifton called her back. After listening to Hill's life story, Lifton advised Hill in no uncertain terms that she had to find her birth mother: she had to resolve these unanswered questions in her life before she could move on. Hill knew Lifton was right, and now she had the money to do it. But she was conflicted. What would the reunion be like? What would her birth mother say to her? Hill continued to spend weeks curled up in bed as she contemplated her next move, feeling alternately depressed and exhilarated that she might finally exorcise her ghosts and answer the question of her origins.

Finally, in 1996, at age forty-one, Hill paid an investigator $3,000 to search for her birth parents. Nine months later, he located both her birth mother, a sixty-three-year-old elementary school art teacher living in Des Moines, Iowa, and her birth father, a lawyer in Albuquerque, New Mexico. The next evening Hill screwed up her nerve. She called her birth mother first. She said, "My name is Hill, and I'm calling about a very personal matter. I was born on March 24, 1955, at the Fairmont Maternity Home in Kansas City." After a very long silence, her birth mother said, "I love you. I've always loved you." They talked for what seemed to Hill a long time, though it was only twenty-five minutes. Soon afterward, Hill flew out to Iowa. The meeting of birth mother and daughter was highly emotional. At first Hill's visit made her feel great joy. But that night, after Hill's mother took her up the narrow attic stairs of her house to a small, clean bedroom, Hill lay sleepless for hours, listening to the droning cicadas and staring at a section of asphalt road shining under a streetlight. She later wrote:

> A loneliness I never bargained for, never thought would be the end of my journey, carves me hollow and black and sick. The only thing that staves it is the sight of the road, it belongs to everyone. It will welcome me over and over, asking only for my feet, never for my courage. All these years I've been a sad question mark to you, while this house where you live has been the only place I could imagine all roads led. All of my life I've been searching for this food, for these people, for this room with its resting place. But now that I'm here, I long for the comfort of the road. I long for the road that will take me away from this house where my family has lived a lifetime without me. I leak tears on the clean pillow case, the one you selected for homecoming that mocks me with its confusion and hollowness. I cry for all the wretched longings that are better left unsatisfied. For where do I go now that I've arrived? What do I do now that I find that I've been gone so long, I don't belong here; that I never did?
>
> I wake to light filling the room like slow music. I must have fallen asleep, dreaming of the road. I hear you downstairs in your kitchen, I go back down the narrow stairs. You're baking cinnamon rolls. Rolling them out just like I do. You have plates like mine. We talk. And laugh. And cry, a bit, in the morning brightness of your kitchen. And though this knowledge will seep through and warm my blood slowly, warm my veins like a gathering sunlight on roads and paths interrupted by the roots of the giant trees of my oldest dreams: I have arrived. My longest journey is over.
>
> My own dear mother is found, and the secrets of the universe are mine.[15]

A month later, Hill wrote a postcard to Albert Anella, her birth father. As a handsome Italian-American lieutenant in the U.S. Army, just returned from the Korean War, he had had a year-long, passionate affair with Hill's birth mother, Jane, while they both attended law school in New Mexico. Anella had trouble with Jane's parents and left. He never saw her again and had no knowledge that Helen Hill even existed. Nevertheless, after receiving Hill's letter, he called her immediately. He was stunned but happy. He said—according to Hill, "with a voice like Al Pacino's"—"Your mama was the love of my life. You were a love child."[16]

Reuniting with her birth parents erased Hill's internal conflicts. Just as important, it also freed her to look beyond her own personal issues and to become involved in the adoption reform movement. Until then Hill had never joined any of the numerous adoption search groups. Now, in the spring of

1997, she joined the Oregon Adoptive Rights Association (OARA), a regional branch of the American Adoption Congress (AAC). After three meetings, however, she stopped attending. Hill recalled that at her initial meeting at OARA she was "attacked by a searcher woman as soon as I walked in the door." The "searcher woman," it turned out, was Darlene Wilson, a volunteer searcher for OARA and longtime member of OARA's board of directors. She was certified and licensed by the state of Oregon to conduct confidential intermediary (CI) searches for a $400 fee.[17] Hill was offended by the woman's zealousness and by what seemed to Hill an obvious conflict of interest. Here was an adoption reform organization whose purported goal was to open the records with a searcher on its board of directors who profited financially from keeping the records closed. If adoption records were ever truly open one day, CI searchers like Wilson would be out of a job.

Hill swallowed hard, ignored Wilson, and continued to attend OARA meetings, but she did not find what she was looking for. The OARA meetings felt to her like therapy sessions. Members stood up, recounted in detail their happy reunions, and were greeted with applause. But these accounts were matched by other members' accounts of horrendously difficult situations, which were greeted by silence. Hill noticed that quite a few people were silent and looked dejected throughout the meetings. What bothered Hill was not OARA's ideology, which emphasized search and reunion and the psychology of the trauma of adoption. She, of all people, understood the necessity of adopted adults to make that journey, and in years to come she never completely shared Bastard Nation's ideological contempt for the "woundies." All things considered, she was glad that she had joined OARA and believed that it was doing good things for adopted adults. What bothered Hill was that OARA appeared to be apolitical: politics was not discussed at meetings and the organization was not proactive at the legislative level.

An unexpected consequence of joining OARA was Hill's discovery of Bastard Nation (BN). During an OARA meeting Hill attended in 1997, one of its members said, "Man, I was surfing the Web and I found this amazing and irreverent and funny as hell organization called Bastard Nation. They are totally into proactive civil rights: Let's just get our birth certificates." Hill's immediate reaction was "Wow. And humor, too?" She went home, logged on to BN's Website, and "started laughing my ass off." She found the group "brilliant" and was drawn to them. Soon thereafter, she joined BN, and although she had never used e-mail before, she was soon a regular on the group's e-mail list, Bastards E-mail Special Training (BEST). Through BEST, Hill found out that BN was planning to hold its first-ever conference that July in Chicago. She

Helen Hill, chief petitioner of Measure 58.

decided to offer an art workshop—which, she recalls with a typical self-deprecating comment laced with optimism, "turned out pretty pitiful, but I didn't have my political chops quite up yet."

Hill's words belied her unerring political instinct, inspired by author-activist Randy Shaw, the convention's keynote speaker. Hill had flown to Chicago looking for political direction, to find out what she could do. She was tired of adoptees complaining that they did not have access to their adoption records and failing to act politically on the problem. Here in Chicago she felt a difference in the air among the BN attendees, an eagerness to effect change. Hill sat in the front row when Shaw spoke. Drawing on his recently published book, *The Activist's Handbook,* Shaw talked about grassroots activism and praised the ballot initiative, by which he meant "a new law or resolution proposed and placed on the ballot by citizen petition, and enacted directly by popular vote."[18] He viewed the initiative as an effective method to control political elites and dismissed criticism of the initiative process from those who feared that it was dominated by special interests and wealthy corporations. Hill thought Shaw was a "fabulous" speaker and felt as though he was talking directly to her.

As she listened to Shaw, Hill began to imagine the possibilities of running an initiative campaign in Oregon. She knew that Oregon was a very initiative-friendly state. Other thoughts tumbled through her mind: Oregon was a state where human-interest stories and matters of the heart played well at the polling booth. It had a thoughtful electorate. And best of all, she thought, it was not yet controlled by a lot of people with money. It probably would not take much money to win an election, she mused. All one had to do was do it! During the question-and-answer session following Shaw's presentation, Hill asked him about the feasibility of running a ballot initiative campaign for adoptee rights.[19] After the talk, while Bastard Nation members staged a protest march through downtown Chicago, Hill peppered Shaw with questions about the possibility of launching an initiative campaign. When Hill mentioned that she was from Oregon, Shaw "became tremendously excited," Hill recalled, and said, "My god, Oregon is an initiative-friendly state! Why don't you start one?"[20] Shaw's reaction gave Hill a tremendous bolt of confidence.

The 1997 Bastard Nation conference was notable for Helen Hill for another reason, for it was there that Hill met Shea Grimm. The two would become the team that was largely responsible for Measure 58's victory.

IN MANY WAYS, Shea Grimm was unlike Helen Hill. She was born in Nebraska to a German mother and a Native American father (who abandoned her mother when informed of the pregnancy), and was placed for adoption with a couple who, as it turned out, were close to divorce. Indeed, they separated when Grimm was a toddler. Consequently, she has few memories of her adoptive father. Grimm grew up in a small town in Nebraska with her adoptive mother; when Grimm was still a child, she and her mother moved to Nashville, Tennessee.[21] Grimm's experience with adoption revelation was also different from Hill's. Though she grew up in an age of secrecy, Grimm always knew she was adopted; there was no trauma. Her schoolmates and friends did not taunt her for being adopted, and her Native American heritage was not a problem for her at school. Grimm recalls, "I passed pretty easily for white, and I was kind of surprised that when I moved to Nashville and my first schools there were largely black, I moved easily into the mixed race groups as well."[22]

From her elementary school days, Grimm was a rebel with a highly developed political consciousness. During those years, Grimm became the "bane of the principal's existence" for regularly organizing petitions and leafleting over bad food, insufficient recess time, and restrictive dress codes.[23] Grimm recalls being crushed when Ronald Reagan defeated Jimmy Carter for the presidency. "I remember feeling guilty, but being happy, when Reagan got shot, because I thought that meant that Carter got to be President again." Her rebelliousness was also evident at home. Grimm never got along with her adoptive mother and at around age fourteen ran away. A love of horses attracted her to work at racetracks and eventually Grimm joined the polo circuit, working as a groom first in the United States and then for almost a year in Italy and Spain. It was one of the happiest times of her life.[24]

At age sixteen, Grimm became tired of living abroad, returned to Nashville, and attended the University School of Nashville, a private, college prep high school. She focused on the humanities and arts, especially drama, and graduated at age eighteen.[25] Grimm also got involved in local theatre and took acting lessons at the Tennessee Performing Arts Center. Early in her studies, she discovered Saul D. Alinsky's *Rules for Radicals* and Simone de Beauvoir's *The Second Sex*, both of which had a "fairly profound influence" on her.[26] Her senior year was a momentous one: she had been accepted to the University of California at Santa Cruz where she intended to go to film school when she fell in love with a musician. Grimm's college plans were put on hold while the couple married and moved in with her mother, who had moved back to Nebraska. They hoped to save enough money to move to the West Coast. Grimm attended the University of Nebraska and gave birth to her first child, China. Grimm and her husband eventually left Nebraska and wound up in Seattle, where Grimm waited tables and attended the University of Washington. She graduated with a BA in political science and American Indian studies.

During her college years, Grimm worked for many radical causes, including Greenpeace, the American Indian movement, and Chicken Soup Brigade, a Seattle nonprofit providing food and services to people with HIV/AIDS. She also attended pro-choice rallies and joined the AAC. In the early 1990s, Grimm searched for and found her birth mother.[27] It took her two years to find her. The only information Grimm had was that she probably had been relinquished for adoption in Omaha, Nebraska, in the 1960s. Grimm somehow secured a directory containing the names of about one hundred attorneys practicing in that period and began calling them one at a time, asking whether they had handled any adoption cases in the month and year that she was born. Near the end of the list, one attorney answered, "Yes." Much to Grimm's surprise, he also told her the mother's name. Grimm quickly dialed directory assistance, but the number was unlisted. She then called the operator, told her it was an emergency, and asked the operator to call and tell the person who answered to call Grimm's number. The plan worked. Grimm's birth mother called, and Grimm said, "I think you're my mother." Although her mother sounded shocked at first, Grimm reported that they had a good talk. Grimm stated, "She had never told anyone."[28] Several years later Grimm and her birth mother searched for and found Grimm's father. Like so many other adoptee–birth parent relationships, Grimm's relationship with her birth parents "is pleasant, but not close. They are more like distant relatives."[29]

Grimm went on to attend the University of Washington Law School and gave birth to two boys, Israel and Max. She continued to wait tables and picked up some paper routes. Grimm was different from the other law students. For one thing, she had little desire to practice law. To her, "law school was more about the intellectual exercise rather than any desire to be a lawyer." Another thing that set her apart was that she would breast-feed her son in classes, which was seen as a radical feminist act at the time. Through her studies, Grimm felt she learned a lot of law and that she evolved "as a person." Though she was "not too crazy about lawyers," she loved "the concept of American law" for "the idealism inherent in our legal system. It's very free of cynicism as it is constructed. That's probably hurt it in lots of ways, but I think the concept is a marvelous one. From the 'jury of one's peers' to the presumption of innocence to the burden of proof being on the state, I think it's really a glorious thing."[30]

During law school, Grimm began exploring the new technology of the Internet. In the early 1990s, she became active on the Prodigy adoption bulletin boards. By 1993, Grimm was participating on the Usenet news group <alt.adoption> and had created the first adoptee-rights Website in existence.[31] For a perspective on how innovative Grimm's Internet ventures were, consider that in 1994 the *Internet Yellow Pages* had no listings for "adoption" except for a notation for <alt.adoption> in the appendix. Just two years later, the search engine Alta Vista revealed 200 sites on the Web devoted exclusively to the issue of adoption records. Grimm was one of the first to see the potential power of the Internet to spur adoption reform. By 1996 she was using the pages of the AAC's newsletter, the *Decree,* to inform its members about the Web's virtues and directing them to the best adoption reform sites. Grimm stated that the most obvious advantage to using the Web was its ability "to distribute large and varied information on a single topic to a huge group of politically active, affluent individuals." Another advantage was the ability of adoption reform organizations or individuals to contact congressional representatives, state governments, and the media. The Internet was especially valuable, Grimm asserted, because it allowed media representatives to contact responsible adoption reform groups, who could quickly counter inaccurate information in adoption stories. Letting her thoughts run wild, Grimm imagined the unlimited potential of the Internet: "From the personal dramas of searchers, to the activities of organizations like the American Adoption Congress, to state grassroots legislative activity, it's all here, on the Net. What we do with this opportunity is in our hands and in our modems."[32] Here Grimm planted the seeds that would grow to become Bastard Nation.

During the early years of Grimm's participation on the Internet, she continued to attend AAC meetings. Her experience at a Washington state branch would have momentous consequences for Bastard Nation and the adoption reform movement. Unlike most new AAC members, who were politically naïve and inexperienced in the ways of searching for original family members, Grimm was a political radical who was a feminist and had worked in the environmental, peace, antipoverty, and American Indian movements. She had been strongly influenced by civil rights leader Malcolm X, indigenous peoples activist Leonard Peltier, and feminist Gloria Steinem. Grimm admired them for their refusal to compromise their principles under any circumstances, a trait she herself would demonstrate again and again in the fight for unconditional access to adoption records. Grimm felt no need to search for her birth parents; at that point she had already gained all the information she needed for a reunion. What attracted her to the AAC was its local leader, "a great lady named Jean Pelto." According to Grimm, Pelto opposed the confidential intermediary system and the disclosure veto, and was "very much an old-school Jean Paton type of lady."[33] Pelto became Grimm's political mentor and plunged her into adoption politics, regularly appointing Grimm to stand in for her in meetings she could not attend.[34]

Grimm ran for AAC state representative on a platform opposing the confidential intermediary system. Her opponent, in conformity with AAC policy, ran on the opposite side of this issue. Grimm won the election, but it was voided when the AAC's regional director discovered that her dues had lapsed. For Grimm, it was not difficult to figure out what happened. "It was a fairly transparent sham. I was a radical and the AAC didn't want to piss off the intermediaries who were very big in the organization at the time, so I was dispensed with." Although Grimm greatly respected the AAC's president, Kate Burke, she was disappointed that Burke had not reinstated her as the victor. Grimm believed that Burke "was great for the AAC, a charismatic and visionary leader, but she wasn't really interested in the nuts and bolts and let some power-hungry lower echelon members take over so she could concentrate on the media appearances and more glamorous stuff." From this, Grimm's first experience with the AAC's political machine, she took two lasting lessons. She would never again trust the motivation of the AAC's leadership, which, she had decided, seemed more interested in personal aggrandizement than adoption rights. And she became "totally radicalized" on the issue of confidential intermediary systems. She now viewed confidential intermediary systems as

utterly corrupt and parasitic, existing only to line the pockets of the intermediaries themselves. Grimm would never compromise on the right of adult
adoptees to unconditional access to their adoption records.[35]

In 1996, Grimm's interest in the Internet and radical adoption reform dove-
tailed when she became one of the founding members of Bastard Nation and
quickly assumed a position of leadership. Soon Grimm was editing *Bastard
Quarterly*, the organization's newsletter, where she expressed her opposition
to legislation that in her view compromised adopted adults' right to their
records. In 1997, Grimm wrote that she had discovered everywhere a new,
"ingenious compromise" that the adoption reform movement had seized upon
"with alarming enthusiasm": disclosure or contact vetoes, legal provisions
that allowed birth parents and adoptees to veto the release of identifying information to the requesting parties. It was "ingenious" because under the name
of adoption reform, the practice lulled adopted adults into thinking that their
records were being opened to them when in reality it was discriminatory to
adoptees as well as being often ineffective and costly. In the context of Tennessee's open records law, then before the Sixth Circuit Court of Appeals,
Grimm argued that contact vetoes were the functional equivalent of restraining orders. Moreover, the Tennessee law provided for criminal penalties for
an adoptee who violated the veto, making it particularly noxious to Grimm
because, unlike a restraining order, "contact vetoes are orders issued without
a cause, and without a remedy. Adoptees have no opportunity to take advantage of due process and face their accuser. These vetoes make adoptees a suspect class, slapping them with orders of protection based solely on their
adopted status, and perpetuating the nescient notion that contact between
adoptees and their birthfamilies is fraught with danger." In short, "The right
to know had won, only to be supplanted by this trampling of the adoptee's
right to due process and equal protection under the law."[36] Grimm was not
tilting at theoretical windmills. Particularly galling was the defeat of an
unconditional open adoption records bill in the Oregon legislature that Grimm
blamed on Delores Teller, reunited birth mother, president of the Oregon
Adoptive Rights Association (OARA), and northwest regional director of the
American Adoption Congress. Grimm would never forgive Teller for supporting legislation that contained a disclosure veto amendment rather than a
pure open records bill.[37]

FROM START TO FINISH, Helen Hill and Shea Grimm were equal partners in
the campaign for Measure 58. Hill would be the public face of Measure 58:
she was ubiquitous on television and radio talk shows, and in published inter-

views; beloved by the measure's advocates; denounced by the opposition. Grimm chose to remain out of the public eye throughout the campaign, invisible in articles that featured Hill and in accounts of Measure 58.[38] She preferred to work behind the scenes, avoiding the camera and the on-the-record statement. She disdained personal glory, believing that only the cause mattered. In Helen Hill and the idea of a ballot initiative, Shea Grimm had found a new way to advance the rights of adopted adults. Together, the two women believed they could do the impossible: qualify a ballot initiative in Oregon for the November 1998 election.

4

Qualifying the Initiative

Helen Hill had reason to believe that she chose the right state in which to launch Measure 58. A hundred years earlier, at the turn of the twentieth century, Oregon was in the forefront of the Populist and Progressive reform movements. The Populists, a political party dominated by western farmers, believed strongly in grassroots, direct democracy; that the people could not be corrupted in a way that legislatures could be; and that the initiative process would make government more honest, efficient, and responsive. Reformers then believed that "the initiative's main purpose was to curb governmental abuses."[1] In 1902 Oregon became the third state in the Union (after South Dakota in 1897 and Utah in 1900) to approve a constitutional amendment containing the initiative and referendum. Two years later, Oregon made history by being the first state in the nation to vote on and approve the first two initiatives ever to appear on a state ballot.[2] In the following decade, in a fever of direct legislation, notes political scientist Richard J. Ellis, "Oregonians voted on over one hundred statewide initiatives and popular referenda."[3] In 1906 alone, Oregon voters put ten initiatives on the ballot. Seven passed, none by less than a 72 percent margin, including four constitutional amendments.[4] These four amendments, the first passed by any state in America, galvanized Progressive reformers across the country to campaign for passage of the initiative, resulting in successful reforms in the states of Delaware (1906), Oklahoma (1907), Maine (1908), and Michigan (1908), and during the same period in cities such as San Francisco; Grand Rapids, Michigan; Des Moines, Iowa; and Wilmington, Delaware.[5] In 1912, Oregon voters set another national record that still stands today, placing twenty-eight initiatives on the November ballot.[6] By 1918, nineteen states, almost all of them west of the Mississippi River, had adopted the initiative as part of their state constitutions. Today twenty-four states, and many cities, have adopted the initiative.[7]

Even during the first decade of its existence, proponents and critics noted both the strengths and the weaknesses of the initiative process. Proponents, such as Progressive reformer C. Frederick Howe, enthused that Oregon was "the most complete democracy in the world." The editor of *Hampton's Mag-*

azine boasted that "Oregon has shown the way by which the people may deliver themselves from the control of Big Business."[8] Indeed, many successful initiatives in Oregon strengthened the democratic process (for example, permitting the election of a U.S. senator by the voters; allowing for recall of public officials; establishing a presidential primary) and fostered progressive causes (levying gross earnings taxes on express, telephone, and telegraph companies; increasing appropriations for the University of Oregon; establishing the Eastern Oregon Insane Asylum; instituting an employer liability law).[9] But, as Ellis notes, there was also the minimalist rationale: the initiative was seen as " 'a safeguard of politics': one which citizens would only need to deploy infrequently to keep politicians in check."[10]

By 1912, however, critics were denouncing the initiative process—or what was now referred to as "the Oregon System." Allen Eaton, for example, wrote that Oregonians could "do anything in politics that they please to do. There are practically no restraints upon their power." He agreed with the initiatives' proponents that Oregon was "without doubt the most democratic democracy in the world, if we mean by democracy a state where the people have absolute power."[11] Unlike the proponents of the initiative, however, Eaton believed that the consequences of the initiative process were bad for the body politic. Initiative campaigns were costly, inviting corruption. They weakened the Oregon constitution by entirely destroying the safeguards of the amendment process, for they allowed no review process and permitted a minority of voters—a mere 8 percent—to make a measure law. Eaton also held that the laws passed were often unwise, because the voters, lacking intelligence, understood neither the laws proposed nor their own interests. Finally, Eaton argued that there was too much room for petition fraud, especially in falsifying signatures.[12]

Nevertheless, a majority of Oregonians continued to consider initiatives democracy in its purest form. Throughout the twentieth century, Oregon remained a leader of the initiative process. It used the initiative more than any other state in the Union; it had the highest average initiative use (5.5 per general election)[13] and the second most statewide initiatives on the ballot in a single year (37 in 1912).[14] Helen Hill and Bastard Nation, it would seem, had the right strategy and the right place.

But only on the surface. If they had looked closely at statistics or researched the issue more deeply or been less radical, they might have had second thoughts. For in recent decades, initiatives in Oregon have struggled to receive voter approval. Between 1976 and 1992, for example, Oregonians voted on fifty-seven initiatives, of which thirty-nine were statutes and eighteen were constitutional amendments. Voters approved only 35 percent of the initiatives and 28 percent of the constitutional amendments. Similarly, Hill and the leaders of

BN might not have been so confident about their fundamental message to the electorate—that adoptees' unfettered access to their original birth certificates was a civil right—had they been aware of how badly civil rights initiatives had fared nationwide. Of the seventy-four civil rights initiatives that U.S. citizens voted on between 1959 and 1993, 78 percent went down to defeat.[15] Oregon's own record was mixed. In 1988, voters approved Measure 8, an antigay measure that overrode an executive order directing state agencies not to discriminate on the basis of sexual orientation.[16] Four years later, however, Oregon voters defeated Measure 9, another antigay initiative; but in the wake of its defeat, antigay laws sprang up in numerous local jurisdictions.[17] Even the basic liberality of Oregon voters was questionable. If Bastard Nation was counting on Oregon's liberals to look favorably on their initiative as tearing down the govenmental walls of secrecy, like the Freedom of Information Act, they had not come to terms with the highly popular, influential—and ultra conservative—Bill Sizemore, Oregon's leading initiative sponsor. In the 1990s, Sizemore successfully spearheaded initiatives that blocked the expansion of commuter railways, cut property taxes, reduced public employees' teachers pensions, and abolished a regional government.[18]

Unaware of Oregon's weak and illiberal track record on initiatives in general and civil rights initiatives in particular, Hill left Chicago supremely confident that getting an adoptee rights initiative on the ballot in Oregon would be a snap. She figured it would take some time and some money. But Hill believed in the power of the Internet. Her plan was, first, to utilize BN's Oregon database, then to contact all of Oregon's search organizations, such as the Oregon Adoptive Rights Association (OARA).[19] She would write the initiative, file the necessary papers, round up an army of adoptees and birth mothers to gather signatures on the streets, and "boom, the initiative would be on the ballot." Tempering her optimism was the issue of money. Thanks to her adoptive father's inheritance, Hill had the money, but she had to give a lot of thought to whether she wanted to spend it on the initiative. She had no idea how much the total campaign would cost; she estimated it at about $20,000. Weighing the possibilities, she decided "to go for it."[20]

What Hill did not know was that most campaigns today are run by "The Initiative Industry," as journalist David Broder has dubbed it, and cost anywhere from $500,000 for a statute to $900,000 for a constitutional amendment. The first phase of an initiative campaign, which typically includes extensive legal service, a statewide poll, input from focus groups, and advice from a campaign consultant costs between $50,000 and $100,000.[21] In fact, these campaigns are so expensive that one consultant typically asks what Broder calls the "million-dollar" question: "Where's your million dollars?"[22]

Hill and Bastard Nation hardly had the money to pay for the first phase of the process, much less hire a professional firm to run the entire campaign.

Hill's vision was to run the initiative campaign solely with volunteers on a high-tech basis. She operated out of her basement, with the Internet her constant companion. Along with incurable optimism, Hill had a capacity for endless work and the power to inspire in others a dedication to the cause of adoption rights. According to her own account, she worked twelve hours a day, every day of the week, for the fifteen months that it took to qualify the initiative for the ballot and see it to victory.[23] A number of Oregon volunteers and the indispensable political and legal advice of BN Executive Committee member Shea Grimm aided her in the first phase of the campaign.

Initiative campaigns are often won before voters even see the measure, and Initiative 46 (as Measure 58 was first designated) was no exception.[24] Key to an initiative's success is the clarity of its title and the language in the body of the initiative.[25] Hill had definite ideas about the ballot measure, which were in accord with this tenet. She envisioned a measure that was so simple and so direct—basically one sentence long—that "no one could possibly vote no for it." When it came to writing the initiative, Hill and Grimm proved to be an effective team. From Redmond, Washington, Grimm wrote the first rough draft of the initiative and sent it by e-mail to Hill, who, in her basement in Nehalem, Oregon, rewrote and edited it. She then e-mailed it back to Grimm, who replied immediately with suggestions and word changes.[26] The final product had two sentences; a long one and a short one tacked on at the end. The short one read, "Contains no exceptions." It was added to ensure that no one would change the wording of the initiative before or after it had been passed by the voters.[27]

There were a few disagreements. Grimm, who was trying to get an open adoption records bill through the Washington state legislature, modeled the initiative on her piece of legislation. This would have made the wording of the initiative more complex, however, and Hill would have none of it. Grimm eventually conceded the virtues of simplicity. Also, Grimm proposed that adopted adults be defined as those who had reached their eighteenth birthday. Hill agreed with Grimm in principle: eighteen-year-olds did have the right to their original birth certificates. But she thought voters would be more likely to support the initiative if the age was twenty-one; Hill's pragmatism was one of the reasons Measure 58 succeeded. Hill reasoned that adoptees' having to wait the extra three years would not be that difficult. On the one hand, she felt, adoptees would be patient because the knowledge that their birth certificates would soon be in their possession would enhance their dignity; and on the other hand, she thought that voters might worry that if eighteen-year-olds

received their birth certificates and found their birth parents they might aban-
don their adoptive families in favor of their newfound birth families. Hill
knew this was highly unlikely, but she did not want to give the opposition a
chance to make this sort of argument. The initiative as written, then, called
for adopted persons age twenty-one years and older to be granted access to
their original, unamended birth certificates.[28]

By the end of July 1997, Hill and Grimm had produced a draft ballot
initiative:

> Upon receipt of a written application to the state registrar, any adopted
> person 21 years of age and older born in the state of Oregon shall be
> issued a certified copy of his/her unaltered, original and unamended
> certificate of birth in the custody of the state registrar, with procedures,
> filing fees, and waiting periods identical to those imposed upon non-
> adopted citizens of the State of Oregon pursuant to ORS 432.120 and
> 432.146. Contains no exceptions.[29]

Unknown to Grimm,[30] Hill crafted a draft ballot title on her own:

> Measure gives voters the opportunity to include and recognize adult
> adoptees as citizens with rights equal to all other non-adopted citizens
> born in the state of Oregon, who, having a direct and tangible interest,
> are guaranteed issuance of a certified copy of their original birth certificate
> as set forth in Oregon Statute 432.120. Measure will amend Oregon
> Statute 432.230, Section 2.[31]

The effort was unnecessary, and unnecessarily wordy, since Oregon election
law mandated that the attorney general write initiative titles, and that they not
exceed ten words.[32] In retrospect, Hill blamed the length and convoluted nature
of the draft ballot title on her unfamiliarity with the law and her inexperience.
Her instincts, however, were good: even attorney Warren Deras, the future
opposition leader to the intitiative, counseled his clients to add a title just in
case the attorney general needed guidance. And ultimately, it did no harm.[33]

Writing the ballot measure and title would prove comparatively easy compared to qualifying it for the ballot. First, the prospective initiative petition
had to be filed at the state capital in Salem. In preparation for what in Hill's
mind was a daunting task, she bought a suit, which, she said, "felt terribly
uncomfortable after almost twenty years of wearing the casual attire of the
artist and teacher." Her motivation for purchasing business clothing was
understandable. Hill was filled with the importance and responsibility of the
task she had assumed, and she believed that when dealing with state political
officials she should be dressed respectfully. On August 8, 1997, she arrived at

the secretary of state's office in Salem with her daughter, Raine, and all the required documents, including one announcing the founding of a political committee, which she dubbed "Open '98," and naming herself as treasurer.[34] Not only was such a committee legally required in order to raise money to finance the initiative; it also gave the campaign an identity for supporters to rally around. Once Hill entered the secretary of state's office, she was chagrined to discover that all the clerks were wearing jeans. Hill laughed at herself and began to relax a bit.

Within two weeks Hill, as chief petitioner, received a draft ballot title sent to her by Hardy Myers, the state attorney general. If initiative campaigns were won partly on the content and clarity of the title and the text of the measure, it was also true that the way the state's attorney general worded the initiative's summary and the "results of a 'yes' vote" statement and the "results of a 'no' vote" statement were very important to an initiative's success. In Oregon, these sections, as well as the initiative's title, were written by the attorney general. Theoretically, the attorney general reads the chief petitioner's initiative and then writes a clear, impartial, legal title; a summary of the measure; and statements informing the public what the results of voting for or against the measure would be. In practice, the attorney general has what amounts to the power to make or break an initiative through helpful or pejorative or confusing language in the title or summary. Whatever Myers's motivation, in Hill and Grimm's eyes the draft ballot title for the initiative was a disaster. Although it was a big improvement over Hill's convoluted title, the attorney general's wording was confusing and potentially very damaging: "REQUIRES ISSUING CERTIFIED OREGON BIRTH CERTIFICATE COPY TO ADULT ADOPTEES." Over the phone and by e-mail, Hill and Grimm furiously prepared an appeal, requesting that the word "original" be added before the word "certified," since adopted Oregonians could already receive certified copies of their birth certificates.[35] Unless the word "original" was added, lawyers would argue after the initiative passed that what the law really meant was that adoptees should be issued a certified copy of their amended birth certificate, not the original. This would, in effect, nullify the initiative.

Two other problems remained. Oregon's attorney general was also required by law to write two 25-word statements describing the result of a yes vote and a no vote and a summary of the initiative of not more than 125 words.[36] The draft ballot title's "RESULT OF 'NO' VOTE" statement read in its entirety: " 'No' vote leaves availability of identifying information for adult adoptees to voluntary adoption registry." The summary section of the draft ballot also incorporated information about Oregon's voluntary adoption registry. The inclusion of Oregon's voluntary adoption registry strongly suggested that the attorney general viewed the initiative as a means for adoptees to search for their biological families.

In response, Hill and Grimm wrote Myers and requested that all references to Oregon's voluntary adoption registry be omitted from the two sections. They argued that bringing up the availability of identifying information in the voluntary adoption registry was irrelevant to the main issue in Initiative 46. The initiative was not designed to facilitate searches or reunions, as was implied by mention of the voluntary adoption registry. Rather, Initiative 46 was "designed to restore a fundamental civil right to adult segment of the Oregon population; the right to access one's own, private, original birth documents." Moreover, they argued, many adopted adults had already successfully searched for their birth parents and still had a right to their birth certificate. Still others desired to obtain their birth certificate but had no intention of searching for their biological family members. Hill and Grimm suggested that if the opposition to the initiative wanted to argue that Oregon's voluntary adoption registry was sufficient to release identifying information, the *Voters' Pamphlet* was the place to do it. But, they concluded, it hardly seemed appropriate for the state of Oregon to be making the argument for the opposition in the wording of the ballot measure.[37] Still, the attorney general had a point. One consequence of an Initiative 46 victory, whether intended or not, would be the revelation of identifying information to adopted adults, and that would inevitably lead to an increase in searches for birth parents.

Others also commented on Initiative 46. As part of the Oregon's initiative process the secretary of state distributed the draft ballot title to the chief petitioners, the legislative assembly, the state capitol press room, and any interested party who subscribed for $10 to an initiative mailing list.[38] Two people requested changes to the draft ballot title. Like Hill and Grimm, Catherine M. Dexter, an adoption attorney of the Portland law firm Dexter & Moffet, found Initiative 46's title misleading because it did not identify whether the original birth certificate or the amended birth certificate was to be given to requesting adult adoptees. She too suggested that the word "original" be added to the ballot title.[39]

The other response to Initiative 46 came from Portland attorney and adoptive father Warren C. Deras, who would later be at the center of the opposition to Measure 58. At age fifty-three, Deras was a seasoned political professional, well versed in election and initiative law, and with an intense interest in adoption. He had adopted two girls: Megan in 1980 and Jennifer in 1982. He was born at Langley Field, Virginia, but grew up in San Francisco, where he attended public high school. After graduating in 1966 from the University of California at Berkeley, he attended Yale Law School. Two

Warren C. Deras, treasurer of Concerned
Adoption Professionals, the first
opposition group against Measure 58.

years later, he married his wife, Rosemary, dropped out of law school, and
enlisted in the U.S. Army. Deeply conservative and alienated by Yale's liberalism during the height of the antiwar movement in America, Deras's military
service was an act of both patriotism and defiance. In 1969–1970, Deras
served in Vietnam as an infantry sergeant. Still, he loved the law, and when
his tour of duty was over, Deras returned to Yale Law School. He received his
law degree in 1972 and went into private practice, primarily in estate planning and probate law, in Portland.[40]

Deras plunged into local and state politics. In 1974, he ran for Republican state representative from District 8—at the end of the Watergate scandal.
He lost. That year, Deras would note in retrospect, was "not a year to be the
Republican nominee." That same year, however, Deras made his mark in legal
circles, through a significant constitutional law decision. In *Deras v. Myers*
(1974) the Oregon Supreme Court became the nation's first appellate court
to rule that campaign spending limits were unconstitutional because they violated free speech rights. (The U.S. Supreme Court came to the same conclusion in *Buckley v. Valeo* in 1976.) As a result of *Deras v. Myers*, Deras's star
rose high in the Oregon Republican Party. For the next two decades he served
part-time in a number of highly important political positions, including as the
party's legal counsel, as treasurer and legal counsel to various political committees, and as a member of the Governor's Advisory Council on Legal Aid.
Deras later served as chairman of the estate planning and probate committee

of the Oregon State Bar for two sessions and wrote significant portions of the probate code.[41] Because of his disagreements with some legislative proposals, he had done some writing in the area of adoption law as well. Deras specifically objected to lawmakers' efforts to prohibit all private placements of infants and to institute elaborate preplacement study requirements, which would, in his opinion, make adoption much more costly. He also urged the legislature to rein in unlicensed paid intermediaries who were extensively advertising for adoptable infants in the classified section of the *Oregonian*.[42]

At the time of Initiative 46, along with his private practice, Deras was a special assistant attorney general for the state of Oregon, doing probate work for the Oregon Department of Justice. He also did some paid work in the political area, including election law. As a result, he was on the secretary of state's mailing list to receive copies of ballot measures as they were filed. Periodically he would see one that interested him and offer a comment. Initiative 46 interested him a lot.[43]

Deras's objections to the draft ballot title and results portions of the initiative merit close attention not only because he would become an important leader of the opposition but also because parts of his arguments would eventually become central to the attack on it. Deras interpreted the purpose of Initiative 46 not as a civil rights issue but rather a disingenuous means to obtain the names of birth family members. He wanted the title of the ballot changed to reflect what he interpreted to be the primary purpose of the initiative. As Deras pointedly noted to Donna Birkey, head of the Elections Division, it was to "require disclosure of birth parent information to adoptees over age 21," which would in effect "prohibit the common practice of confidential adoptions." Moreover, Deras believed that Initiative 46 violated several Oregon adoption laws by being retroactive, applying to adoptions in the past about which birth parents had been promised confidentiality. Consequently, he proposed that the draft ballot title be reworded to read: "PROHIBITS KEEPING NAMES OF BIRTH PARENTS OF ADOPTEES CONFIDENTIAL." Deras suggested that the "RESULT OF 'YES' VOTE" statement should be rewritten as: " 'Yes' vote allows adoptee over 21 to receive confidential information identifying birth parents." And he wanted the "RESULT OF 'NO' VOTE" statement to read: " 'No' vote leaves identity of birth parents to voluntary disclosure." In addition, Deras made substantive changes to the summary portion of the draft title ballot. He expanded the original summary written by the attorney general by adding "open adoptions" to Oregon's voluntary adoption registry as means adoptive and birth parents already had to make available family information. Deras's proposed summary also pointedly noted that the initiative "would require the state registrar to issue Oregon adoptee over the age of 21 a copy of birth certificate disclosing birth parents." Finally, Deras mentioned the issue of retroactivity and the fact that the initiative applied to birth parents who in the past had been assured of confidentiality.[44]

The attorney general reviewed all the comments submitted in response to the draft ballot title for Initiative 46. On September 10, 1997, Myers sent Initiative 46's certified ballot title to Colleen Sealock, director of the Elections Division. The initiative had met all the preliminary requirements for filing; Hill could now begin to collect signatures to qualify the initiative for the November 1998 ballot. In the letter accompanying the certification, Deputy Attorney General David Schuman noted that changes had been made to the "caption, result of 'yes' and 'no' vote statements, and summary in response to the comments and our further review of the measure." The result was a resounding victory for Hill and Grimm of Bastard Nation. The suggestions of all four of the commentators—Hill, Grimm, Dexter, and Deras—had been taken into account. The title of the proposed initiative now specified that an adoptee could obtain a copy of his or her *original,* unamended birth certificate. And although the attorney general did not accept Hill and Grimm's suggestions verbatim for changing the "yes" and "no" vote statements and summary, he did accept their substance. Completely removed from the statements was any mention of Oregon's voluntary adoption registry. In contrast, Myers had dismissed the rest of Deras's proposed changes because they were "overly broad and argumentative."[45]

The importance of the attorney general's favorable review can hardly be overemphasized. Had Deras prevailed at this point, Hill and Grimm would have been forced to file an appeal to the Oregon Supreme Court to review the ballot title, a time-consuming process that would have prevented Hill from beginning to collect the tens of thousands of signatures needed to put the initiative on the ballot. Bastard Nation's success compounded Deras's earlier mistake of not filing a ballot title contest and attempting to tie up the initiative as long as possible in the Oregon Supreme Court.[46] Instead, as Deras admits, he totally underestimated the initiative's proponents: "Frankly, I didn't see this as a serious measure. I didn't anticipate that there would be someone [with] either the money or the organization to collect the signatures." Deras's long experience with initiatives played him false when it came to this case. "You see a lot of measures filed and very few on which signatures are actually collected. And I looked at this and I thought, 'This isn't serious.' So I sort of let it go."[47] Deras's overconfidence allowed Hill and Grimm to dodge a bullet. With the initiative certified by the secretary of state, Hill and her Oregon workers immediately set out to collect the 73,321 signatures needed to qualify Initiative 46 by July 2, 1998, for the November general election.[48]

During the filing of the prospective initiative, Hill had to decide whether she would hire paid or volunteer petition circulators to gather the signatures.[49] Historically, when initiative campaigns sprang from grassroots activists, a dedicated army of volunteers, usually connected with organizations like temperance leagues, churches, unions, teachers associations, or third-party political organizations, circulated initiative petitions. But modern initiative campaigns, which allow only 90 to 150 days to collect signatures, have led to the demise of volunteers. In the past two decades, professional signature-gathering firms have been responsible for practically all of the successful drives to place initiatives on the ballot.[50] Though they are expensive—costing anywhere from $20,000 to $200,000—paid petition circulators get results.[51] Dan Kennedy, president of a Colorado signature-gathering firm, boasts, "We handle everything. You just give me the petitions and we'll get them back to you, filled out. We've got it down to a science."[52] A 1988 study of a California signature-gathering firm, Kimball Petition Management, revealed that of fifty-three initiative campaigns that had retained its services, all but one reached the ballot.[53] By the 1990s, not only business corporations, but even reform movements like environmental, consumer, and campaign finance groups, resorted to such firms.[54]

Costly, results-oriented initiative campaigns have, however, corrupted the process. Studies have revealed that in their haste to gather signatures, paid circulators are often dishonest, misrepresenting the measure's substance, adding fictitious names, and occasionally forging names from the local telephone book. Other studies have revealed that by emphasizing speed over explanations of the initiative, paid petition circulators mislead a majority of the voters, who tend to sign petitions without having read them.[55] Hill had very definite ideas on this subject. She and other social activists hated that the petition system in Oregon permitted paid signature-gathers.[56] For Hill, it took the integrity out of the grassroots initiative campaign and turned it over to mercenaries who were in it only for the money. Hill wanted Initiative 46 to be the one Oregon initiative whose petition drive qualified for the ballot through the work of dedicated volunteers.

As the initiative drive began to pick up steam, Hill realized that she could not manage it alone. With advice from Shea Grimm, she added to her Open '98 committee five or six dedicated adoption rights activists. The group met weekly in Portland to coordinate campaign activities, trade ideas about new media opportunities and places to collect signatures, and work through problems. The committee, composed of adoptees and birth mothers, was both Hill's tool and sounding board.[57] By December 1997, the pattern of the drive to qualify Initiative 46 for the ballot had been set. Committee members, including Hill, were the nucleus of about one hundred volunteer petition circulators. The committee advertised in the media, at Oregon Adoptive Rights Association (OARA) meetings, and over the Internet for additional volunteers. The volunteers collected signatures where there was heavy foot traffic: at Fred Meyer supermarkets, for example, or in the front of movie theatres. They were especially successful at the Saturday Market, an open-air farmer's market and bazaar that was crowded with Portland shoppers every weekend. In addition, Hill organized a number of rallies, including one on December 23, where Initiative 46 advocates held a signature-gathering candlelight vigil at Pioneer Courthouse Square. There they introduced their new mascot, Max, a golden retriever, who, according to Hill, because he had access to his records, knew more about his pedigree than Oregon's adopted adults did.[58]

By early February 1998, the campaign was in full swing. At committee meetings, suggestions were made to add signature-gathering sites such as bowling alleys, county libraries, Powell's Books (Portland's most popular bookstore), Portland International Airport, and even the Rose Festival Parade. Media coverage was supportive, and the group considered placing ads on local cable access channels (they eventually did so). That month, Hill ran a weekly ad with the slogan "Got Records? Max Does" in the *Oregonian*'s Metro section. Bumper stickers with the slogan "YES on 46" and T-shirts stating "EQUAL RIGHTS FOR ADULT ADOPTEES!" were also available. Cable and local television stations had run a story about Initiative 46, and in March radio talk show coverage was anticipated to begin. The committee was also planning a big rally in Pioneer Square in late March.[59] The initiative drive appeared to be off to a successful start.

But there were several troubling signs. In mid-January, OARA decided to restrict Hill and her companions' activities. OARA's actions were surprising. Although Hill had stopped regularly attending OARA meetings, she and one of her Oregon Committee members, Linda Corbin, a birth mother, had resumed attendance once the initiative drive had begun. They set up tables in the back of the meeting with T-shirts and bumper stickers, gave talks about Initiative 46, and handed out petition sheets to members who volunteered to collect signatures. This went on for some time until Delores Teller, a birth mother and president of OARA, through an intermediary, asked Hill and Corbin to stop talking about the initiative at the meetings. Teller said that there had been so many complaints that OARA's board of directors had reached the conclusion that "our members want to focus on issues of healing, reunion and support." She told Hill that her group could set up their table in the hallway at 6:30 P.M. but had to leave before the OARA "support groups [began] at about 8:15."[60] Hill did not believe that OARA members had complained of her advocacy of Initiative 46 at the meetings. Instead, she interpreted her silencing as a hostile act fomented by OARA board member Darlene Wilson, the state's confidential intermediary records searcher. If adoption records were open, Hill reasoned, Wilson's source of income would dry up. Resentful at being muffled, Hill never returned.[61]

More seriously, in early February, alarm bells sounded over the dearth of signatures being gathered. The problem seemed to lie with the volunteer collectors. What Hill did not expect was the lack of cooperation within the adopted adult and birth mother community itself. Initially, she was surprised at the difficulty of recruiting volunteers. She had expected a mighty army of Oregon adoptees and birth mothers to rise up, both as volunteer petition circulators and as signers, but was taken aback when hardly anyone turned out. Later, after gaining some experience with the campaign, she came to realize that signature gathering was no amateur activity. It was an art, a science, and a bare-knuckle sport. Volunteer circulators of a controversial initiative had to have thick skins to withstand the coarse and insensitive remarks often directed at them. Many of the adoptees who circulated Initiative 46 petitions, including even Hill herself, were not prepared for opponents' insensitivity. Once, while she was petitioning, a man had shouted at Hill, "Your mother got rid of you for a good reason. That's all you need to know."[62] For a time, Hill felt devastated by that experience. She just wanted to go home and hide. And she was not the only one who felt that way.

Committee members became more and more alarmed. In mid-February there was a showdown of sorts. Committee members demanded to know how many signatures had been collected. Hill, as the keeper of the signatures, revealed that there were only 13,000. The committee members bluntly told Hill that the present system was not working and that the initiative would never be qualified for the ballot by using volunteers. The only solution was to raise money and pay people to get the signatures needed. Despite her idealism about qualifying the initiative using only volunteers, Hill was also a pragmatist. She herself had seen this coming and was mentally prepared for it. Back in December 1997, in her role as Bastard Nation's state director for Oregon, she stated in her monthly report that if the initiative had not garnered 40,000 signatures by February she had already "made the commitment to switch gears." She would "refile [with Oregon's secretary of state] to pay circulators, and perhaps even turn over the job to one of the professional paid circulation companies that have sprung up here in Oregon. To hell with it, I say. All I care about is that this initiative gets to the ballot. And with a Bastard National at the helm, there *is* no fooling around. [Initiative] 46 will be before the voters or I'm not a Bastard. And God knows I am."[63] Hill thus abandoned her ideal of qualifying the ballot with volunteers and used her own money to hire paid petition circulators.

Some Circulators For This Petition Are Being Paid

The person obtaining signatures on this petition is being PAID.

PETITION FOR STATE ☐ INITIATIVE ☐ REFERENDUM MEASURE

SIGNATURE SHEET

PETITION I.D. _____

THIS IS A STATE PETITION. SIGNERS OF THIS PAGE MUST BE REGISTERED VOTERS IN

COUNTY ONLY. _____

TO THE SECRETARY OF STATE OF OREGON:

We, the undersigned voters, request this measure be submitted to the people of Oregon for their approval or rejection at the election to be held on _____ , 19 _____ . A full and correct copy of this measure was made available for review and we have not previously signed a petition sheet for this measure.

(INSERT CAPTION OF BALLOT TITLE OR SUBJECT IN TITLE OF ACT) _____

	SIGNATURE	DATE SIGNED MO./DAY/YR.	PRINT NAME	RESIDENCE ADDRESS STREET AND NUMBER	CITY OR POST OFFICE	ZIP CODE	PRECINCT (IF KNOWN)
1.							
2.							
3.							
4.							
5.							
6.							
7.							
8.							
9.							
10.							
11.							
12.							
13.							
14.							
15.							
16.							
17.							
18.							
19.							
20.							

CIRCULATOR'S VERIFICATION

STATE INITIATIVE/REFERENDUM MEASURE PETITION

I, (print circulator's name) _____ , hereby verify every person who signed this sheet did so in my presence and I believe each person is a qualified voter in the State of Oregon (ORS 250.045).

THIS VERIFICATION MUST BE SIGNED BY THE CIRCULATOR.

SIGNATURE OF CIRCULATOR _____

SHEET NUMBER _____

CIRCULATOR'S ADDRESS (street, city and zip code) _____

The initiative petition. Helen Hill hired paid signature gatherers when volunteers failed to gather a sufficient number.

Also motivating her to hire professional signature gathers was the negative experiences she and the other volunteers had had with boorish members of the public. Hill decided that "it would be impossible and perhaps even wrong to ask our limited volunteer force to do the bulk of the petitioning, to essentially wear their hearts on their sleeves and confront the public en masse with an issue that is deeply personal and, in many cases, unresolved." Now she defended the paid signature gatherers, whom she had once denounced as corrupters of the political process, as public servants and paragons of democracy. She wrote, "Far from decrying a group of citizens' concerted effort to put an issue before a vote of the people by any lawful means necessary, I believe we should support this kind of active participation, for citizen participation is the true essence of democracy."[64]

Hill turned to Bastard Nation for financial aid. She told the Executive Committee that Initiative 46 would fail to make it to the ballot unless it received a large infusion of money. She requested help. In response, the message Hill heard from BN's leadership was: "No, you are on your own. We can't send you any money. Although we wholeheartedly support you in what you are doing, we have no money." Although disappointed, Hill rationalized that BN must have a lot of individuals approaching the organization to request funding claiming that they were going to reform this or protest that—"Saturday activists," she called them—and BN probably thought Hill was one of those who would eventually give up when things got hard. In this respect, Hill did not fault BN; many others also thought she would quit when things got tough. Still, Bastard Nation's refusal to contribute a significant sum of money to the initiative rankled Hill.[65]

Despite the lack of financial support, Hill was determined to get Initiative 46 get on the ballot even if it meant spending her own money to pay for the professional petition circulators. She now knew, however, that rather than her original estimate of $20,000, the cost might rise to $100,000 or more. Thanks to her late adoptive father, Hill had the money, but she had to decide whether she should deprive her children of their inheritance in support of the initiative. When she inherited the money, Hill had immediately invested it in safe, conservative, low-income bonds for her children. She now worried about her children's financial future in the face of her decision to finance the initiative petition drive. She and her financial adviser decided to move the money into the stock market, investing in high-yield, risky stocks. Hill was fortunate: this was the bull market of the late 1990s, and her gamble paid off. In nine months, the return on her investment paid for almost the entire campaign.[66]

Undaunted by the lack of financial support from her erstwhile allies, Hill plunged ahead. Toward the end of February, Hill and her Open '98 committee hired professional petition circulators and agreed to pay them fifty cents a signature. But this created a new set of problems. Hill was paying and supervising the petition circulators herself, a huge managerial job that consumed her time and energy. Complicating her oversight of the petition circulators was the threat of new burdensome bookkeeping tasks, required to avoid charges of fraud.[67] By late February, it had become clear to Hill that the job of running the initiative petition drive—overseeing the media events, supervising the signature-gatherers, keeping the financial records and administrative books—was too much for one person, even with the help of her Open '98 committee. Hill proposed to the committee that she should hire a petition manager to oversee the day-to-day activities of the initiative drive. The committee readily agreed.

Donna Harris, the person eventually hired, Hill credited with turning the whole initiative drive around and was key to getting Initiative 46 qualified for the November ballot. Hill and Harris liked each other from their first meeting in a Portland restaurant. Although Harris herself was not a member of the adoption triad, her business partner, Parker Bell, was an adoptee. The two women had much in common. Both were single mothers with a teenage child. Hill never finished college; Harris, too, had never earned a degree, although she had attended several Oregon community colleges. Neither had pursued a career in her youth. Harris had worked sporadically as a secretary and at different psychiatric hospitals in entry-level positions. "I never found anything I liked," she said.[68] Also like Hill, but more deeply involved, Harris was a political activist. Politics was her passion. She laughingly sums up her college days by saying, "I kind of neglected my grades while I was saving the world." In 1991, at age thirty, while student body president of Portland Community College's Southwest Campus, Harris had run a statewide initiative campaign to get a new library built at the main campus. She and her signature gatherers collected 80,000 signatures in three months. The following year, she worked on the "Save the Salmon" initiative to ban gill-net fishing in the Columbia River.

In 1995, Harris went to work for Bill Sizemore's group, Oregon Taxpayers United. Like Hill, Harris was an optimist, though unlike Hill she was young and gullible. She believed media stories that painted Sizemore as the Robin Hood of Oregon, saving the elderly from high property taxes, and considered it a giant step up in the political world to be counted as one of Sizemore's loyalists. Harris worked long and hard on five initiatives and one referendum for Sizemore, qualifying three initiatives and the referendum for the ballot.[69] By her own account, some of the initiatives, like property tax relief, were easy to qualify because "everyone wanted their taxes lowered."

But others, like the initiative that would prohibit public employee unions from raising political money via paycheck deductions, she found stressful to work on. Harris received death threats while running the union dues initiative; in retrospect, she regretted her involvement. In addition, the longer she worked for Sizemore, the less she admired him. As she recalled later, "Instead of being Robin Hood, I found him to be more like the Sheriff [of Nottingham]." Disillusioned, Harris left Sizemore after the 1996 election campaign and started her own company, Creative Campaigns.[70] When she applied for jobs with liberal initiative campaigns, however, her past employment with the conservative Sizemore haunted her. Harris believed that she was turned down repeatedly because of her past employment: she might be a Sizemore spy who would sabotage the campaign. Thus it was that in January 1998, at the start of the initiative drive season, that Harris was in the office of the secretary of state, flipping through the initiative log, looking for a campaign she would be interested in working on. Among the few letters she sent out offering her services was one addressed to Helen Hill.

Hill responded. The two met and they talked intensely at the Portland restaurant, with Linda Corbin and Parker Bell in attendance. Hill immediately established "a real bond" with Harris and after the meeting said to Corbin about Harris and Bell, "I really like those folks." Corbin agreed. Hill had a gut feeling that "these were real people, they weren't some slimy business money-heads." Shortly thereafter, they signed a contract giving Harris a salary of $5,000 a month for the five months left in the petition drive, plus ten cents a signature.[71] Hill would later give Harris a bonus of $5,000 at the end of the initiative petition drive.

Despite her strongly positive first impression, Hill needed to develop a sense of trust in Harris; after all, they were strangers, and a lot was riding on Harris's shoulders. Harris earned Hill's trust through her intensity and devotion to the cause of adoption rights. She took her responsibilities very seriously; she felt that Hill was entrusting her not only with the money to run the initiative petition drive but also the hopes and dreams of all the people who were counting on them to qualify the initiative. Harris remembers wondering, "What if I failed on my end? That was very motivating." She received phone calls constantly from adoptees wishing her good luck. Many would add, "I hope you get on the ballot because I want my birth certificate." The same sentiments greeted Harris when she went out collecting signatures. Voters would say, "Oh, I'm adopted," and "Thank you so much." Harris felt responsible not only to Hill but also to "it seemed liked half the state."

Most of all, Harris earned Hill's trust by the results she soon delivered. Harris received no orders or directions; Hill left the nuts and bolts of the initiative petition drive to the more experienced Harris, who had her own two-pronged strategy for running the campaign. One of Harris's smartest ideas was to stop concentrating on heavily populated Multnomah County, especially the Portland area, which was very competitive and thus more expensive for gathering signatures. Instead, she concentrated on collecting signatures from every county in Oregon. Harris believed that the campaign for votes began not after the initiative qualified for the ballot but the minute the petition drive began. She reasoned that since signature gatherers spent time explaining the issue to voters who signed the petitions, those voters were won over during the initiative qualifying process itself.

Harris chose five experienced and energetic signature gatherers she knew personally and sent them with others around the state. Some of the experienced petition circulators pulled in over 1,000 signatures a week, an extraordinary number. There were bad periods also. One week, the petition circulators collected only 6,000 signatures. The next week, however, they got 15,000 and the next, 19,000. Harris recalls that through good times and bad Hill was always there, "very encouraging and motivating." When the secretary of state verified the signatures, only 30 percent came from Multnomah County, and voters from thirty-five of Oregon's thirty-six counties were represented. The petition drive had undoubtedly been carried on with more efficiency and less cost because it was easier to obtain signatures from outside Multnomah County.

The second prong of Harris's strategy was to plan on submitting the signatures two months ahead of the state's July 2 deadline. Oregon's election law mandated that once 100 percent of the required number of signatures had been collected—in the case of Initiative 46, that was at least 73,261—the chief petitioner must submit them to the Elections Division of the secretary of state's office for verification. Signature sheets had to be sorted into separate stacks by county, each numbered sequentially. After receiving the signature sheets, the Elections Division would verify the signatures through a statistical sampling procedure to determine whether the initiative contained enough valid ones to qualify for the ballot.[72] One reason that Harris wanted to submit signatures early was to avoid the terrible stress that accompanied the frenzy of collecting signatures up until that last week and then dashing off to the secretary of state's office, as she had been forced to do in the past. More importantly, she had participated in petition drives where the secretary of state had disqualified the initiative for the ballot because an insufficient number of the signatures were deemed valid. It was a sickening feeling after working so hard. But Oregon's election law permitted signatures for an initiative to be submitted early, with collecting of signatures allowed to continue while the verification process went forward.[73] Submitting their signatures early would be a great advantage for Initiative 46 advocates; they would find out before the deadline what their validity rate was and have the opportunity to make up the difference, if they had to.

On Thursday morning, May 22, Hill walked beside Max, the campaign mascot, who was pulling a wagon loaded with petitions bearing 86,422 signatures up the ramp to the state capitol for verification at the Elections Division of the secretary of state's office.[74] It was the first submission for the November ballot and took political experts by surprise. Most had expected Bill Sizemore, the political pro, not Helen Hill, the rookie, to file first.[75] The next day, Harris sent six paid petition circulators and some volunteers out to collect more signatures. Harris and Hill were in constant communication, sometimes two or three times a day. Harris's admiration for Hill's hard work and determination increased as the campaign wore on. Hill found Harris's intense devotion inspiring. By then, Harris had become so committed to the cause of adoptee rights and to Hill personally that, she recalls, "[I] never felt like I could do enough for the campaign. If I worked twelve hours in one day on the campaign, I always felt guilty if I didn't do more."

For the next month everyone involved in the petition drive waited nervously to hear from the secretary of state's office. Adding to Hill's worries was news from Delores Teller that the legal counsel of the American Adoption Congress (AAC), Fredrick F. Greenman, had some concerns about Initiative 46. Hill e-mailed Greenman, requesting an opportunity to discuss the initiative with him.[76] Greenman, a partner in the firm Deutsch Klagsbrun & Blasband, who had reunited eight years earlier with his out-of-wedlock daughter, was a strong advocate of adoption reform. He donated his time to the AAC and was the senior attorney on the legal team fighting to open adoption records in Tennessee via *Doe v. Sundquist.*[77] Greenman called Hill and then wrote her confirming his discouraging news: he had recommended that "the AAC should not participate in the petition process." It was not a matter of the ultimate goal of the initiative—to open original birth certificates to adult adoptees. Both Hill and the AAC were in agreement about that. Rather the AAC had serious doubts about Hill's tactics. Greenman said that the AAC worried that the initiative "will be vulnerable to appeals to prejudice and dishonest sound bites, and a possible loss may damage adoption reform" at the national level. In short, the damage that could be done by a highly publicized defeat of an initiative campaign run by amateurs outweighed the potential gain. Nevertheless, Greenman assured Hill that if Initiative 46 qualified for the ballot, the AAC would support it and he personally would be glad to help in any way he could.[78]

But the bad news from the AAC faded quickly. Hill and Harris soon had a much more serious matter to worry about. On June 19, Secretary of State Phil Keisling issued a news release announcing that Initiative 46's "petition currently *does not* contain enough valid signatures to gain ballot access."[79] They were short by 4,554 signatures—6.2 percent of the 73,261 needed. Harris's petition circulators, who had been collecting signatures for several weeks, now went into high gear, picking up an additional 8,858 signatures, which Hill turned in to the Elections Division on July 2.[80]

Reporting back to Bastard Nation on her "day in the trenches," Hill described her "highs and lows." The state's "papers and radio stations and television stations" were swarming over the chief petitioners; an interview Hill gave, in which she emphasized civil rights, aired twice that evening on Oregon Public Broadcasting. She also took part in a TV interview with an adoptee and her adoptive mother about the initiative that ran later that week on the five o'clock news. But the effort to qualify the initiative had came at a high price. Hill wrote: "Folks, I'm so excited I can't sleep. I have no stomach left from worrying about it all, these last few weeks. . . . I'm a total burnt out noodle of a shadow of my former self . . . gads how can folks do this shit for a living?" Hill also expressed conflicting views on whether Initiative 46 would make the ballot. On the one hand, she expressed confidence that "we KNOW we are on" even thought she knew she was "a real rookie" and therefore found it difficult to figure out the timing of things. On the other hand, Hill expressed doubts: "Just knowing everything is a done deal, all signatures are handed in and there is no chance to hand in any more, that's scary. Though we covered our bases well and have been told 'unofficially' that we are on, still, I want that official letter."[81] Hill need not have worried. The extra signatures proved to be more than enough. On July 9, Hill triumphantly announced to the press that the adoptee rights initiative had officially qualified for the November 3 ballot.[82]

Helen Hill had accomplished what few had thought possible. But this was only the first step. Now came the electoral campaign itself. Hill appointed her comrade-in-arms Harris as campaign manager. They would soon find themselves under constant attack by what felt like relentless opposition from almost every sector of society.

5

The Rise of the Opposition

The supporters of Measure 58 were not surprised by the opposition to the initiative; the idea of opening adoption records has long been controversial.[1] The opposition group that Helen Hill and Shea Grimm feared most was the National Council for Adoption (NCFA).[2] Founded in 1980, the NCFA was a nonprofit, nonsectarian organization originally made up of sixty adoption agencies. It soon became the fiercest, most effective opponent of opening adoption records through its legislative lobbying to block state laws that sought to liberalize adoption records statutes.[3] The organization's success at thwarting open adoption records legislation was due to the NCFA founding president and strategist-in-chief, forty-four-year-old William L. Pierce. Born and raised in Nebraska, Pierce graduated with honors in 1958 from Benedictine College in Atchison, Kansas, and after a variety of jobs—insurance broker, stockbroker, columnist, newsletter editor—found his vocation in social welfare and child care. In 1966, in the midst of President Lyndon B. Johnson's Great Society, Pierce became the director of Statewide Neighborhood Youth Corps, a part of Iowa's Office of Economic Opportunity. Four years later, Pierce joined the prestigious Child Welfare League of America (CWLA) as the director of a day care project because, he says, he was "outraged at the failure of the child welfare field to stick to decent standards." With the merger of the Florence Crittenton adoption organization into the CWLA, Pierce became immersed in adoption issues, visiting the organization's branches and publishing its monthly newsletter. During his ten-year stay at the CWLA he would rise to its second highest position, associate director.[4]

The original purpose of the NCFA was to oppose the Department of Health, Education, and Welfare's Draft Model State Adoption Act, which had been published on February 15, 1980. NCFA officials singled out three provisions: one that would retroactively open sealed adoption records; one that gave unmarried fathers rights to thwart the placement of his child; and one that legalized "independent"—nonagency—adoption, an adoption accomplished by a doctor or lawyer. These three sections of the Draft Model State Adoption Act, Pierce and NCFA officials believed, constituted a radical threat to

William L. Pierce, president of the
National Council for Adoption,
which tried to aid groups opposed to
Measure 58.

adoption practice and policy in the United States. In setting forth NCFA's ten goals, the group's founders made number two "to make the Federal 'Model State Adoption Act' acceptable or stop it."[5] Beginning his operations in the increasingly conservative climate during the new political administration of President Ronald Reagan, Pierce, at the head of NCFA's lobbying effort, had been quite successful in striking the offending passages from the revised act, which was made to emphasize adoption for special-needs children, the original charge from Congress.

For the next two decades, adoption reform leaders, as well as the rank and file, would see Pierce's fingerprints, real or imagined, on pending state legislation to open adoption records. Bills that seemed destined for passage somehow lost their sponsors or never came out of committee; sudden amendments were added that gutted a bill's meaning; meeting rooms and times were mysteriously changed so key witnesses were not present to testify, making a bill go down in defeat.[6] Oregon, they hoped, would be different. Still, they worried. Even before Helen Hill took pen to paper and with the assistance of Shea Grimm wrote Initiative 46 back in July 1997, Hill wanted to keep news of the measure quiet because she was "afraid of attracting the NCFA . . . guys before we have a nest of $$$, a group of dedicated petitioners, and a healthy base of signatures."[7]

Hill and Grimm's instincts were good, but their fears were unfounded. By February 1998, Pierce and the NCFA were aware that "a petition drive was under way" in Oregon to open adoption records. But the NCFA was too busy with other activities to become involved in Oregon. When Measure 46 came up at NCFA's board meeting it was placed on the "non-action items for discussion" part of the agenda. Pierce, however, was alarmed by the failure of the board to take a more active role. He warned, "chances are that those who want a ballot measure will buy enough signatures to force a vote. This will be a new and expensive challenge to NCFA." He suggested that the NCFA might have to mount a "a counter-campaign."[8] But although Pierce would increase the number of his inquiries about the initiative in June 1998, the NCFA did not send any resources or operatives to Oregon until early October of that year. In effect, first Initiative 46 and then Measure 58 would be allowed to grow and flourish while the NCFA was busy with a multitude of other projects, ranging from tax-subsidized adoption legal cases and international adoption to opposing court-enforced visitation and recruiting new agencies to join its organization.[9]

Likewise, Portland attorney Warren C. Deras had been caught unawares when the secretary of state certified Initiative 46 for the November 3 ballot. "The next thing I read in the paper," he recalled, "the signatures had been filed for this measure, and lo and behold it looks like there's a real serious thing happening here, which was a surprise."[10] Deras would not be caught napping again.

The next step after certification was for the secretary of state to appoint a five-person committee to write the *Voters' Pamphlet* explanatory statement.[11] The committee wrote a draft explanatory statement, which, like the draft ballot title, was circulated to the state legislature, the state capitol Press Room, and individuals on the secretary of state's subscription mailing list (this included Deras). On July 29, 1998, the committee held a hearing at the state capitol in Salem to receive comments. Deras was one of the few who showed up. He expressed concern over what he saw as the inaccuracy of the draft explanatory statement. He charged that it incorrectly stated Oregon law, failed to explain the legal context in which the initiative operated, and did not identify what he believed to be the initiative's primary objective: "to allow [the] adopted person to find out the identities of their birth parents."[12] Deras's comments fell on deaf ears. On August 3, adoption attorney and committee member Catherine Dexter faxed Deras the final version of the explanatory statement for the *Voter's Pamphlet:*

> This measure changes existing law to allow an adopted person 21 years of age or older to obtain a copy of the person's original birth certificate. Current Oregon law prohibits the release of an original birth certificate which may provide birth information to an adopted person without a

court order. The law currently requires that upon receipt of a decree of adoption or a report of adoption from a court, the state registrar shall issue a new birth certificate unless the court, the adoptive parents or the adopted person requests otherwise. The new birth certificate may not provide accurate birth information and the original birth certificate shall not be subject to inspection except by court order.

This measure requires that upon receipt of a written application the state registrar shall provide a copy of the original birth certificate which may provide accurate birth information to an Oregon born adopted person 21 years of age or older. This measure requires that the procedures, filing fees and waiting periods for certified copies of original birth certificates be the same for requests by adopted persons as for non-adopted persons.

This measure applies to persons adopted in the past or in the future. There are no exceptions to this measure.[13]

Deras, still troubled by the wording, decided not to let the matter rest. Final *Voters' Pamphlet* explanatory statements were reviewable by the Oregon Supreme Court. Once an explanatory statement was written, Oregon law permits any dissatisfied person to petition the state Supreme Court to correct an explanation that is not impartial, simple, understandable, or accurate.[14] On August 5, Deras sought allies in this enterprise, but his friends at Oregon Right to Life, the largest anti-abortion group in the state, had decided not to take "a stand either way" on Measure 58 and declined to participate.[15] Similarly, Robert J. Castagna, attorney for the Catholic Archdiocese, was in agreement with Catholic Charities' policy recommendation of neutrality on Measure 58 and was uninterested in petitioning the Supreme Court.[16] As a result, Deras was alone in filing a contest to the explanatory statement. He did not have high expectations of success. The standard for review was very limited. If the explanatory statement substantially complied with the statute, even though it in no way was the best explanatory statement there could be, the Supreme Court customarily refused to intervene and change it. But Deras felt he had to do something about the explanatory statement, which he considered one of the most persuasive devices in the initiative campaign's arsenal. He later recalled himself thinking at the time: "Gee, that's so awful and so politically disastrous, if that's in the *Voters' Pamphlet,* we've got to take a shot at trying to fix it. And I took a shot."[17]

Deras found himself racing against the clock. He had received Measure 58's explanatory statement from Dexter on Thursday, August 3; the Supreme Court challenge had to be filed by Monday, August 7. Working feverishly, Deras finished his brief that Sunday night. In the memorandum of the oral argument that Deras delivered before the Court, he argued that the "fundamental problem" he had with the explanatory statement was its inaccuracy. It did not "correctly explain the difference between an original birth certificate of an adoptee and the amended birth certificate." Instead, it stated that the amended birth certificate "may not provide accurate birth information" and the original birth certificate "may provide accurate birth information." Deras emphatically denied that this was the difference between the two birth certificates and labeled the description of the amended certificate "a loaded pejorative" because it falsely described the amended birth certificate as not accurate. The amended birth certificate, he argued, had to be filled out according to existing Oregon statutes, which left no justification for suggesting that it contained inaccurate information. The explanatory statement also claimed twice that the only way a birth certificate could be released was through a court order. Deras disputed the accuracy of this claim, noting that Oregon law "expressly provides for access to original birth records by agencies operating voluntary adoption registries." He proposed an entirely new explanatory statement, which emphasized that Measure 58 violated the statutory right to privacy and was unconstitutional because it violated the secrecy provisions of adoption records.[18]

At first, Hill and Grimm did not take Deras's challenge to the explanatory statement seriously. Why should they? Except for an article and a letter to the editor or two during the initiative petition drive, there had been hardly any serious opposition to Measure 58. Two months before Deras filed his lawsuit against the explanatory statement, an event had occurred that reinforced their optimism. In June 1998, after doing her first morning talk-radio show from Portland, Hill excitedly sent an e-mail message to Bastard Nation that the show's moderator "had tried to get someone to speak in opposition to the measure and they couldn't find anyone!" She added that the show had been a huge success.[19] But two weeks later, almost as an omen of the difficulties that lay in the future, Hill had "the world's worst talk radio show experience" that an adopted adult ever had, she reported, with a hostile talk-show host, hostile callers, and insufficient time to reply.[20]

When Grimm heard about Deras's "lawsuit" from Hill, she tried to remain upbeat. Grimm was not even sure if it was a serious threat; she felt there was a possibility that the Oregon Supreme Court might not hear the case until after the election or might dismiss it outright. Still, Grimm worried; at the very least, the measure's supporters would find Deras's action "very distracting." She was suspicious of Deras's motivation, concluding, "I simply have to believe that Warren is tied to the NCFA in some way. He's been on our ass since Day 1." BN leaders could not believe that there might be opposition to Measure 58 from citizens independent of the NCFA.[21]

Nevertheless, Hill and Grimm could not ignore the legal challenge to the explanatory statement. Deras had to be taken seriously. By August 13, Hill, with help from Grimm, had hammered out a memorandum in opposition to Deras's petition, countering him at almost every point.[22] She denied Deras's basic claim that the explanatory statement was inaccurate, grounding her argument in the right of privacy that the "Oregon Revised Statutes, the Oregon Bill of Rights, the Oregon Constitution or the U.S. Federal Constitution expressly recognized." Hill continued her attack. Citing as her authority the recently decided case in the Sixth Federal Court of Appeals, *Doe v. Sundquist* (1997), which, with a contact veto, gave adopted adults in Tennessee access to their original birth certificates, Hill declared that the right of secrecy that Deras claimed was "constitutionally nonexistent."[23]

Shea Grimm also denied that the explanatory statement was "potentially misleading," noting the balanced nature of the committee of five and its procedural fairness and responsiveness to the public. She argued strenuously that both original and amended birth certificates were characterized by inaccurate information, and found Deras's discussion of adoption reunion registries "irrelevant."[24] After filing their memoranda, both Hill and Grimm had to prepare to make brief oral arguments before the Oregon Supreme Court on August 18.

Deras, too, had to prepare for the oral argument before the high bench on August 18. He also had to complete two crucial tasks for opposing Measure 58, which were due in the secretary of state's office before the deadline of 5 P.M. on August 25.[25] He needed to write a statement against Measure 58 that would be placed in the *Voters' Pamphlet*. Casting about for allies, he contacted the Boys and Girls Aid Society of Oregon (BGAS). Founded in 1885, it was the oldest, largest, and most respected adoption agency in the state. As he explained to BGAS social worker Evelyn Lamb, the statement could be filed by individuals or committees, but it had to be accompanied either by a fee of $300 or a petition with 1,000 signatures of registered Oregon voters.[26] Deras was enthusiastic about the potential his *Voters' Pamphlet* arguments would have for defeating Measure 58. He believed that "the *Voters' Pamphlet* was tremendously influential among Oregon voters as a source of information on candidates and measures. You've got to be in the *Voters' Pamphlet* to be serious."[27]

The other task facing Deras before the August 25 deadline was to form a political committee to oppose Measure 58. Deras set up a meeting with the BGAS. There he found himself speaking to an interested and sympathetic audience. The BGAS's involvement in public advocacy was not surprising. All through the first half of the twentieth century and into the 1960s (when the agency was the first in the United States to engage in transracial adoption) the BGAS had been a national leader in adoption policy and practice.[28] BGAS executive directors wrote legislation, testified as expert witnesses, and introduced laws. However, with the increasing use of ballot initiatives in public policy areas, the BGAS's influence had waned. In 1992, under the leadership of Executive Director Michael H. Balter, the BGAS would undergo a total reorganization, recommiting itself to public advocacy in the political arena against poverty, racism, and sexism, which the organization believed to be the deeper social forces responsible for blighted communities and damaged children. This new policy proved hard to put into practice. In several attempts to advocate for divisive ballot initiatives, BGAS personnel were unable to agree among themselves on a position; when they did agree, they often discovered that the agency did not have the financial resources or infrastructure to mount an effective campaign. Still, Balter, the board of directors, and agency personnel believed that advocating for public policy was part of being a professional social worker.[29]

As he appeared before the BGAS, Deras was unaware that the agency had paid close attention to Initiative 46 and during the initiative petition drive had began a long internal conversation about the initiative. As the oldest adoption agency in the state, involved in tens of thousands of confidential adoptions, Balter believed that BGAS had "a unique point of view that would or should be listened to." By March 1998, the BGAS had formed an internal committee led by eight-year veteran social worker Nancy P. Simpson, manager of the Adoption Unit, asking the question "Should we be taking a stand on Measure 46?"[30] The answer would take months to decide: participatory advocacy took time; all of the agency's personnel had to be consulted and a consensus arrived at; and then the decision had to be brought before a meeting of the board of directors, which met on a quarterly basis.

One of the first groups to meet to discuss whether the BGAS should take a stand against Initiative 46 was its Adoption Unit. The immediate response to the initiative among the adoption workers was negative; they questioned both the merits of the initiative and Helen Hill's motivation. In a memo circulated to BGAS personnel, Lauren Greenbaum and Lynn Schroeder, both members of the Adoption Unit, outlined their case. They wrote, "A woman named Helen Hill has been gathering signatures to a measure on the ballot that would immediately open all adoptees' birth certificates. She has been unwilling to send a copy of the measure to the agency, once it became clear that we were not in support of her agenda." They also stated that "Ms. Hill was not open to discussing the rights of birthparents or the availability of search services. She insists this issue is around civil rights not search laws."

Nancy P. Simpson (left), manager of the Adoption Unit of the Boys and Girls
Aid Society of Oregon.

Greenbaum and Schroeder wondered "if she may have a hidden agenda
around birthparents who refuse to meet under current search laws." Still,
according to the memo, the real problem was not Hill's motives, but that the
initiative established "no guidelines for birthparents to refuse to have their
names revealed nor would it allow birthparents to have the same access to
the information as adoptees would have." The two adoption workers also
denounced the initiative for not mentioning the history of adoption:
"specifically, birthparents of 20, 30, or 40 years ago were assured that their
privacy would be protected and many still wish that it continue to be." They
concluded that "it would be devastating if this measure were to pass."[31]
Clearly, at least at this stage, the BGAS Adoption Unit was adamantly
opposed to Helen Hill and Initiative 46.

Part of the BGAS's internal development and public advocacy process,
however, was to understand all points of view, which meant, according to Balter, that you invited and listened to people you disagreed with. Rather than
relying on Initiative 46 brochures to develop an opinion about the initiative,
Balter believed it was important to hear directly from Helen Hill or her representative. He hoped that bringing Hill in to speak would begin a process of
identifying where there existed mutual points of agreement between the BGAS
and initiative advocates and where exactly the two disagreed. Balter also

Lauren Greenbaum, lead adoption
clinician of the Boys and Girls Aid
Society of Oregon.

hoped to clear up some questions about Bastard Nation's involvement in what
he and other BGAS personnel considered outrageous actions, such as calling
birth mothers "birth whores."

In April 1998, Hill spoke to the Adoption Unit and other interested BGAS
members. Hill was a very effective speaker. Putting a human face to the cause
of open adoption records resulted in many of those in the audience finding
the cause more reasonable. They also began to understand that if certain individuals within Bastard Nation used language like "birth whores," it did not
necessarily mean that Hill and the members of her campaign endorsed it.
Bringing in Hill to speak also proved to be a crucial step toward moving the
BGAS away from its oppositional way of thinking about Initiative 46 and to
get back to its "best practice child welfare orientation." Or, as Balter said, it
made the agency focus on the question "how does public policy get made,
rather than 'this is no good because Helen is nuts.' "[32] She clearly was not.

In addition, the BGAS manifested a second form of involvement with Initiative 46 by reaching out to Oregon's other adoption agencies. Balter did not
believe that public policy was made or "executed by lone rangers, either as
individuals or as institutions." He modestly discounted the BGAS's influence:
"We may think we are very important but most of the larger society is going
to say 'Who?' " His instinctive tendency, from an institutional point of view,
was to look for allies to support the BGAS's opposition to the initiative.[33] In
Oregon, most of the major adoption agencies belonged to an umbrella organ-

ization known as the Coalition of Oregon Adoption Agencies (the Coalition), which was made up of about twenty-nine agencies.[34] In May, Balter brought the issue before the Coalition, seeking support for placing a statement against the initiative in the *Voters' Pamphlet*. The ensuing discussion was heated. In the end, the Coalition voted down the BGAS's motion and decided to remain neutral. The reasons for the decision were complex, but they essentially resulted from the revolutionary demographic and social changes that had been going on in American adoption during the prior thirty years. Many older, established adoption agencies were inactive or were shutting down. In their place, and present at the Coalition's meeting were agencies that specialized in international adoptions or open adoption, or agencies that simply felt it unwise to take a public stand on a divisive issue. But the Coalition's vote was only a temporary setback for the BGAS. By July, when Initiative 46 qualified for the November ballot, there was no question that the BGAS would oppose the initiative. It just was unsure how to do it openly, because it still needed its board's approval.[35]

Then Deras entered the picture. At the August meeting, Deras expressed concern about Measure 58 and the apparent lack of any overt opposition to it. He wanted to know what the BGAS was going to do. Deras felt that the BGAS had existed for a long time and was respected in the community, and that adoption professionals would provide a stronger voice in opposing Measure 58 than his would.[36] To make their voice heard, Deras explained, he would contribute $300 to offset the fee for the *Voters' Pamphlet* statement. Deras also asked whether they would be interested in setting up a political committee. The importance of such a committee, he outlined, was twofold. First, not a penny could be raised in an Oregon political campaign without forming and registering a political committee with the secretary of state (like the one Helen Hill formed prior to starting the initiative petition drive in August 1997). Second, a political committee gave one visibility, an identity, and an entity for followers to rally around and support. Without a political committee, an opposition campaign was often leaderless, amorphous, and ineffective.[37] Nancy Simpson remembers the group's looking around almost in wonder and thinking, "Oh my God, this could be something big!" The opportunity had been totally unanticipated. Deras stated that he would assume the duties of treasurer, do all the legal work, and file the financial reports with the state. His goal was to enlist the BGAS in the ranks of the opposition to Measure 58.[38] He was unaware that the BGAS was just then looking for a means by which its people could oppose the initiative and yet not be openly identified as part of the agency.[39]

Deras found the BGAS members maddeningly slow in making up their minds on whether they were going to form a political committee. He thought they were free agents and did not realize, nor was he told, how deeply Simpson and the others were enmeshed in the BGAS structure of participatory advocacy. Also unknown to Deras, neither Simpson nor the Adoption Unit had the authority to speak for the entire organization. For her part, even though Simpson knew that Deras's offer was the answer to the BGAS's dilemma of what to do about Measure 58 while waiting for the board to give its approval (which could not take place until September), she had to bring the proposal back to the agency for internal debate and approval.[40] When Deras finally received approval from Simpson and members of BGAS's Adoption Unit, it was the day before the August 25 deadline. Deras ended up literally faxing the paperwork to the secretary of state's office to get it in on time.[41] Deras named the political committee Concerned Adoption Professionals (CAP), with himself as treasurer and the BGAS's Nancy Simpson director.[42]

Just twenty-four hours later, Deras's life became even busier. Word had gotten out that Deras was the point man for the opposition to Measure 58, and he was inundated with phone calls and faxes. On August 25, Judith Van-Duzar of the League of Women Voters Guide Committee gave Deras thirty-six minutes to choose a group of statements in opposition to Measure 58 that were acceptable to him for the group's planned Mock Election video. Van-Duzar warned him that it was his only chance to have any input into the video program. The League of Women Voters also wanted him to vet its arguments for their own *Voters' Pamphlet,* which the organization issued every election year.[43] Despite the time pressure, Deras was happy to oblige.

Two days later, on August 27, the Oregon Supreme Court handed down a decision modifying Measure 58's explanatory statement. Overall, Deras viewed it as a victory. The Court held that, as Deras had argued, the explanatory statement's references to the relative accuracy of the original birth certificate and the adoptee's amended certificate were defective and that the explanatory statement's description of current law was insufficient. In the 6–1 decision, Judge Michael W. Gillette, writing for the majority, noted that the purpose of the measure was to make the original birth certificate available to adult adopted persons; the accuracy or inaccuracy of either the original or amended birth certificate was irrelevant to the measure's purpose. He also stated what Deras argued, and Hill and Grimm had conceded: that the sentence: "Current Oregon law prohibits the release of an original birth certificate which may provide birth information to an adopted person without a court order" was insufficient because Oregon law provided such information to adoption agencies that operated voluntary adoption registries. The Court's solution to the insufficiency of the sentence was to strike the words "which may provide birth information" from the sentence and insert the word "such" after the word "to" so that the sentence read: "Current Oregon law prohibits the release of an original birth certificate to such an adopted person without a court order."[44] The Court certified the following explanatory statement as modified on Measure 58 for inclusion in the *Voters' Pamphlet:*

> This measure changes existing law to allow an adopted person 21 years of age or older to obtain a copy of the person's original birth certificate. Current Oregon law prohibits the release of an original birth certificate ~~which may provide birth information~~ to such an adopted person without a court order. The law currently requires that upon receipt of a decree of adoption or a report of adoption from a court, the state registrar shall issue a new birth certificate unless the court, the adoptive parents or the adopted person requests otherwise. ~~The new birth certificate may not provide accurate birth information and the original birth certificate shall not be subject to inspection by court order.~~
>
> This measure requires that upon receipt of a written application the state registrar shall provide a copy of the original birth certificate ~~which may provide accurate birth information~~ to an Oregon born adopted person 21 years of age or older. This measure requires that the procedures, filing fees and waiting periods for certified copies of original birth certificates be the same for requests by adopted persons as for non-adopted persons.
>
> This measure applies to persons adopted in the past or in the future. There are no exceptions to this measure.[45]

Deras was pleased by the news that the Court had concluded that "two of petitioner's arguments are well taken." Announcing the decision to the BGAS's adoption lead clinician, Lauren Greenbaum, he noted that "the Court took the critical action I wanted, deleting the 'accurate' vs. 'not accurate' distinction." Although he was disappointed that the Court did not substitute anything, such as voluntary adoption registries, as an option that existed for adoptees to gain access to their birth information, he explained to Greenbaum that the Court's inaction was due to its reluctance to get involved in the political process. It did not surprise him, and he cited Judge Robert D. Durham's dissent as evidence. In any case, it did not matter because Concerned Adoption Professionals would make those arguments and explain the differences between the two types of birth certificates, "if the average voter reads that far." What was important was the victory in Court: "We got what we needed," he said.[46]

But Shea Grimm recognized, rightly, that the Court's decision was a victory without substance for the opposition. Although the Court sided with

Deras in modifying two sentences of the explanatory statement, Grimm noted that the end result was actually to the supporters' advantage. The Court's refusal to add Deras's argument about voluntary adoption registries to the explanatory statement left the committee's draft intact. The changes simply made its purpose clearer to the voter. In fact, Grimm could not help gloating to Patty Wentz of *Willamette Week* that the Court had found Deras's arguments on these issues "not well taken."[47] She felt that Deras had suffered a clear defeat, which he failed to recognize.

Concerned Adoption Professionals would prove a remarkably weak and ineffective political committee. In the age of the Internet, it remained technologically behind the times, never even having its own Website. Deras was content to use Bastard Nation's Website, <www.plumsite.com/oregon>, which he viewed as merely a free clipping service for newspaper editorials.[48] Nor when he was organizing CAP and constructing arguments for the *Voters' Pamphlet* did Deras ever solicit large sums of money or elite political support, two imperatives if a ballot initiative was to win, or be successfully opposed, at the polls.[49] His initial instinct had been to approach Oregon's religious and social institutions that he perceived as being supportive of confidentiality in adoption—for example, Oregon Right to Life, Catholic Charities, and the Boys and Girls Aid Society of Oregon—rather than political figures. Nevertheless, he must have been gratified that, almost immediately after the Oregon Supreme Court's decision in late August, first-term Democratic governor John A. Kitzhaber, dubbed "Dr. No" for the record number of bills he vetoed at the previous session of the legislature, came out in opposition to Measure 58. Kitzhaber's aide attributed the governor's hostility to the measure to the fear that it would make women less willing to place children for adoption.[50]

Most Measure 58 advocates denounced Deras as a fanatic, but in reality he was less a true believer than a concerned adoptive parent and a dedicated citizen who used his legal skills to oppose an initiative he strongly disagreed with. He was politically and financially conservative, and it showed in the way that he ran the campaign against Measure 58. The campaign Concerned Adoption Professionals waged against Measure 58 was conceptually small; Deras sought neither a mass base of supporters nor a large number of contributors. The total membership of CAP was never more than twelve, and most of them came from the BGAS, with the addition of a few adoption lawyers, most of whom were Deras's personal friends. Although friends and associates promised to contribute $50 or $100 at one time or another, somehow the money never came through. Deras never contemplated running a conventional campaign based on media ads and big money. He explicitly ruled out direct advertising because of a lack of funds, and he restricted CAP's budget to $500.[51] Deras may thus be seen as old-fashioned, a gentlemanly throwback to another era.

Personally, Deras was not a charismatic leader. He was honorable, intelligent, self-effacing, hard-working, highly moral, and scrupulously honest, but he preferred his administrative role as the treasurer of Concerned Adoption Professionals to the idea of asserting himself as the powerful head, or spokesman, of the group. As BGAS adoption worker Nancy Simpson later observed, "We did not find a dynamic leader; he was not a passionate person, and we were very passionate about this."[52] His commitment to adoption law and the protection of birth mothers' privacy had thrust Deras forward to sound the alarm against Measure 58, write comments to Oregon's attorney general, petition the Oregon Supreme Court, and prod citizens to organize against Measure 58 in a political committee. Principle and deadlines explain Deras's prominence in the early months of the campaign against Measure 58. But in his heart of hearts, Deras was uncomfortable in that leadership role. He viewed his role as treasurer as telling CAP members "what the schedules were, filing the forms that had to be filed. But I didn't want to intrude upon the policy side of how the argument [that went into the *Voters' Pamphlet*] should be based."[53] He did not like appearing in the spotlight. He did almost no public campaigning against Measure 58 and regularly refused to appear before the media. When asked to come down to a radio booth or TV studio—and he often was—Deras passed the request on to someone in the BGAS, much to the annoyance of the members of the Adoption Unit. They were unprepared for taking on the role of media representative and resented the time lost from their important work as adoption workers.[54] Deras became almost invisible after his appearance before the Oregon Supreme Court on August 18, except for a brief appearance on October 4 on the TV program *Town Hall,* and a published letter or two in the *Oregonian*. Instead of leading the troops, Deras reveled in administering the legal business of CAP, emphasizing its financial accountability. He took special pride in the monthly financial reports he made to the secretary of state's office, accounting for contributions and expenditures for every individual in CAP. His prime goal, which he accomplished, was to keep CAP spending below $500, thus allowing the political committee to avoid having to file a much more complicated set of documents.[55]

CAP's weak leadership, however, was not simply the result of Deras's conservative personality and financial philosophy. He guided the opposition's campaign with a strong political philosophy, which he was proud of. He believed that "the nature of a contest like this should have people on both sides who were totally unfamiliar with the political process." Deras favored grassroots democracy on both sides; but when he looked back on the Measure 58 campaign what he saw was "totally ineffective grass roots. I mean there was no effective political campaign."[56] Experts in the field have observed that grassroots movements are indeed composed of "ordinary people, the rank and file, who start and lead movements, working in concert to change things." They are trying to right wrongs, alter social norms, and change laws in a world dominated by corporations, governments, universities, and the media.[57] Thus, it was ironic that Deras viewed the opposition to Measure 58 as a grassroots movement when in fact it was headed by Oregon's leading social and religious institutions and many of its political leaders, who, like himself, were respected lawyers. What Deras meant by grass roots was that neither side put massive amounts of money into repetitive media ads—the type that win initiative campaigns. Deras also meant that because Measure 58 was not a pocketbook issue, like taxes, few people would pay attention to it. Consequently, the voters would make their decisions based on very little information. According to Deras, it was thus critical to present the small amount of information that voters would receive—the ballot title, the explanatory statement—in a way that was favorable to his side. But because he favored what he called "grassroots democracy" and simply refused to raise money for big media campaigns, he boasted that the CAP's was the more "effective campaign" financially because "we didn't waste money on direct advertising." Deras admitted that he had no choice to do otherwise, since "there wasn't enough money do an effective direct advertising campaign so you don't waste money on that" and that the adjective "effective" is relative, since Measure 58 was ultimately victorious at the ballot box and in the courts. Deras felt that the most effective use of money was to spend it on the people who directly affect voters' decisions: newspaper editorial boards.[58]

By mid-September newspaper editors were demanding that Deras send them background information on Measure 58 so that they could take a stand on the initiative.[59] According to Deras, editorial boards at election times considered the least controversial races first and built up to the important ones—with their endorsement for president of the United States published last. Initiative endorsements worked the same way: from least to most controversial. In the case of Measure 58, some of the newspapers wanted to deal with it early because they felt it was not very controversial. At the same time, Deras was receiving calls from women who had placed children for adoption but had never told their husbands and families and they were extremely anxious over the measure. One woman "in an absolute panic" phoned Deras and told him she had been raped, had relinquished the child for adoption, and now had been contacted by the adopted adult who wanted to know who the father was. Deras felt overwhelmed. He recalled, "I didn't know how to deal with this! I had the politics on one hand and these heart-wrenching calls on the other. In the meantime, I'm trying to practice law."[60] Deras pressed on and did the best he could.

Under pressure from a number of editors, including Salem's *Statesman Journal,* to meet deadlines, Deras fired off a packet of documents outlining the position of Concerned Adoption Professionals. To editorial page editor Dick Hughes of the *Statesman Journal,* he summarized the opposition's campaign in a single page entitled "Summary of Arguments against Measure 58."[61] First, it said, the initiative would "retroactively nullify promises made to thousands of Oregon women who had given up infants for adoption that their identities would remain confidential." Second, if Measure 58 were enacted future birth mothers, unable to be assured of confidentiality, would be more likely to choose against adoption in Oregon and go to another state where confidential adoption exists. This would reduce the "already limited supply of adoptable infants in Oregon to couples unable to have children." Third, all adoption records, including original birth certificates, should remain sealed in order to protect adopted adults from knowledge of traumatic circumstances, such as rape or child abuse, which may have been the reason for their adoption. Fourth, Oregon law had already mandated voluntary adoption registries, through which interested parties could have access to their adoption records, including medical information. These registries were a better solution to the problem because they respected the rights of all parties in an adoption, unlike Measure 58.[62] In short, retroactivity, reduction of the number of infants for adoption, protection of adoptees' innocence, and voluntary adoption registries were the primary reasons Deras suggested that Hughes should editorialize against Measure 58.

By the third week of September, Deras had managed to send CAP's packet of opposition arguments against Measure 58 to most of the ninety-nine daily and weekly newspaper editorial boards in the state.[63] Whereas the "Summary of Arguments against Measure 58" to the *Statesman Journal* had gone out under Deras's own name, it now went out under CAP's name. That change did not sit well with some BGAS members of CAP. On September 24, coinciding with the BGAS board of directors' long-awaited approval to the agency to oppose publicly Measure 58, Nancy Simpson and Lauren Greenbaum voiced "concerns they wanted to express" to Deras. They stated that while they clearly had the same goal of preventing the passage of Measure 58, "we prefer to keep our position separate." They did not mean to slight Deras in any way, and they were enormously grateful for all of his assistance and expertise in organizing CAP. They even looked forward to continuing to have a mutually beneficial partnership that would lead them to achieving their goal of defeating Measure 58. But they "were upset" at the document entitled "Summary of Arguments against Measure 58." They claimed that they had not previously noticed that Concerned Adoption Professionals was listed as the author of that piece. Simpson and Greenbaum admitted that they agreed with some of the arguments presented. But they made it clear that they objected to the document because the argument was "predominantly your argument rather than ours." In the future, they stated forcefully in conclusion, "we would prefer that you no longer send the summary unless it is clearly marked as information as coming from you."[64]

But there were deeper problems between the two women and Deras, ones that went to the heart of CAP's leadership and philosophy. The problems Greenbaum and Simpson had with the "Summary" brought to a head the questions over Deras's leadership and his position on closed records. The two BGAS adoption workers had had enough. They had noticed what they called "a great deal of confusion from the media personnel to whom we speak" on the issue of "whether you are speaking for Concerned Adoption Professionals." In what amounted to a declaration of independence, Simpson and Greenbaum wanted to make sure there would be no confusion in the future: "We would appreciate it if you would make clear that you are not a spokesperson for us." They conceded that it was necessary to identify Deras as treasurer of CAP, but they wondered whether it might be possible "to remove your name from the letterhead" in order to alleviate the confusion.[65] For the rest of the campaign, Greenbaum and Simpson would identify themselves not as members of Concerned Adoption Professionals, but as adoption workers from the Boys and Girls Aid Society.

What was really at issue between the two parties were "some clear philosophical differences." This was made abundantly clear in a four-and-half-page "Position Paper by Concerned Adoption Professionals" that Greenbaum and Simpson sent to Deras and requested that he include in any future mailings to newspaper editorial boards.[66] Its context was social work, not the law; its guiding principle openness, not confidentiality. The position paper reflected the BGAS's current, liberal adoption principles and practices. It favored open adoption and supported "adoptees' right to have access to information regarding their genetic heritage and birth parents' right to have information regarding the current health and happiness of their children." It enumerated the various existing options that met the needs of adoption triad members. In addition to the statewide voluntary registry for both birth parents and adoptees, there existed a process for assisted search for both birth parents and adoptees with the involvement of a trained social worker. Finally, it noted, all triad members must have the "freedom and power" to decide whether and when they might choose to disclose their identities. "No one member of the adoption triad should be able to override the rights of another member without consent." The biggest contrast between the BGAS contingent and Deras was the position paper's remarkable declaration that "the idea of opening birth certificates is a good one." Moreover, it hoped that future initiatives and legislative action would lead to the "dismantling of the current system of issuing amended birth certificates and the institution of issuing both an unaltered birth certificate and a certificate of adoption." But, the document continued, there must be some acknowledgment in the law of the way things used to be done in times past, no matter how "ridiculous at times" those old-fashioned mores seem now, and "there must be protection for the birth parents who do not want contact."[67]

Although the position paper urged Oregonians to defeat Measure 58, it never did so stridently.[68] In contrast to Deras, who clearly wanted to see the measure defeated, Concerned Adoption Professional's members from the BGAS Adoption Unit concentrated their energy on ways that Measure 58 could be amended. First, they thought "a simple addition" to Measure 58 that allowed birth parents to a contact veto by adopted adults, such as the one in place in Tennessee's recently enacted open adoption records law, was "all it would take" to protect the confidentiality of birth parents. They were refer-ring to the Contact Veto Registry, a counterbalance to Tennessee's 1995 access to adoption records law. The registry permitted parties to an adoption com-pleted after March 16, 1951, to veto contact from other parties to the adop-tion, if they wished, by registering their nonconsent. Once a party had filed a statement of consent or nonconsent, the registry had to notify the filing party whenever an adoptee requested contact. Although the Contact Veto Registry did not inhibit an adoptee's access to birth information, it did protect both adopted adult and birth parent from unwanted contact from other parties to the adoption. A person who failed to comply with a contact veto was subject to civil penalties.[69] Second, the position paper suggested that Measure 58 be amended in the event of its victory, so that it not be retroactive. Adoption made under different laws enacted at different times would still be held to the standard in place at the time the adoption occurred. In other words, original birth certificates from times past would remain sealed.[70] Five days after the release of the position paper, on September 29, the BGAS members of CAP completed a "Summary of Arguments against Ballot Measure 58," which incorporated all their arguments about openness in adoption and amendments to the initiative, including the phrase "the idea of opening birth certificates is a good one," and sent it to Deras, asking him to substitute it for his own "Ar-guments against Measure 58" and include their summary in information pack-ets sent to newspaper editorial boards.[71]

Although there were deep differences in philosophy and leadership style between BGAS members of CAP and Deras, at one level, they did little damage to the working of the group. Deras took no umbrage at Simpson and Greenbaum's manifesto. He viewed the position paper's recommendations for amendments to Measure 58 as naïve suggestions from political amateurs who failed to understand that the wording of an initiative could not be changed once it was proposed.[72] He focused on the fact that they all agreed that Measure 58 needed to be defeated, no matter how feebly they might express this position. As for the matter of leadership, Deras never cared to be the leader of the opposition. He was glad to give up the burden of command and assume more fully his administrative duties as treasurer. He thus agreed to all of Greenbaum and Simpson's concerns. He ceased being a spokesperson for Concerned Adoption Professionals and happily referred all media requests to them, such as when Channel 2 in Portland requested someone to represent the opposition to Measure 58 on its program *Town Hall*.[73] Although Deras appeared on the program, he spoke only once. It was Greenbaum who was front and center, sitting side by side with Hill.[74] In the meantime, Deras continued to send CAP's informational packets, which now contained Greenbaum and Simpson's position paper, though not always their "Summary of Arguments against Ballot Measure 58."[75] For all intents and purposes, Deras and Concerned Adoption Professionals, the political committee he had formed, vanished from public view for the rest of the campaign.

By early October, the Boys and Girls Aid Society had supplanted CAP as the preeminent public leader of the opposition to Measure 58. Simpson and especially Greenbaum were its passionate spokespersons. The agency, having at last received its board of director's approval, was now able to mobilize the institutional resources of the BGAS to support Simpson and Greenbaum's work. Under Deras, the two had had no support from the agency and legally could work against Measure 58 only on a voluntary basis on their own time. Now, not only were the BGAS's rich facilities available to them, but they would be paid to work against Measure 58.[76] Workers at the BGAS switchboard were instructed to direct calls from the public and the media on Measure 58 to Simpson and Greenbaum. The two could now use BGAS offices for media interviews and strategy meetings, and they could use its equipment to make calls and copies, send faxes and e-mail messages, and conduct Internet searches. In addition, the BGAS paid Simpson, Greenbaum, and various other members of the Adoption Unit and support staff $3,897 in wages for the time they spent on Measure 58.[77]

As members of the BGAS got their feet wet in the rough-and-tumble of an initiative campaign, they received a political education, far removed from the world of social work and the idea of "building communities through consensus." In doing so, they developed a visceral dislike of reporters like *Willamette Week*'s Patty Wentz and members of Bastard Nation. The media was the locus of the animosity that BGAS members of CAP felt for Measure 58's leaders and supporters. The first incident occurred at the beginning of September. According to Greenbaum, when Patty Wentz of *Willamette Week* contacted CAP for an interview "we had been really very open with her and really tried to present our side, thinking she was going to put both sides in there." They felt betrayed when Wentz "just took whatever parts she could pull out of context to meet her needs as to the side she wanted to tell." Wentz, said Greenbaum, "twisted everything we said."[78] They did not know that Wentz, an adopted adult and an admirer of Bastard Nation, had been in close contact with Helen Hill and only revealed her own support for Measure 58 with the publication of her story in the *Willamette Week* on September 16.[79] Greenbaum and Simpson had been sandbagged. Greenbaum ruefully recalled that there had been a positive result of that experience: "it made us realize that we needed to be more careful about who we talked to."[80] It also soured BGAS members' view of Bastard Nation, who they concluded were underhanded political players.

Simpson and Greenbaum had been ready to dislike Bastard Nation even before this incident. The very name "Bastard Nation" they found slightly offensive, for it suggested that the group had "not a sense of support for birth parents."[81] Moreover, they were disgusted at the offensive language that some Bastard Nation members directed at birth mothers. While doing research on the Internet, Greenbaum and Michael Balter read e-mail messages from Bastard Nation members in the unmoderated Internet Usenet newsroom <alt.adoption> (which they mistakenly called BN's chat room) that frequently referred to birth mothers as "birth whores" and contained "very vicious, nasty kinds of comments." This glimpse into Bastard Nation's thinking about birth mothers confirmed, intensified, and alarmed BGAS members' reaction to BN. According to Greenbaum, "if these were the people who were going to be getting ahold of birth certificates and tracking down birth mothers, that was going to be awful." It motivated Simpson and Greenbaum to work harder and spurred them on to find some way to protect birth mothers who had been promised confidentiality.[82]

Simpson and Greenbaum's first face-to-face meeting with members of Bastard Nation only reinforced their dislike of the organization. That meeting occurred on October 4 in the Green Room of the *Town Hall* television show. Their impressions were partly due to their youth and political naiveté— Greenbaum was just out of graduate school and had been at the BGAS for just two years—and nothing in either of the women's social work training had prepared them to be political activists. They watched wonderingly as Bastard Nation members raised a ruckus with the KATU-TV production staff, demanding that they be allowed to wear their "Bastard Nation" T-shirts on camera.[83] The resulting tension turned the Green Room into "a little war zone," which, with the proponents of Measure 58 "staring daggers at us," made it an evening Simpson and Greenbaum would never forget.[84]

Though BGAS personnel's handling of media responsibilities was off to a rough start, Deras's strategy of bombarding newspaper editorial boards paid spectacular dividends. Almost every major daily newspaper in Oregon editorialized against Measure 58, keeping up a steady drumbeat of opposition throughout late September and October. What made the editorials especially convincing was their tone, most of which were temperate rather than demagogic.[85] None of them came close to suggesting, as the Uniform Adoption Act had done in 1994, that birth certificates should be sealed for ninety-nine years.[86] Instead, most sympathized with the plight of adopted adults who were unable to have access to their own medical and birth information. Like the BGAS, many suggested amendments to current adoption law to alleviate the problem. But they opposed Measure 58. The *Oregonian*'s editorial of September 23 was typical. The stumbling block to that paper's endorsing Measure 58 was that it was retroactive and thus would "reverse decades of adoption law and break promises of confidentiality that Oregon had made to thousands of women who gave up their children for adoption." The editorial asserted that this would be an injustice to women who had been advised at the time to keep the birth a secret from their families, especially those who were raped or had been victims of incest. These women had kept their secrets, and "Oregon can't change the past." Besides, the editorial continued, adoptees have alternatives. Oregon had established voluntary adoption registries, which were growing larger and more efficient, although, the paper admitted, "they were not perfect" and "efforts to reunite are often frustrating and expensive." Reform was needed, but Measure 58 went too far. The editorial suggested that Measure 58 would be a good law provided that it not be retroactive— that is, if it simply changed adoption law beginning January 1, 1999, and enabled future adoptees at the age of twenty-one to access their birth certificates. If it did that, it "would be worthy of strong support." But of course it did not, and the *Oregonian* concluded that although adoption laws should be changed "M 58 isn't the right way to do it."[87]

Also by October, Measure 58 began to appear in the national media. The interest sprang from a combination of reasons. The issue was politically unprecedented: it was the first time ever that Americans were being asked to

vote on whether adopted adults should have the same rights as other citizens
to access their birth certificates. Moreover, the clash of conflicting rights
between adopted adults and birth mothers had hit an emotional and moral
nerve all over the nation. As early as October 5, the *Boston Globe* ran an editorial criticizing Measure 58 for failing to "acknowledge that a birth mother
or father has rights too, chief among them the right to privacy." The *Globe*
favored a compromise. Under its proposal, adopted adults would gain access
to their birth certificates, but an intermediary—an adoption agency or judge—
would contact the birth parents to find out if a meeting with the son or daughter was desired. It was the *Globe*'s belief that "these reunions will be more
rewarding if they are brokered with respect for both parties."[88] Toward the end
of the month, well-known conservative columnist Mona Charen denounced
Measure 58 for its retroactive nature and for breaking promises made to unwed mothers.[89]

Back in Oregon, by October the opposition to Measure 58 had begun to
spread beyond CAP and the BGAS. The American Civil Liberties Union of
Oregon (ACLU-OR) advised voters to oppose Measure 58 on the grounds
that the "competing civil liberties interests [were] too complex for the initiative process" and suggested that the issue was best left to the legislature. The
ACLU-OR did not mean that the average voter was unable to understand the
meaning of Measure 58, but that adopted adults and birth mothers both had
rights that needed protection, the former in obtaining information about their
medical and birth history, the latter an interest in maintaining their privacy.
The ACLU-OR also raised the issue of "potential ex post facto constitutional
problems raised by changing adoption confidentiality retrospectively."[90] The
Ecumenical Ministries of Oregon (EMO) issued its own *Voters' Guide* rec-
ommending a "No" vote on Measure 58, questioning Hill's Open '98 Committee's equation of a birth certificate with a civil right. The EMO guide also
argued, somewhat illogically, that original birth certificates might be inaccurate or incomplete and that birth mothers sometimes used aliases on birth
certificates. (Lack of data or inaccuracy would seem irrelevant to the issue.)
In addition, the EMO *Voters' Guide* made other arguments against Measure
58, including the familiar ones that Oregon already provided voluntary adoption registries and assisted searches, and that the initiative was retroactive.
EMO felt that the state's present adoption system "respects the interests of
birth parents, adoptees and adoptive parents. This balance and honor of
confidential commitments should be maintained."[91] This was a powerful aid
to the opposition: the EMO *Voters' Guide* would be sent out to over 12,000
people statewide and 1,400 congregations.[92]

Joining the chorus of opposition in mid-October, letters to the editor began appearing in the *Oregonian* denouncing Measure 58. Deras wrote the first. He attacked Helen Hill by name and then unintentionally gave free advertising to Bastard Nation by mentioning its Website address to the *Oregonian*'s readers in his diatribe against BN's urging its members to "debunk" those "idiotic editorials being printed by Oregon regional newspapers." Deras's point was the inability of Hill and her followers "to appreciate the perspective of birth mothers—including rape victims—who wish to preserve the privacy promised them by law when they surrendered children for adoption." For Deras, the "fundamental flaw" of Measure 58 was its failure to appreciate that adoption involved three groups—adoptees, birth parents, and adoptive parents—each of whom had legitimate interests that needed to be protected. Measure 58 gave adoptees alone the right "to break promises of confidentiality made to birth parents."[93]

Lori Mason Namba of Northeast Portland, identifying herself as the wife of an adoptee, rather than a member of the Adoption Unit of the BGAS, urged *Oregonian* readers to vote "no" on Measure 58 because both adoptees and birth mothers had rights: the adoptee, like her husband, had the right to see his birth certificate, and the birth mother had "the right to say whether or not she still wants that privacy." Ultimately, Namba observed, the adoptee "should not have more or fewer rights than his birth parents do."[94]

In contrast to Deras's blast at Hill, Lauren Greenbaum, using her professional title of "Adoption Lead Clinician of the Boys and Girls Aid Society," put forward the agency's conciliatory message, which was in essence that there was not a great distance between those who opposed Measure 58 and those who supported it. Both sides believed that adopted adults had a need to know their history and had a right to their medical records. Both believed that birth parents welcomed the opportunity to talk to the children they had placed for adoption. Both saw little harm in allowing adoptees to have access to their original birth certificates. The only change those who opposed Measure 58 wanted, Greenbaum stated, was to add a clause "allowing those birth parents who prefer not to be contacted to file a notice to that effect with Vital Records." According to Greenbaum the issue boiled down to "being compassionate and considering the needs of others." But each individual, "adopted or not," had the right to decide when or whether to be in a relationship with another individual. That was why Greenbaum urged readers to vote "no" on Measure 58 and expressed the wish that "interested parties should work together to design a balanced initiative that considers all parties' needs."[95]

On October 12, the office of secretary of state published the state's official *Voters' Pamphlet,* a booklet required by law to be sent to every post office mailing address prior to election day. It was a crucial document in the campaign for Measure 58 because for voters who read it, especially for those out-side the Portland area, it was a major source of information on the initiative. In addition to the official text of Measure 58, the *Voters' Pamphlet* informed citizens of the consequences of voting "yes" or "no" on the initiative, the fi-nancial impact on state or local government expenditures or revenues, paid arguments for and against the initiative, and an explanation of how the ini-tiative would work in practice. A "yes" vote, the pamphlet explained, would require the state of Oregon to issue adult adoptees a copy of their original Oregon birth certificate upon request. A "no" vote would retain the confiden-tiality of original birth certificates unless a court were to order disclosure. The financial impact on the various levels of government was said to be none. Unfortunately for opponents of Measure 58, the *Voters' Pamphlet* contained ten arguments in favor of the measure and only three in opposition. In addi-tion, voters would see the arguments in favor of Measure 58 first. That meant that voters would have to do a lot of reading before they got to the arguments against the measure.[96]

The three arguments against Measure 58 in the *Voters' Pamphlet* over-lapped. The eleven female adoption professionals from the BGAS, including Simpson and Greenbaum, signed the first one, which was paid for by CAP. For tactical reasons, Deras's name was absent: he would purchase his own argument for $300 and make it appear that there was a third more opposi-tion than really was. CAP's argument reminded voters of the shame and stigma that surrounded having a child out of wedlock decades earlier and how back then it was almost impossible for those women to consider parenting their children alone. They had made the "wrenching decision" to relinquish their babies for adoption and did so with the clear expectation that their iden-tities would be kept confidential. Adoption agencies assured both birth par-ents and adoptive families of confidentiality services. "Many birthparents took, or intended to take, this secret to their graves," wrote the adoption workers. Implicit in this argument was that Measure 58 violated the retro-active promise of confidentiality that adoption agencies had made to birth parents. Times had changed, adoption practices had evolved, and there now existed options, ranging from adoption registries to assisted search for both adoptees and birth parents, that respected the rights of all parties in the adop-tion triad. The signers opposed Measure 58 on the familiar grounds that "there are no provisions in this measure allowing birthparents to veto either the disclosure of their identities or potential contact from the adult adoptee." But the CAP adoption workers added a new wrinkle to their argument, one that they had not raised in public from mid-August, when this text had been composed, to mid-October, when it appeared in the *Voters' Pamphlet*. They complained that under Measure 58 there was also "no way for birthparents to access current identifying information about the children for whom they planned adoptions." They believed that all members of the adoption triad deserved "equal respect and courtesy" and for that reason the principle of equality must govern them all: "Services offered to one of these parties should be offered to the others."[97]

Not surprisingly, Warren Deras approached opposition to Measure 58 from a legal point of view. He argued that Measure 58 would destroy a critical part of Oregon's adoption laws, which had a dual system, characterized by confidentiality and tempered by flexibility. Here Deras was referring to the fact that an unwed woman could choose to have an open or a confidential adoption. If she chose open adoption, she maintained contact with the adoptive parents. If she chose a confidential adoption, the adoptive parents received essential medical information, but the biological and adoptive parents had no contact. In order for confidential adoption to function, Oregon law sealed adoption records—original birth certificates, court records, and adoption agency records. The problem with Measure 58, according to Deras, was that it would "destroy the system of confidential adoption, breaking promises made to women over many years that an adoption would help permanently put behind them acts ranging from rape to a moment's indiscretion." He believed that the flexibility in confidential adoption came from lawmakers' wisdom in designing voluntary adoption registries, where biological parents and adult adoptees could register their wish to meet. If both registered, they were introduced with the help of trained social workers. Existing law thus gave interested parties access to sealed adoption records. Deras urged voters that "Oregon should preserve choice."[98]

The third and final argument in opposition to Measure 58 in the *Voters' Pamphlet* came from Steven Dahl, who represented a group called Friends of Adoption. Like Deras, Dahl argued that the Oregon legislature had provided well for all parties involved in an adoption. Also like the others, he argued that the flaw in the argument of proponents of Measure 58 was that it was wrong "to assume that any one individual has a greater right to information in adoption than another." Dahl added that Measure 58 removed protection of personal choice and the right to privacy precisely because it disturbed the carefully crafted legislation that put all parties in adoption on an equal footing and required that all be contacted and give their consent prior to any personal information being released. Thus, Measure 58 sought to create a new "right" by destroying the right of privacy and personal choice. Measure 58 was seriously flawed, Dahl concluded, and it must not pass.[99]

By mid-October, the opposition's campaign against Measure 58 was in full swing. And if the standard for success was the number of newspaper editorials opposed to the initiative, the numerous endorsements of its position from political leaders and social and religious organizations, letters to the editor, and cogent arguments in the *Voters' Pamphlet,* the opposition looked exceedingly strong. But if the standard was public support, their position looked shakier. Polls showed the opposition behind.[100] Also worrisome, hardly anyone was writing to the newspapers in opposition to Measure 58. In fact, after the three letters to the editor in mid-October—with only one from a citizen not connected to CAP—no one wrote a letter to the *Oregonian* in opposition to Measure 58 during the rest of the campaign.

In fact, the opposition campaign was plagued by problems, some inherent. For example, the group most interested in seeing Measure 58 defeated was birth parents (really almost entirely birth mothers), whose privacy would be affected by its victory. But birth mothers faced an inherent dilemma that kept them from participating against Measure 58: How did they participate in a public political campaign on an issue when by doing so they compromised the privacy they were seeking to protect? Birth mothers came to Deras's office complaining that newspapers refused to publish their anonymous letters. Deras thought this an understandable policy from the newspaper editors' perspective, but it certainly left the public in the dark about the opposition's viewpoint, at a time when the initiative's supporters were waging an active and effective campaign of letters to the editor. In addition, Deras, ever the stickler for accountability and following initiative law, was forced to tell potential birth-mother contributors that contributions over $50.00 had to be reported to the secretary of state's office, where they would become part of the public record. Even contributions below $50.00 had to be recorded and could be inspected by supporters of Measure 58 at any time. Deras sympathized with the birth mothers who decided not to contribute even small sums of money to CAP: "Who wants to be exposed to an organization like Bastard Nation, which would delight in 'outing' a birth mother who wants privacy, a category frequently referred to as 'birth whores' in their web postings."[101] In the end, few birth mothers voiced publicly their opposition to Measure 58.

An exception to the passivity of most birth mothers during the Measure 58 campaign was the one-woman crusade of "Cindy," the pseudonym of a birth mother who had been raped. She first appeared on the October 4 *Town Hall* television show, wrapped in deep shadow, her voice distorted by a voice synthesizer to protect her privacy. Cindy's presence and her story were impossible to ignore. She filled the screen and in a low, harsh, gravelly voice told a compelling story of being brutally raped, having had a reunion with the daughter she relinquished for adoption, and feeling betrayed by that daughter, who wanted to meet her father—Cindy's rapist. Cindy was the person whose testimony had sent the rapist to prison, and she was terrified that he might return to harm her and her family. It was for that reason that she opposed Measure 58.[102] But even Cindy's brave crusade could not make up for the letter writers and public support that the opposition needed.

The opposition to Measure 58 exacerbated its weakness by refusing to accept aid from outside Oregon. By the start of October, Measure 58 had attracted the active intervention of the National Council for Adoption (NCFA). Alarmed by poll numbers that showed Measure 58 leading by a substantial margin, NCFA's president, William L. Pierce, decided to offer his assistance to defeat it. Although he had never met Deras or his CAP colleagues, Pierce telephoned him, Michael Balter, and Nancy Simpson. Pierce needed no introduction; his reputation as the most prominent national anti–open adoption records figure over the past twenty years preceded him. After talking with the three Oregonians, Pierce faxed them a number of memoranda containing arguments, suggestions, and information he believed would be useful in combating Measure 58.[103] On October 1, for example, Pierce sent Deras a few arguments to use against the adoption reform movement's claim that there was a psychological need for search and contact between adopted adults and birth parents and a statement debunking the notion, also advocated by the adoption activists, that that over 90 percent of birth mothers did not object to an adoptee's receiving identifying information. In both cases, Pierce criticized the unscientific nature of the methodology used to arrive at these conclusions.[104]

A week later, Pierce faxed Deras additional arguments to use against Measure 58. His materials took a more extreme position than Deras's and much more so than the BGAS's. Along with the conventional opposition arguments, such as denunciation of the initiative's retroactivity, Pierce emphasized that the consequences of Measure 58's passage would be to undermine respect for the law in general. Using the "slippery slope" argument, he also claimed that a Measure 58 victory would embolden adoption reform activists "to demand total access to agency, attorney, and court records."[105] Pierce also sent Deras the text of the favorable decision NCFA had received in the Tennessee's Court of Appeals (before it was overturned by a higher court).[106] Finally, based on his experience in 1985, when NCFA fought a major battle over retroactive opening of adoption records in California, Pierce urged Deras to calculate the financial liability of each of Oregon's adoption agencies should Measure 58 pass. Once Deras had arrived at the figures, he should take them to the agencies that would, Pierce suggested, immediately recognize the financial jeopardy they were in and join the opposition to keep the initiative from passing.[107] Nancy Simpson recalled that Pierce offered to pay the salary of an additional staff member.[108]

CAP paid no attention to Pierce. And Pierce's arguments were strikingly missing from a new color brochure Deras compiled. Deras's new publication simply contained some information from Oregon's laws about birth parent secrecy and the state's voluntary adoption registries on the outside, and, on the inside, four newspaper editorials that opposed Measure 58, including the *Oregonian*'s "Oregon Must Keep Its Word."[109] Deras sent Pierce a copy of the brochure and in a cover memo wrote sarcastically, "Just think, for a mere $675,000 I could send this flyer to 1,000,000 voter householders in Oregon. There are about 1,900,000 voters. I assume you have the cash sitting in your petty cash drawer."[110] In fact, while Deras always respected Pierce, he sometimes doubted the wisdom of his advice. He could not imagine why Pierce had sent him the Tennessee Court of Appeals decision. Deras mused, "Perhaps he thought because I was a lawyer I'd be interested in court decisions." But, Deras thought, he was an estate and probate lawyer; he did not litigate. Why should he be interested in such matters? Moreover, Deras thought Pierce was simply wrong to use legal arguments in a political campaign. Deras's experience had taught him that it was particularly ineffective to argue that an initiative was unconstitutional: citizens did not like to be told that what they wanted to do was unconstitutional.[111] And Deras never crunched the numbers on potential adoption agency liability or tried to enlist agency support using such an idea. Finally, after consulting with Balter, Simpson turned down Pierce's offer to pay for an additional staff member to work on the campaign against Measure 58.[112] In short, the opposition to Measure 58 generally spurned Pierce's suggestions and offers of help, and the NCFA had little effect on the campaign.

Though financially weak, internally hobbled, losing at the polls, and refusing help from external allies, the organized opposition to Measure 58 never expressed a sense of urgency during the last two weeks of the campaign, a period that should have been marked by intense activity. Instead, the last appeals against Measure 58 that Oregonians living in the most populated area of the state had the opportunity to read before entering the polling booth were published fully one week before the election. One of them appeared on October 28 as an op-ed piece in the *Oregonian;* Nancy Simpson, in her role as adoption program supervisor, wrote it for the Boys and Girls Aid Society of Oregon. This article at least had the virtue of consistency. It argued, once again, that Measure 58 infringed on the birth parents' right to privacy that adoption agencies had promised them at the time the decision had been made to place the children for adoption. Today many options for openness in adoption were available including a process for the release of nonidentifying information, a statewide voluntary registry for both birth parents and adoptees, and a process for assisted search for both birth parents and adoptees with the help of a trained social worker. Simpson struck one new note in her use of the phrase "civil rights," a term that had become identified with the supporters of Measure 58. Simpson pointed out to the readers of the *Oregonian* that the initiative did not give "equal rights or opportunities to birth parents so that they could learn the current identities of their birth children." Simpson objected repeatedly to the failure of Measure 58 to provide balance for all parties to an adoption; instead, she asserted, "all the power and opportunity is given only to the adoptee."[113]

Two other articles appearing in the *Oregonian* during this next to last week before the election powerfully personalized the issue of birth mothers' right to privacy by using the example of Cindy. After her appearance on *Town Hall,* Cindy had tried to publicize the cause of birth mothers' right to privacy, but had been thwarted at every turn. Especially frustrating was the *Oregonian*'s refusal to give her equal time to counter the complimentary article it had written about Helen Hill, even after Cindy had written a long personal history and sent it to Spencer Heinz, the reporter who wrote the Hill story. But on October 25, Cindy at last found a sympathetic listener. She had called Margie Boulé, an *Oregonian* columnist, and Boulé took up the cause of Cindy and birth mothers against Measure 58.[114] Boulé described Cindy's vicious rape, her feelings of powerlessness in the maternity center, the initial reunion with her daughter by letter, and how her daughter wanted to meet her birth father because, according to Cindy, "her adoptive mother didn't believe I had been raped." Boulé quoted Cindy as saying, "I don't want my family hurt, and I know that man is dangerous. It's not that I'm closing the door to my daughter. If she needed anything medical, even a bone marrow transplant, I would do that. But I need to be protected. The Oregon measure is starting a nationwide movement. If voters in her state opened birth records, it would be like another rape. Again, I would have no rights, no voice, no choice. I would be violated all over again."[115] Four days later, Boulé again used Cindy's story to excoriate proponents of Measure 58 for being selfish people who "don't care; they just want what they want for themselves, without regard of the harm it might cause others." Boulé made clear her position: she believed that adult adoptees have a right to know who they were and that Oregon should open its adoption records. But "in case of documented rape," Boulé went on, "there should be some kind of safeguard, a system in which a victim of rape can be asked if she wants her name or the rapist's name withheld. Women who've been raped have suffered enough, sacrificed enough to give life to children conceived by a brutal crime. They do not need to be revictimized."[116] Letters by the hundreds poured into Boulé's office praising the columns. Many writers mentioned how they had never thought of the issue in such terms and how Boulé had made them decide to change their vote.[117]

Toward the end of the campaign, when it would have maximum effect, the national media once again swung its spotlight on Measure 58. Here too, the issue of birth mother's privacy was prominent and personalized in emotional terms. On October 26, Cindy was interviewed on NBC's *Today Show,* first shown with her back to the camera, walking down a street, and later in shadow. Cindy told the national audience that she feared that if Measure 58 passed, the man whom she sent to jail could track her down. "It terrifies me, it really does," she said. "I feel I can't keep my family safe."[118] In addition, both host Matt Lauer and Portland attorney and adoptive father Frank Hunsaker argued that Measure 58 violated promises of confidentiality made to birth parents.[119]

Even with media attention and at least one birth mother's activism, the message against Measure 58 was apparently not moving enough voters. Polling data in late October revealed that Measure 58 held a 54-to-35 percent advantage, with 11 percent of the Oregon electorate still undecided.[120] During the closing days of the campaign there was an odd silence in the opposition camp. Perhaps they were imagining the celebration preparations being made by the supporters of Measure 58.

6

The Bastards Strike Back

Bastard Nation's campaign strategy for passage of Measure 58, run by
Helen Hill, Donna Harris, and Shea Grimm, was a mixture of happen-
stance, planning, and counterattacks on the opposition. An example of how
chance affected the campaign occurred in early July 1998 when Delores Teller,
reunited birth mother, president of the Oregon Adoptive Rights Association
(OARA), and northwest regional director of the American Adoption Congress, took it upon herself to become a spokesperson for Measure 58 and campaign for it behind the scenes. Ultimately, Teller was not successful in
converting opposition organizations to support Measure 58. Yet ironically,
she would be hailed as one of the chief architects of Measure 58's victory.[1]

Bill Bosset, past president of the OARA, suggested to Teller as early as March
1998 that if Measure 58 was to win it was important that Oregon's adoption
agencies, registry program, and Vital Statistics office support it. By June, Teller
had decided, without discussing the matter with Helen Hill or Bastard Nation,
that it would be her role to "open the dialog between those people" and Measure 58 advocates.[2] That opportunity presented itself on July 9 when the Boys
and Girls Aid Society of Oregon (BGAS) invited her, during its fact-gathering
period, to speak before its board of directors about birth mother confidentiality. The BGAS was particularly interested in how other states, such as
Alaska and Kansas, which permitted adoptees access to their birth certificates,
handled these issues. Teller promised to contact the state officials requesting
guidance, which she subsequently did.[3]

Teller came out of the BGAS meeting feeling that she had been "effective
in providing them information," which reinforced her intention to target other
people and organizations. In the next several months, Teller was a whirlwind
of energy and purpose: she made countless phone calls, attended many meetings, wrote dozens of letters, and published a few articles. She went to the state
capitol and met with Edward Johnson, state registrar and head of the state
Department of Human Resources, and his staff. There Teller met resistance
from officials in the Bureau of Vital Statistics. They complained that "it would
be too much work for them to go get birth certificates. They would have to get

Delores Teller, president of the Oregon
Adoptive Rights Association.

them in the basement." Teller admits she was not quite ready for this level of
hostility. Nevertheless, she dutifully wrote down all their questions, queried
the Alaska and Kansas Vital Statistics offices about how they handled releas-
ing original birth certificates to adopted adults, and wrote back to their Oregon counterparts with the relevant information "so that when the law came
into effect they would know."[4] Teller also called Oregon Right to Life, the
state's oldest, largest, and most comprehensive anti-abortion organization. A
spokesperson informed Teller that the organization was going to remain neutral on Measure 58 because it did not believe that opening adoption records
would have any effect on abortion rates. Teller was quite surprised at this decision: it was axiomatic among adoption activists that anti-abortion religious
organizations staunchly opposed open adoption records legislation because
they believed that unwed mothers would chose abortion rather than adoption
if adoption records were open.[5]

Teller was elated at the progress she was making. She began to rethink
some of the advice she had been given. Teller had been warned not to approach Catholic Charities of Oregon because it was a hopeless cause: the
organization had been opposed to open adoption records for many years. As
recently as October 1997, Oregon Catholic Charities communications director Heather Kmetz had publicly reiterated the organization's opposition, stating that the agency was likely to oppose the initiative because it was
retroactive, and would thus require revealing the names of women to whom
the state had promised confidentiality. In fact, according to Kmetz, the women

who came to Catholic Charities signed a contract with the organization guaranteeing their privacy.[6] She predicted that if the initiative became law, adoption agencies like hers would use all their power to fight it in court. But Teller was not to be deterred. On July 15, armed with an alleged quotation from the Pope, "Every child has a right to know his or her parents and to the right to preserve his or her identity,"[7] Teller decided to call Paula Lang, Catholic Charities' recently appointed Pregnancy Support and Adoption Services program manager.[8] Five weeks later, Teller had a two-hour lunch with Lang, which she viewed as a triumph: "I was thrilled to find her open to my opinions." When Catholic Charities announced it would not oppose Measure 58, Teller attributed its decision to her influence.[9]

The importance of Teller's activities to Catholic Charities' decision to remain neutral on Measure 58, however, was in reality less than she believed. Large, nonprofit institutions do not make decisions as the result of a two-person lunch; their decision-making process is far more complex, difficult, and time-consuming. In the case of Catholic Charities, the decision to remain neutral on Measure 58 began when Communications Director Heather Kmetz was quoted in the October 1997 *Willamette Week* denouncing the initiative without having consulted with or secured authorization from anyone else in the organization. This set off alarm bells throughout Catholic Charities, because the organization had a prescribed process for responding to public policy initiatives, which had not been followed in this case. Usually the Executive Committee of the board evaluated public policy issues and then consulted with the Oregon Catholic Conference, which was the public policy arm of the Church. None of this had been done; consequently, Kmetz was reprimanded.[10]

Kmetz's impetuous action galvanized Catholic Charities' public policy review process. After the *Willamette Week* article was published, Catholic Charities Executive Director Dennis Keenan received a call from the director of the Oregon Catholic Conference, Robert Castagna, who wanted to know if Catholic Charities had taken an official stand. Keenan told him no, and referred Castagna to Lang. Castagna proceeded to pepper Lang with a series of questions: Will Measure 58 increase abortions? The Church could not support a position that might lead to an increase in abortions. What about the promise made to women? Will this hurt them? Will there be lawsuits against Catholic Charities? Castagna suggested that Lang research and answer these questions. Lang personally favored open records and Measure 58. But Catholic Charities did not share Lang's views. The organization would eventually take a neutral position. Lang was not bothered by that. She said, "The neutral stance made so much sense to me. Even though I personally was going to vote in favor of Measure 58 and believed in it, I did not want Catholic Charities to take a stand in favor. I thought the neutral stance was the right moral stance because I wanted all women who had worked with us to be served by us and not to be concerned about coming to us."[11] On July 15, 1998, Lang wrote the memo that officially justified the organization's position. She noted that "because Catholic Charities is acutely aware of the tremendous emotional impact of being 'found' without giving permission and the equal devastation of 'not finding' a birth member, we propose taking a *neutral position* on this ballot measure. We feel great commitment to those brave women who chose life for their child under the promise of anonymity, yet we also have great compassion for those adult adoptees who have been cut off from information regarding their biological family." Lang's memo was reviewed and approved by Douglas Alles, Director of Social Services, and Executive Director Keenan, and then sent off to Castagna. Thus, on the very day that Delores Teller contacted Lang, and five weeks before Teller had lunch with her, Catholic Charities had already hammered out an official policy of neutrality on Measure 58.[12]

For Teller, the ostensible breakthrough with Catholic Charities "was a really pivotal moment for me," defining her role in the Measure 58 campaign. It was then that she realized that the key to changing opinions was letting people talk about Measure 58 and voice their fears about this law—fears that Teller found were almost always rooted in the issue of birth mother confidentiality. Teller created what she referred to as "my program." The beginning of a meeting consisted of letting the opposition group talk for at least fifteen minutes. Then Teller would demand that the group listen to her, a birth mother, "because they needed to hear from someone who wasn't depressed, wasn't angry, wasn't a mad adoptee, wasn't what they considered a whiny spoiled adoptee or whatever, and who could be warm, articulate, happy, and listen to them." Teller believed she had "got it down to a science, what I was doing." At that point, she said, "I just called everybody." In the following months, Teller contacted Executive Director Robert Roy of the Waverly Children's Home, the American Civil Liberties Union of Oregon, Governor John Kitzhaber, and Warren Deras. Her program had little effect.[13] Each either maintained their opposition to or eventually came out against Measure 58.

In mid-July, while Teller was busy lobbying the opposition, Helen Hill sat down with Donna Harris—newly promoted to Measure 58's campaign manager—to map campaign strategy. Looming large was the need to get arguments in favor of Measure 58 into the *Voters' Pamphlet* before the August 25 deadline. They coupled this imperative with a "vote yes" drive. They set up booths at all the state's county fairs and at other popular places, such as Fred Meyer stores and public libraries, as they had done earlier. This time, the goal was not to qualify the initiative for the ballot, but to encourage voters to vote "yes" in November and to sign petitions. Every 1,000 signatures collected would, in accord with Oregon election law, allow Hill and her Open '98 Committee to place an argument for free in the *Voters' Pamphlet* and avoid paying the $300 purchase fee.[14] Optimistically, Hill and Harris hoped that they could collect enough signatures by this method to get ten arguments into the *Voters' Pamphlet* before the deadline.[15] They managed to get only one—another demonstration of the worth of paid signature gatherers.[16]

During the first week in August, Grimm met with Hill in Portland, also to discuss strategy for the upcoming campaign. Uppermost in Grimm's mind was getting out the adopted adult search-and-support-group vote—groups like the Oregon Adoptive Rights Association (OARA), the Triad Connection, and the Adoptee Birthfamily Connection, which, in the eyes of Bastard Nation, were less concerned with legislative issues and more with reuniting birth family members. How could getting these groups to the voting booth be done most efficiently? Perhaps setting up carpools would help. When would be the best time to do that? Hill told Grimm that most of Oregon's voters voted by absentee ballot three weeks before the election. This forced Grimm to rethink her original ideas. If what Hill told her was true, there was no need for the traditional last week push for votes as in other states. Even better, this fact could work to Measure 58's advantage, especially if William Pierce and the NCFA were unaware of it. Grimm concluded that in light of Oregon's absentee ballot system, Hill and Bastard Nation should run most of their media ads in early and middle October.[17]

While in Oregon, Grimm also helped Hill and Harris with their arguments for the *Voters' Pamphlet*. They still faced the challenge of getting additional statements supporting Measure 58 into the *Voters' Pamphlet*. Eventually they would be quite successful. Against the opposition's three, supporters of Measure 58 would have ten arguments, and six of the ten would emanate either from Hill's Open '98 committee or from Bastard Nation. The average Oregon voter, however, would not be aware of the provenance of the arguments. Besides the statement earned by 1,000 voter signatures, both Hill and Harris each purchased a spot in the *Voters' Pamphlet*. Harris did not identify herself as the campaign manager of Measure 58 for either the free or the paid argument. Similarly, Donna Martz, a resident of Texas and a Bastard Nation member, purchased a spot for an argument, but she did not identify herself as being from out of state or as a member of Bastard Nation.[18] From her home in Redmond, Washington, Shea Grimm used the Internet to provide leadership and ideological direction to the Bastard Nation Executive Committee and others as she drafted, edited, and wrote two additional *Voters' Pamphlet* arguments.[19] The proponents' strategy thus made it look as though nine different groups or individuals instead of just one or two were willing to spend $300 each to persuade Oregon citizens to vote for Measure 58.

The *Voters' Pamphlet* statements, though written in August, would not appear until mid-October, when the secretary of state was required to send the booklet to every post office mailing address prior to election day.[20] How would voters learn about Measure 58 before then? Media ads cost extraordinary amounts of money. Hill had little money left. She withdrew another $20,000 from her account in September only to find that prices for ads on network TV had tripled from the last time she had inquired.[21] Hill bought time on cable television instead. She would eventually spend tens of thousands of dollars on TV and radio ads, outspending the opposition many times over.[22]

The only consistent media ally in Oregon for BN and Measure 58 was the alternative newspaper the *Willamette Week,* with a circulation of 80,000.[23] The paper's position was due in no small part to its reporter Patty Wentz, an adopted adult, who favored Measure 58. Throughout the campaign, she kept in close contact with Hill and Grimm.[24] On September 16, 1998, Wentz personalized the *Willamette Week's* cover story on Measure 58 by beginning with the words "I am adopted."[25] She described her adopted childhood as one long lie, from the time her adoptive parents had told her that her "real parents" had died in a car accident to the discovery that her birth certificate had been altered to make it appear as though her adopted parents were her original parents. According to Wentz, even her first name was a lie: she later learned that her birth mother had named her Rebecca. She searched for her birth parents, but found only unsatisfying nonidentifying information. Wentz's message to her readers was that Measure 58 was the answer to the pernicious pattern of adoption secrecy.[26]

Along with the support of *Willamette Week,* Bastard Nation members rebutted any and all of the media's opposition to Measure 58. Their strategy took a variety of forms. They would schedule media appearances, but they would also counterpunch instantaneously with an onslaught of e-mail messages to newspaper editors, hammering home their message of equal rights for adoptees. By setting up Bastard Nation's Website as command central, the proponents of Measure 58 made theirs the first political initiative campaign conducted from the Internet. In August 1998, a month after the initiative qualified for the ballot, there appeared a link on BN's Website with the heading "Contact Oregon Newspapers," containing the names, addresses, phone numbers, fax numbers, and e-mail addresses of the major newspapers in Oregon (divided into two categories, weeklies and dailies). Most important were the e-mail addresses of the "Letters to the editor" department of every Oregon newspaper.[27] Linked to this Web page was a "Frequently Asked Questions" page about Measure 58 that provided BN members with answers to common, anticipated questions. For example, to the question "Will access to OBC's [Original Birth Certificates] cause a birthparent to try and reclaim the child?" BN members were advised to answer: "Access to the OBC is only available to adult adoptees who have reached the age of 21."[28] In addition, on the same Web page as the "Frequently Asked Questions" was a link to information containing numerous facts, statistics, legal precedents, and opinions that letter writers could use in rebutting what BN members considered unfair media stories. When a negative article or editorial appeared, a BN member would notify the group of its existence by posting the entire article, or by linking the Web address for the piece to BN's Listserv, BEST. This allowed the entire membership to read the offending piece the same day it was published and to respond immediately with facts ready at hand, drawn from BN's Web page.

BN unleashed its letters-to-the-editor campaign in response to the *Oregonian*'s September 23 editorial attacking Measure 58. On the same day as the editorial, both Helen Hill and Shea Grimm sent e-mail communications to the *Oregonian* and also posted them to BN's list. In response to the editorial's contention that Measure 58 reversed decades of adoption law, Hill argued that the 1957 law sealing adoption records was unconstitutional. She also noted that before 1957 adoptees had had the right to access their original birth certificates. Measure 58 therefore was simply intended to overturn an unconstitutional law. Hill challenged the heart of the opponent's attack on Measure 58: that the state of Oregon had made a promise of confidentiality to birth mothers. She did this by raising the question of evidence. "No birth mother out of the thousands who have contacted this campaign in support of this measure can remember wanting, or being offered, any such promise" she wrote.[29] Grimm pointed out that the intent of sealing adoption records was not to protect birth parents, but "to insulate the adoptee and the adoptive family from the 'stigma of adoption.' "[30] By 8:30 the next morning, Damsel Plum had posted the *Oregonian* editorial to the BN list under the subject heading, "URGENT: Letters to Oregonian needed ASAP." She claimed that the paper "had now come out against the measure on the bogus grounds of implied birthmother confidentiality." Plum urged BN members to write, fax, or e-mail letters in support of Measure 58 and debunk the false notion that birth mothers were promised permanent anonymity from their birth children. The state had "no business supporting the lies of random unscrupulous agencies or lawyers. Ending lies, shame, and permanent secrecy in adoption is good for adoption." Plum ended by rallying the troops with: "Let's not be silent! Make your voice heard! Please. Thank you."[31] Rally they did. More than a dozen letters surged on to the BN discussion list and into the *Oregonian* editorial offices over the next two days. However, the *Oregonian* did not publish any. In fact, the paper allowed its editorial to stand unopposed for five days. Finally, on September 29 it published a birth mother's letter in support of Measure 58.[32] Hill was ecstatic.

The letter was written by Patricia Florin of Ashland. Florin was one of Hill's hardworking "Oregon people," who had been in the rank and file since the very beginning of the initiative campaign. Florin recounted her reunion with her sixteen-year-old daughter and wrote eloquently of what a profound experience it had been. She was now in a birth parent support group and had done extensive research on the subject. In regard to the promise of confidentiality, and contrary to the *Oregonian*'s editorial, Florin claimed, "it was usually implied, rarely stated, and never written down." She went on, "If [birth mothers] had had a choice, they would have chosen to keep their children, have an abortion, or have an open adoption."[33] Hill forwarded Florin's letter to the BN list, calling it "one of the finest letters I have ever read," and telling BN members that she had told Florin that "she had perhaps single-handedly done more for the campaign than any one person out there. We had a good cry."[34] Hill's feelings were no doubt heartfelt, but of course one published letter (out of the dozen or more sent) would not sway the public and did not bode well for a victorious campaign.

Bastard Nation's difficulty in getting its message across in the *Oregonian* was not unusual. One of the harshest commentaries on Measure 58 appeared in the *Medford Mail Tribune*. Medford, located near the Oregon-California border, had grown up with the railroads in the 1880s and evolved into a modern-day timber town; it is home to some 60,000 residents. Veteran columnist Russell Sadler, who taught journalism and environmental studies at Southern Oregon University in Ashland, claimed in the October 4 *Mail Tribune* that the initiative would open "all Oregon adoption records—past, present and future—to public inspection." It would break promises of confidentiality and promote abortions. He asked "whether Oregon law should be changed to respond to the need of the Me Generation to recover their Inner Child by ferreting out their birth parents. Does Oregon law say yes to those demanding 'I want my Mommy' when some Mommies do not want to be found?" Sadler referred to Measure 58 advocates as "adopted children" and used the term "open adoption" when he meant open records.[35]

No other column in the entire initiative campaign got under BN members' skin as Sadler's did. Joanne Nichols's response to Sadler was typical: "I have never before read more misinformation in one article—all carefully calculated to push every emotional button."[36] She provided BN's membership with two e-mail addresses for the paper. Helen Hill also weighed in and urged the BN membership to "hit this one extra hard."[37] BN members from Washington, Alabama, Pennsylvania, New Jersey, Montana, and Ohio wrote letters debunking every issue raised in Sadler's column.[38] Correctly, they denied that Measure 58 would open all adoption records to the inspection of the public, pointing out that the initiative would open only the original birth certificates to adopted adults twenty-one years or older upon request. David C. Ansardi, coordinator of the group Adoption Truthseekers and also a BN member, rebutted Sadler's skewed psychological profile of Measure 58 advocates by asserting that "we are competent citizens just like everyone else, and so are our birthparents. It may surprise you that we are fully capable of exercising our liberties to freely associate with other people and can work out our interpersonal relationships just like everyone else."[39] Montana's Tom Clement, citing Oregon's Right to Life research, refuted Sadler's claim that open records led to an increase in abortions.[40] Mary Anne Cohen, a birth mother and co-founder of *Origins,* a national birth mothers' group, found Sadler's piece "one of the most ignorant and misinformed articles I have ever seen." Like other BN messages, Cohen's emphasized that Measure 58 did not force anyone to search or have a relationship with anyone else if they did not want it. Rather, Measure 58 was about civil rights for all adopted adults in Oregon.[41]

But, like their experience with the *Oregonian,* BN's letter-writing campaign was a failure: the *Mail Tribune* printed none of the messages. The paper printed no response to Sadler's column or Measure 58 for two weeks. Then on October 16, two pro–Measure 58 letters were published, one from Medford and the other from Ashland. Ashland's Lorie Anderson corrected Sadler's inaccurate claim that Measure 58 would open all adoption records for inspection to the public. Medford's Paul B. Robinson wrote a hearty endorsement of Measure 58 on the grounds of equal rights, without any reference to Sadler's column. No other letters to the editor about Measure 58 would appear in the *Medford Mail Tribune* for the rest of the election.[42] Hill praised Plum and BN for using the Internet to get out "blast emails and blast faxes asking for people to write into newspapers," but complained that this tactic led to accusations from newspaper editors "that this was an outside agitated ballot measure and it was starting to harm us. . . . Oregonians hate nothing more than that."[43]

BN members never gave up their letters-to-the-editor campaigns, however, and sometimes they found a forum. The *Bend Bulletin* was one of them, perhaps because in this city of 50,000 residents, located in the middle of Oregon and east of the Cascade Mountains, the biggest business was tourism, and Bend was less parochial in its outlook than many other urban areas in the state. The city's paper had urged a "no" vote on Measure 58, citing the initiative as an invasion to birth mother privacy and an incentive for unwed mothers to choose to have an abortion. It praised the state's Voluntary Adoption Registry, concluding that "this system is sensible and we can see no reason to change it."[44] BN members were late in responding, so none of their letters were published. But the *Bulletin* later published a news article about Measure 58. In response to this article, three out-of-state BN members wrote letters to the editor that were published.[45]

On October 8, with negative editorials buzzing around their heads, BN was faced with a new attack, from the American Civil Liberties Union of Oregon (ACLU-OR). The organization advised voters to oppose Measure 58 because, among other things, the competing rights of adoption triad members made the issue too complex for the initiative process.[46] New Jersey–based BN member Mary Anne Cohen denied that adoptee civil rights were "a complex concept requiring bevies of lawyers and legislators to untangle. It is a simple matter of human dignity, justice, and equality under the law. Adult adoptees are simply asking for the same right that the rest of us have—to obtain a copy of their own original birth certificate—and then do with it what they wish."[47] Many BN members believed that the ACLU-OR should have been on their side; most were surprised it was not. As Cohen observed, "The ACLU of all groups should be in the forefront of supporting this simple civil rights issue."[48] Shea Grimm was especially critical of the ACLU-OR's contention of "the potential *ex post facto* constitutional problems raised by changing adoption confidentiality retrospectively." She reminded the ACLU-OR of its ignorance of the fact that the original law to seal the records in 1957 was applied retroactively and no one raised constitutional issues then.[49] Other BN members responded with the organization's typically abrasive humor. The Executive Committee's Damsel Plum rejected the idea that adoptee civil rights was too complex by informing the ACLU-OR that they were "out of [their] gourds and seriously out-of-touch if [you] think that a handful of self-interested legislators is more capable of assessing civil rights than the general electorate of Oregon." Plum then informed the organization that she would be "calling all my family and friends this weekend to tell them to tear up their ACLU cards. Your administration has clearly been taken over by some muddy-headed bureaucratic farts. You wouldn't know civil liberties if they jumped into your lap and started humping on your leg, you idiots. . . . And thanks for protecting the rights of those nazis and KKK folks."[50] But once again, BN's on-line letter-writing campaign was futile. The ACLU-OR never changed its recommendation to vote "no" on Measure 58.

This first week of October brought a share of doubt and questioning to BN's campaign for Measure 58. The negativity—from Governor Kitzhaber's refusal to endorse Measure 58 back in August, to the increasing opposition from groups like Warren Deras's Concerned Adoption Professionals and more recently the Boys and Girls Aid Society of Oregon, coupled with what seemed like a never-ending stream of hostile newspaper editorials and now the ACLU-OR attack—was beginning to take a toll. One small sign of BN's faltering confidence showed up on October 5. In an effort to bolster members' spirits, the Executive Committee, after having held the information for two months, decided to inform the membership that the AAC was endorsing Measure 58.[51] Any sign that someone supported them, even an adoption reform group that BN held in contempt, seemed good news. Inside BN, members' remarks and actions also belied their outward confidence and revealed other signs of doubt. On October 8, on learning from Julie Dennis that the *Eugene Register-Guard* had come out against Measure 58,[52] Shea Grimm wrote, "Shhhheeeesh, is there a paper that HASN'T come out against the Measure?" Grimm asked Dennis if she knew when the *Willamette Week*'s positive editorial was due out, adding, "We sure could use some good news." Still, Grimm rallied the troops. She urged them that "now is NOT THE TIME to let up" and instructed them to "just send your previous letters to the editor to the *Register-Guard* with some customizing."[53] Similarly, Cynthia Bertrand Holub, an Executive Committee member, said she "was getting the teensiest bit concerned over all the opposing editorials," but had her confidence restored by Hill, who reminded her that Oregon newspapers railed against the physician-assisted suicide initiative also, but to no avail.[54]

When August "Toff" Philippo, one of BN's most thoughtful members, asked the e-mail list what would happen if Measure 58 failed to pass, his question met impassioned response. Helen Hill summed it up best: "We are in a win-win situation here. We have galvanized many more people, we have publicized our issue, we have gathered the signatures of over 95,000 people in support . . . we have been on radio, television and in the newspapers, we have furthered the revered name of Bastard Nation, we have proved we can get organized and have a powerful voice, we have gotten adoption professionals to admit on television and radio that we have excellent points, that the system SHOULD be changed, we have accomplished an incredible amount."[55] Damsel Plum agreed with Hill and asserted that BN was "turning the tides." She continued, "just wait until adoptees all across America and Canada are freed from the bounds of pathologizing psycho-bullshit which has plagued adoption reform, yea, these past 2 decades." Then, Plum prophesied, an adoption reform movement holding up the banner of civil rights for adoptees would triumph.[56]

In truth, the situation was never quite as dark as it seemed. At the very end of September, the *Oregonian* published a number of letters in favor of Measure 58 from adoptees and an adoptive parent.[57] On October 2, the *Boston Globe*'s Adam Pertman wrote a long front-page article sympathetic to Measure 58. In it, he featured Helen Hill, identified as BN's Oregon director, and Bastard Nation, which he characterized for the first time as "the largest and most vocal adoptee activist organization in the country."[58] Damsel Plum immediately reproduced it on the BN e-mail discussion list with the endorsement "It's a very good article, people."[59] The same day, the *Oregonian*'s veteran staff reporter Spencer Heinz wrote a sympathetic portrayal of Helen Hill and Measure 58, calling it "the most thought-twisting, heart-wrenching-no-easy-answer issue of this Oregon election season."[60] On October 4, the television show *Town Hall* featured advocates of Measure 58, including Helen Hill and Shea Grimm; opponents, such as Lauren Greenbaum, Michael Balter, and Warren Deras; and ordinary triad members. A segment called "Man on the Street," in which a crew member solicited citizens' views of Measure 58, revealed overwhelming support for adoptee rights. Reporting back to the Executive Committee, Grimm said she was pleased by the show. She wrote, "All in all, it went very very well. Score one big [one] for our side. . . . I give it an 8, and I am fairly convinced that none of these people care enough about opposing the measure to spend any money or launch any kind of media campaign. Unless Bill [Pierce] or Warren [Deras] starts stirring the pot (and it's a little too late to do so), I think we may just coast this thing to victory."[61]

By October 10, BN's spirits had begun to lift. An unexpected favorable editorial from Salem's *Statesman Journal* elicited from Helen Hill the subject line "an endorsement at last," to which she added, "I say, I say hooray."[62] The next day Grimm reported the "good news" she had received from Hill of a poll taken by the *Oregonian* showing that Measure 58 was "supported by 54 percent of voters, with 35 percent opposed, and 11 percent undecided." Other polling data found that "about 70 percent of Oregonians preferred voting by mail." Grimm concluded that "it's unlikely anything will occur in the next few weeks to derail that support."[63] The poll predicting Measure 58's victory in November could hardly be better news.

The icing on the cake was the *Willamette Week*'s formal endorsement on October 14. It denounced the state of Oregon for operating "a system of secrets and lies" for forty years. It argued that promises of confidentiality made to birth mothers were made without the adoptees' consent and that the reasons for confidentiality were not clear. The editorial also declared that "there are times when promises should be broken." It compared laws sealing adoption records to restrictive real estate covenants that promised "white homeowners that blacks and Jews would not be able to move into certain neighborhoods." Moreover, it cited studies concluding that the majority of birth mothers welcomed contact from their offspring. As for voluntary adoption registries and mutual intermediary systems, "it forced the state into the role of permanent nursemaid between adults. Yes, Measure 58 forces one to weigh the rights of adoptees to his true birth certificate against a birth mother's right to privacy." But for the editor of the *Willamette Week* it was not a difficult choice: "We come down squarely on the side of the adoptee." [64] Referring to the *Willamette Week*'s editorial, Grimm exalted on BN's e-mail list: "Now Here's an endorsement! . . . This editorial comes right out and says HOWDY and oh by the way, Vote YES! I love it!" [65]

During the last week of the campaign, however, BN lost control of the campaign's message. The arguments began to focus on the rights of birth mothers to their privacy, not adoptees' civil rights. BN leaders found themselves on the defensive, unprepared to counterattack the opposition's relentless reiteration that Measure 58 would abrogate promises that adoption agencies had given birth mothers to keep their identity confidential. Throughout the election campaign, the BN leadership had never taken these arguments seriously, dismissing them on the grounds that the promises had never been given and refusing to recognize the emotional power of the claim with the public, whether or not there was any truth to it.

The reasons for BN's ignoring the opposition's main argument are complex. Besides not wishing to stray from their own ideological party line and not wanting to give credence to their opponents' message by repeating it, proponents of Measure 58 harbored deeper reasons for rejecting a concern for birth mothers' rights to privacy. From the very beginning of the adoption search movement, some adopted adults harbored resentment toward their birth mothers, whom they viewed as having callously abandoned them. Fueling BN's dislike of birth mothers was the refusal of Concerned United Birthparents, the largest and most influential national birth mothers' organization, to support Measure 58 because it did not permit birth mothers' access to birth certificates, only adopted adults. [66] But an even more specific reason for Measure 58 proponents' blindness to the issue of birth mothers' claim to privacy was Shea Grimm's opposition to birth mothers' having a prominent role in what she considered an adoptee rights issue. [67] As she told Hill, "I am opposed to birthmothers having central positions in open records for adult adoptees. Part of the goal here is to empower adoptees and to cease having other people speak for us or do our work." [68]

Now, near the end of the campaign, *Oregonian* columnist Margie Boulé's anti–Measure 58 columns, based on the experiences of Cindy and other birth mothers who were rape victims, urged some sort of protective system by which these women would not be "revictimized." Without such a mechanism in place,

Boulé was clearly advocating a "no" vote on Measure 58.[69] Combined with Cindy's appearance on what was a clearly sympathetic national TV program (the *Today Show*), Hill began to fear the effect of the media on public opinion. With her pulse on Oregon voters, Hill detected a groundswell of sympathy growing for Cindy's plight. Would voters imagine that the birth father, a convicted rapist, would use Measure 58 to find out Cindy's real name and try to harm Cindy and her family? And, by extension, would voters conclude that they should vote "no" on Measure 58 to protect the confidentiality of all birth mothers who in the past had relinquished children for adoption?[70]

Hill sought advice from Grimm—though she may have felt a little ambivalent about seeking out Grimm on this issue. She was well aware that Grimm "had a real thing against birthmothers—all of them." Grimm had frequently advised Hill to get Linda Corbin, Hill's loyal companion, who had been with her through thick and thin, "off the [Oregon] Committee—get her out of there, she's a birthmother."[71] Hill had none of those problems with birth mothers. She had even come to like Delores Teller and appreciated her behind-the-scenes campaigning for Measure 58. But confronted by the Boulé columns, Grimm did not let her ideology or personal dislike of birth mothers get in the way of politics. She recognized that on the street "the word is this Boulé article is really hurting us."[72]

Grimm e-mailed Hill and made two points. First, she observed that in cases of rape, the name of the rapist, even if he is not prosecuted, would not appear on the birth certificate. Enlarging on this point, Grimm wrote that Measure 58 would have nothing to do with birth mothers being sought out by rapists one way or another. Why? According to Grimm, because "The names of birthfathers who were rapists, or indeed ANY birthfathers, do NOT appear on original birth certificates unless the birthmother CHOOSES to put him there." Second, Grimm pointed out that if, as Cindy claimed, she prosecuted the rapist, then he already knew her name "because of the constitutional requirement that the accused be allowed to face his accuser. You cannot file charges anonymously."[73] Grimm's arguments rang true, and Hill expected they would give voters pause. Hill decided to run a full-page ad in the *Oregonian* with the names of birth mothers who supported Measure 58. The idea for the ad came from Jane Edwards, a fifty-six-year-old Salem attorney, new to adoption activism, who had recently reunited with her birth daughter.[74] As was her habit, Hill ran the idea by Grimm. She e-mailed her, "I'm thinking full page ad is the best way to go, with all these bmoms," supporting Measure 58. Grimm was noncommittal, showing neither great enthusiasm nor strong criticism. In general, she agreed with the idea, made helpful suggestions, and continued to give Hill important advice throughout the process of creating the ad.

Hill took it from there. She committed near $10,000 for the ad and contacted thousands of birth mothers through Sunflower Birthmothers, an international group connected by the Internet. Like BN, these birth mothers wanted to gain access to birth records for adopted adults; but they also wanted biological parents to have access to information concerning the welfare of their children. Their response to Hill's call for action was overwhelming. Within days Hill received over a thousand birth mothers' names in support of Measure 58.[75] At her campaign headquarters in a Kinko's in Northwest Portland, Hill spent the next several days without sleep, verifying the identities of the birth mothers who responded and pasting up the ad for the *Oregonian*. Hill's design was brilliant: five hundred signed birth mother statements run together one after another in support of either Measure 58 or open adoption records. She was in the middle of trying to fit them all on a single page when Delores Teller came running in with a photograph of five birth mothers who supported Measure 58, which she suggested should be placed in the middle of the ad. Teller, on her own, had hired the photographer, recruited the five birth mothers (one of whom was herself), and paid the photographer.[76] Hill "thought it was a damn good idea. It personalized it. It made you see faces. I was very grateful to her for that."[77] Hill's creative design coupled with the five birth mothers staring out from the middle of the page appeared under the caption: "Over 500 Birthparents say VOTE YES on Measure 58." Those who read the statements, set in tiny type, could not help being moved. Sherryl Wilkens wrote, "My son was born as a result of rape and I am willing to speak to anyone in support of Measure 58." Alicia Lanier wrote, "I was forced to surrender my daughter in 1975. I support completely Measure 58." The full-page ad ran in the Sunday edition of the *Oregonian* on November 1 and was well-placed, right after the editorial and op-ed pages.[78] With the publication of the birth mother ad, media electioneering for Measure 58 was, for all intents and purposes, over.

During the last week of the campaign, BN members flew into Oregon, and Hill rented a wing of the Rose Manor Motel, on the outskirts of Portland, for them to stay in. Hill herself, along with her Oregon workers and members of Bastard Nation, went to Portland's upscale Mallory Hotel to hear the election results on November 3. That evening, as they milled around waiting for the election results, everyone was excited and expressed confidence in victory.[79] Outside the state, the feeling was similar. In Philadelphia, BN Executive Committee member Cynthia Bertrand Holub wrote, "This is it, folks. I am so exited I can barely stand it. We are making history—we already HAVE made history, focusing so much national attention on the rights of adoptees. . . . I know we will win. I just know it. But no matter what the results show, we have won."[80] Holub was echoed by BN member David C. Ansardi in Alabama: "Whatever happens today, the Fight for Measure 58 had been a huge victory in the adoption community! The tide had changed!!! This is the one that is going to start the domino effect!!!!! I'm ready to see that first domino (Oregon!!!) tumble over!" Still, the vote was not in, the results were unknown, and most Measure 58 advocates also shared a tinge of doubt and probably agreed with Ansardi's comment: "Is that the sound of one BIG HUGE collective inhale all over the country today?????"[81]

By morning, the results were in. Measure 58 had triumphed, beating the opposition by what the early editions of the *Oregonian* described as a "narrow margin" of 54 to 46 percent. This would eventually grow, after all the absentee votes were counted, to the official victory margin of an impressive 57 to 43 percent. Joy swept across the adoption reform community nationwide. Alabama activist Ansardi reported to Bastard Nation how he wished everyone could have seen "the whoops and hollers on our own [Internet] BAMAdopt mailing list last night, people saying they couldn't sleep, champagne bottles popping in front of the keyboard of an Alabama adoptee in Sacramento, CA, and all of the resounding cries for 'Alabama's Next! Alabama's Next!' I am sure that those cries are echoed in states all around the country today because, thanks to your leadership, WE HAVE DONE IT!!!!!!!!! People now believe that it CAN be done!!"[82] Another BN member wrote:

> I'm overcome. . . . I can't help but wonder how it would feel to walk into a courthouse and ask for original birth certificate and actually receive it. The piece of paper I have been denied for so long with such venomous intensity. To not have a bespeckled county clerk tell me, 'That's confidential' or 'Your birth is none of your business' or even the classic, 'Why would you want that? Didn't you have a good adoption?' I try to fantasize about NOT wanting to strangle a total stranger for spewing such tripe. . . . Instead, I see myself simply paying the same fee for that small piece of paper as any non-adopted citizen. And, to even spice it up a bit, the clerk may even say, 'Have a nice day.' Refreshing don't you think? . . . This fantasy that so many of us have played over in our heads will be a reality for kindred spirits in Oregon. Can you imagine?[83]

Helen Hill put it more succinctly: "We are being reborn into integrity and honesty."[84]

The happiness of Bastard Nation members and other adoption activists derived not only from the personal advantages that might be reaped from passage of Measure 58 but also from its historical significance. The passage of Measure 58 was a milestone in the history of the adoption reform movement.

As Hill observed, "We're making history here tonight."[85] It was the first time in U.S. history that an initiative to restore the right of adopted adults to request their original birth certificate had been attempted and had been victorious. It was the first time that a sealed adoption records law had been repealed in the United States. It also demonstrated that, at least in Oregon, the general public supported opening records to adult adoptees. Measure 58 was also groundbreaking because it framed the issue of adoption reform in terms of civil rights and equal protection of the law rather than in terms of psychological needs or medical necessity.[86]

All of these were reasons for proponents of open adoption records to celebrate. But what particularly excited adoption activists was the idea that, as Damsel Plum put it, "the passage of Measure 58 in Oregon signals the beginning of the end of state sanctioned lies and secrecy in adoption."[87] Hill viewed it as part of a "trend whose time had come" and announced that there were plans in the works for possible ballot measures in Nevada, Montana, Colorado, and New Mexico. Grimm promised to introduce an open records bill in Washington State.[88] Around the country, adoption activists believed that passage of Measure 58 heralded the beginning of a sweeping state-by-state revolution that would finally give adopted adults access to their adoption records. As Linda Shipley of the Philadelphia Adoption Congress Internet Panel put it: "Oregon today, and tomorrow the world."[89]

7

The Legislature Weighs In

The morning after the election, Shea Grimm and Helen Hill were among the few people who had considered the possibility of a court or legislative challenge to Measure 58. On November 4, even as she celebrated Measure 58's victory, Grimm announced to Hill and Bastard Nation's Executive Committee that it was "back to work." She was going to spend the week with lawyers "preparing for the likely attempt by the opposition to halt M58 with a temporary court injunction." Grimm also stated that "Oregonians and Bners" had to start planning for the likelihood that the Oregon legislature would try to amend Measure 58 with contact veto legislation, a law making adoptee contact of a birth mother a felony if she had prohibited contact.[1]

One of the lawyers Grimm consulted was Thomas McDermott, who had volunteered to defend any court challenges to Measure 58 pro bono. McDermott was a Portland attorney who had adopted two boys. The initiative had first come to his attention in September 1998 when he read *Willamette Week* reporter Patty Wentz's cover story, "Bastard." Although one of his sons had been adopted in the traditional system of closed records, McDermott began to consider "the importance of my son having more information about his background and where he came from." What particularly struck McDermott about Wentz's article was that Warren Deras, a lawyer and an adoptive father like himself, was leading the opposition to Measure 58. Deras's status as an adoptive parent really bothered McDermott: "My initial gut reaction was, wait a minute, this is bullshit. . . . I felt like it really gave adoptive parents a bad name—that we would all be viewed as sort of co-conspirators in maintaining the secrecy." He immediately called Wentz for Hill's telephone number. Hill invited McDermott, who brought along his children, to appear on the October 4 *Town Hall* program, which featured both advocates and opponents of Measure 58. One of the highlights of the show was McDermott's fourteen-year-old son making a strong, articulate plea in support of adoptee rights. Afterward, Hill, advised by Grimm that there might be a court challenge to Measure 58, buttonholed McDermott and asked him whether he

Thomas McDermott, the Portland attorney who defended Measure 58, with his son.

would be willing to help. Without realizing what he was potentially volunteering for, McDermott replied, "Oh sure, I'd be willing to do that."[2]

The other attorney with whom Grimm conferred, and who would work with McDermott, was American Adoption Congress (AAC) legal adviser Frederick F. Greenman, who had offered to write the legal brief pro bono. Grimm remained suspicious of Greenman, despite what she interpreted as his personal "mea culpa" about the AAC's stand on Measure 58, but she thought his help a good idea because it took "a lot of pressure off of Thomas while giving us a lead counsel we can better trust."[3]

In discussing the opposition to Measure 58 after the victory, Grimm for the first time downplayed the importance of the National Council for Adoption (NCFA). She reported that the NCFA was having financial problems and that its board of directors had resolved several weeks earlier to cease presenting the organization's own briefs in legal cases. Instead, it would put its name to other people's cases, if it approved of them. For Grimm, this meant that William Pierce and the NCFA "will probably be behind the scenes, but they're not going to head-up any court effort." Who then would be the opposition's lead attorney? Grimm thought it would be Warren Deras, past leader of Concerned Adoption Professionals, mainly because it would not take much money or work to spearhead the initial temporary restraining order hearing against Measure 58.[4] But she ruthlessly rejected the possibility of a Deras victory: "He'll almost certainly lose. . . . (The justices hate him.)"[5] Grimm relished the idea of a contest between McDermott and Deras. Apparently, even before the anticipated temporary restraining order, she announced that McDermott was "going to go ahead and contact Deras with an eye towards intimidating him a little bit. Thomas is a very handsome, high-profile trial attorney. Very L.A. Law. He'll scare the bejesus out of Warren."[6]

Grimm proved remarkably prescient in predicting the opposition's strategy, though she was incorrect about some of the details. She had only to read the *Oregonian* to find out that Measure 58's opponents would seek redress in the Oregon legislature. On the day of the initiative's victory, Lauren Greenbaum, lead adoption counselor for the Boys and Girls Aid Society of Oregon (BGAS), continued the opposition to Measure 58. The *Oregonian* quoted her as hoping that the narrow margin of victory would prompt citizens to lobby their legislators to build in protections for birth parents.[7] The next day, she publicly called on the "upcoming Oregon Legislature to provide procedures . . . more responsive to birth parents' rights to privacy." Greenbaum said she expected that other adoption agencies would join the BGAS.[8] The BGAS planned to encourage the Coalition of Oregon Adoption Agencies, an umbrella group of twenty-nine organizations, to approach the state legislature to amend Measure 58 with a "contact preference form" that when filled out would indicate whether or not a birth mother wanted to be contacted by the adopted adult. The form would then be attached to the adoptee's original birth certificate. Such a law would allow a birth mother to officially express her desire not to have contact with her biological children. Oregon's law would differ from Tennessee's "contact veto form" by not levying civil penalties for violations of the act. Greenbaum and the BGAS believed that "this is the crucial piece that we feel needs to be in place to assure fairness and to give balance to the law."[9]

The legislature, however, did not immediately attempt to amend Measure 58. Instead, a week after the election William L. Pierce, president of the NCFA, announced that advocates of Measure 58 "were going to get a legal challenge from us. We are preparing to file suit." According to Pierce, the Oregon initiative "was a terrible thing because it does not respect the ability of somebody to say no. We've had calls from birth mothers in Oregon, crying 'Help us, help us.'" He went on to argue—just as the opposition had done during the campaign against Measure 58—that Oregon already had a system in place, a mutual reunion registry, in which adoptees and birth parents who wanted to find each other could do so. In addition, Oregon offered "confidential intermediaries" who would contact adoptees or birth parents.[10] But Pierce's announcement was a bluff, and Grimm's information was sound: the NCFA was financially strained, and it would play a minor role in the legal events that followed, filing only an amicus curiae brief to the Oregon Court of Appeals.[11]

Rather than Warren Deras or Bill Pierce, I. Franklin Hunsaker would lead the legal challenge to Measure 58. Hunsaker, a Portland attorney and adoptive parent, had long opposed Measure 58, but he had preferred to work behind the scenes rather than assume a prominent leadership role, at least until late into the election campaign. He first learned of Measure 58 from reading about it in the *Oregonian*. His immediate reaction was, "It's wrong." He called the BGAS, which had been mentioned in the paper, and volunteered his services. Like Thomas McDermott, he was motivated by his adoptive parent status, but in Hunsaker's case he was "an adoptive parent who felt strongly that birth parents have rights."[12] This led to his appearance on the *Town Hall* program. His reputation as a champion of birth parents' rights to privacy continued to grow as he continued to speak out. Hunsaker's first taste of national publicity was his October 26 appearance on the *Today Show,* where he shared the spotlight with Helen Hill and Cindy. His appearance on other talk shows and in the newspapers after the passage of Measure 58 prompted some forty to fifty birth mothers to call him requesting legal action against the initiative. It was then that Hunsaker decided to bring a lawsuit against the initiative.[13]

On November 28, Hunsaker announced that in two days he planned to block Measure 58 by filing a lawsuit against the state, a mere three days

I. Franklin Hunsaker, the Portland attorney who represented birth mothers who challenged Ballot Measure 58.

before the new law was due to go into effect. Hunsaker said he would seek a temporary restraining order in the Marion County Circuit Court in Salem. If granted, it would prevent Measure 58 from going into effect until there was a court hearing in which both parties could be heard.[14] Hunsaker was representing four birth mothers who were suing the state under "Jane Doe" pseudonyms. These birth mothers had filed affidavits stating that they had been promised confidentiality by an adoption agency, a lawyer, a doctor, or in one case by a nun. The affidavits contended that this promise had been instrumental in their decision to relinquish their children for adoption, and that if Measure 58 went into effect it would cause them great harm. As Hunsaker explained to the press: "Our argument is that Oregon law promised the privacy and confidentiality that was the basis of the adoptions, and because this law was retroactive it wipes away those promises. And that's why we believe it's unconstitutional." He also argued in the lawsuit that Measure 58 deprived birth mothers of equal protection of the law, in violation of the Fourteenth Amendment.[15]

Albin W. Norblad was the presiding judge for Marion County. His grandfather had been governor of the state and his father a U.S. congressman. Judge Norblad, however, according to an article in the *Oregonian,* was known "as a maverick among attorneys, Darth Vader to co-workers, and 'The Mean Judge' to the huge number of juvenile delinquents he sent to detention in the 1970s." By "maverick," attorneys meant that he could not be pigeonholed politically. Although generally thought to be conservative, he had upheld a controversial 1994 state law that in effect banned local anti-gay ordinances. All agreed that although Judge Norblad was unconventional, he was a topnotch jurist and predicted that he would be dispassionate and fair in the Measure 58 case.[16] On December 1, Judge Norblad granted Hunsaker's motion for a temporary restraining order and blocked Measure 58 from becoming law. The initiative would remain on hold until legal challenges were resolved under an agreement lawyers for both sides were ordered to sign by Judge Norblad. It was expected that application of the law would be delayed for at least two or three months.[17]

Bastard Nation's response to the temporary restraining order ran the gamut, from reasonableness to intense anger and even a suggestion that civil disobedience might be appropriate. On December 1, Grimm announced on BN's e-mail Listserv that the law would not go into effect, but assured its members that the attorney general's office fully expected to win. In the *Oregonian,* Helen Hill was quoted as saying that she "was deeply saddened for the adoptees out there who have waited so long and have had to endure brick wall after brick wall. This is another brick wall between them and a very simple civil right, which is the right of an adult to his or her own document of birth. Not a hard thing. The right of an adult to have the information that everyone else has."[18] By the next day it was clear that the rank-and-file members of Bastard Nation were taking a much tougher line than their leaders. They railed against the temporary restraining order, expressed their skepticism of the media, and even questioned their own lawyers. One BN member satirized Measure 58's defense team: "So these attorneys we have representing our side are going to stand up and shout 'MOO . . . MOO . . . MOOT' in the courtroom?" Answering his own rhetorical question in the negative, "Marko" said, "I'm ready for civil disobedience." He then went off on a wild riff of fantasy: "Can the public just show up at these [court] hearings (say, dressed in a cracked-egg costume and mooing like a cow every time the plaintiff's attorneys open their mouths)? I want a Johnny Cochran standing up there looking personally insulted and barking 'outrageous' 'insulting' and 'inflammatory' at the judges, and beating his fist on the table."[19]

The advocacy of civil disobedience hit a nerve with a few BN members, and a vigorous discussion ensued. In general, those in favor of civil disobedience urged BN adoptees to ignore the temporary restraining order and refuse to leave the Department of Vital Statistics Office until they received their birth certificate. The BN Executive Committee unanimously rejected this approach. While not ruling out civil disobedience if it proved to be necessary in the future and approving of it in theory, BN's leadership agreed that it was neither the right tactic nor December 3 the right time. Grimm reminded members that "civil disobedience is NOT the goal of Bastard Nation. The goal is adoptee rights in the form of open records."[20] Ron Morgan, BN's California state director, agreed, adding, "We discourage any acts of civil disobedience that break any law of the communities in which we are staging the Rush for Our Records. The cost would simply overwhelm any benefit."[21] On more pragmatic grounds BN Executive Committee member Cynthia Bertrand Holub objected to the use of civil disobedience because it would be "just plain irresponsible to rush into such a thing without serious training."[22] Morgan worried that besides having no training, BN had "no contingency plans in the event of an arrest or other police actions (bail, for instance) and in many cases were not providing direct Bastard Nation site leadership." Other members joined the leadership in condemning civil disobedience.[23] In the end, the cooler heads prevailed. BN's Rush for Our Records demonstration at Oregon's vital records office in Northeast Portland was peaceful, with about one hundred adoptees and supporters turning out.[24]

On December 10, Thomas McDermott, the attorney for Measure 58, filed the first of two motions with Judge Norblad that proved to be perhaps more important than the legal arguments contained in the briefs themselves. He requested "intervenor status" for his clients. This is a procedure under which a third party may join an ongoing lawsuit, providing the facts and the issues of law apply to the intervenor as much as they do to one of the existing contestants. Intervention must take place fairly early in the lawsuit, so as not to prejudice one or more of the parties who have prepared for the trial on the basis of the original litigants. In this case, McDermott had to convince not only Judge Norblad but the state attorney generals, who did not often like intervenors to work on behalf of the state. McDermott persuaded them by virtue of his own standing in the legal community and his assurance that he was not going to make the lawsuit a three-ring circus by having hundreds of people intervene (a situation that occurred in an ongoing Tennessee open records lawsuit, *Doe v. Sundquist,* where three hundred amicus briefs had been filed). McDermott's strategy was to have only a small number of diverse intervenors. In addition to Hill, who would be involved as an adopted adult and the chief petitioner, McDermott asked Hill to enlist as intervenors a birth mother, an adopted adult who did not yet have his records, and the Oregon Adoptive Rights Association—this last, he recalled later, "because I liked the sound of it. It was not Bastard Nation. . . . Oregon Adoptive Rights Association was much more salable to a court than Bastard Nation."[25] In other words, McDermott wanted as intervenors the entire adoption triad, including a birth mother who favored granting adopted adults access to their original birth certificates, and a respected adoption reform group that would enhance their image. Hill did as McDermott asked.

The parties that sought intervenor status were the Oregon Adoptive Rights Association, an Oregon nonprofit corporation with a membership of about 200 (represented by its president, Delores Teller); Helen Hill, chief petitioner for Measure 58; Curtis Endicott, a St. Helens resident and an adopted adult; and Susan Updike, a Scappose resident and birth mother, who welcomed contact from the child she relinquished for adoption.[26] If Judge Norblad approved the motion it would give the intervenors the ability to participate in discovery and exchange of information, cross-examination, and related activities in court. This would give the state more leeway in supporting the defendant's position. The state's attorneys, who dealt frequently with the same judges, had to be circumspect about the kind of questions they asked and concerned about the impression they left. Or, as McDermott put it: "For fear of future cases, they might be stuck then with something that might come back to bite them."[27] Intervenors had no such worries and could act as the state's surrogates. Moreover, if the plaintiffs won, the state would probably choose not to appeal the case; it was always very busy with other matters and usually accepted the decisions of the judge. But if McDermott gained status as an intervenor, he could appeal the case if the defendants lost.[28]

On January 13, Helen Hill quit Bastard Nation following a dispute between herself and Grimm about authorship of Measure 58.[29] Six days later, on January 19, opposing attorneys McDermott and Hunsaker finally met face to face in Judge Norblad's chambers for the preliminary hearing on whether to allow Measure 58 advocates intervenor status in the case. The two men were on opposite sides of the issue, but, ironically, their life stories revealed remarkable parallels. Both McDermott and Hunsaker were Vietnam veterans; both went to law school and received their law degrees in the San Francisco Bay area; both worked at prestigious Portland law firms; both were adoptive parents; and both, angered over Measure 58, volunteered their time pro bono in a legal case that would stretch out for the next year and a half.[30] On January 22, Judge Norblad granted McDermott's motion to allow the defendants intervenor status noting that "they clearly have a strong interest in the outcome and ought to be allowed to bring their theories of constitutionality to the table," thus handing Hunsaker his first defeat.[31]

Meanwhile, a second event was taking place that would have a significant effect on the outcome of the case. During January and February, BGAS's Lauren Greenbaum made good on the BGAS's plan to contact the Coalition of Oregon Adoption Agencies and its legislative committee chairperson, James Wheeler, to begin lobbying the Oregon legislature to amend Measure 58. She began by meeting with Wheeler, the director of Columbia Adoption Services, a private adoption agency; and representatives from two other adoption agencies that were part of the Coalition and pro–Measure 58: Paula Lang of Catholic Charities, and Cathy Stalker, co-president of the Coalition, who represented Holt International Children's Services. Wheeler was a longtime Oregon resident and adoptive parent. In 1968, he had earned his master's degree in social work at the University of Wisconsin; in the next seven years he worked at the Milwaukee County Department of Pubic Welfare, married, had one biological child, and adopted a child from Vietnam. In 1976, Wheeler moved his family to Portland, Oregon, where he joined the foster care program at the Boys and Girls Aid Society of Oregon. Four years later, Wheeler was put in charge of the BGAS's Adoption and Pregnancy Counseling Program, which he ran until 1988, when he left and started his own adoption agency.[32]

Wheeler had been an early opponent of Measure 58, objecting to it on the grounds that it violated birth parents' confidentiality and that Oregon already had laws in place that more than adequately dealt with this issue, such as Oregon's Voluntary Adoption Registry. The BGAS had been the first Oregon agency to start a voluntary adoption registry, and it proved so successful that the state used it as a model. Wheeler recalled that in some 90 to 95 percent of cases the person being sought agreed to be found, and in the other cases the birth parent called back within six months to consent to a meeting. Wheeler's early vocal opposition to Measure 58 had made him a favorite of the local media and also made him the logical choice to be one of the opposition members on the five-member committee that wrote the *Voters' Pamphlet* explanatory statement.

Greenbaum's decision to meet with the Coalition made sense. It was common knowledge that, as Wheeler stated, the Coalition had "a bill or more than one bill introduced in [each legislative] session, which we feel would better adoption in Oregon." Wheeler was especially knowledgeable and skilled in political lobbying, having worked at the job for a decade.[33]

The Coalition members and Greenbaum wanted to provide a solution to the complicated and emotional problem that had dominated the election campaign: how to balance the privacy rights of birth mothers against adopted adults' civil right to access their original birth records. The group quickly agreed to Greenbaum's idea of a "contact preference form." This particular solution was not surprising. Given the political realities, the group had little choice. They knew the legislature would be reluctant to overturn a popular ballot initiative. But, they hoped it might be willing to attach something to the original birth certificate that would protect birth mothers. After the group had agreed on its basic strategy, Wheeler met with House Minority Leader Kitty Piercy in her home to talk about the Coalition's proposal and asked her to sponsor the legislation. Piercy, a Democrat from Eugene and an adoptive parent, readily agreed.[34]

House Bill 3194, the piece of legislation that Piercy's office drafted in mid-March, was the opposition's attempt to amend Measure 58. Several sections surprised both Wheeler and Hill. The opening sentence stated that birth parents were to be notified that an adopted person had applied for his or her original birth certificate. It also specified that in the event the birth parent did not welcome contact, the adopted adult would receive the following note: "Please ask the adoptee to honor this information and voluntarily forgo receiving the original birth certificate. If I decide later that I would like contact, I will register with the voluntary adoption registry."[35] These portions of the draft bill appear to have been the result of a miscommunication between Wheeler and the legislative counsel or between Piercy's office and the legislative counsel,[36] not a deliberate effort to subvert Measure 58. According to Wheeler, the draft amendment that emerged was not what the group intended or wanted.[37]

Nevertheless, the proposed legislation, which by March 24 had been filed and sent to the Human Resources Committee, set off alarm bells for both Shea

Grimm and Helen Hill. Grimm was particularly opposed to the proviso that adopted adults should be asked not to access their birth certificates just because the birth parent did not want contact. According to Grimm, "That guts the intent of Measure 58, and also is rather undignified. It seems to presume that the adoptee cannot have access to their birth identity without violating the birth parent's wishes, as if they are an immature, impulsive child."[38] As she examined it more closely, Grimm concluded that "it's a fucked up bill." She particularly faulted the clause that called for the birth parent to be notified if an adopted adult applied for a birth certificate. Getting to the heart of the issue, she posed a series of questions to Patty Wentz, the *Willamette Weekly* reporter and confidant who continued even after the campaign in her dual role as journalist and committed political activist: "Who is going to search for the birthparents or how long [does] the adoptee [have] to wait for this search to take place, or what happens if the birthparents are dead, or can't be found. Or who's going to PAY for all of this. It just makes it sound like the registrar is going to call up Mr. and Mrs. Birthparent and fax them a form while the adoptee waits patiently at the window. Humph."[39] And who did Grimm immediately suspect was behind this nefarious piece of legislation? Delores Teller and the American Adoption Congress.[40]

Hill was especially alarmed by the clause that required the state to contact birth parents when adoptees applied for a birth certificate. She contacted Grimm for help. Grimm e-mailed her with specific instructions on how to amend the bill. On March 29, armed with various approaches on how to revise the bill, Hill drove to the state capitol in Salem and arrived there just before closing time. Upon being refused entry and believing that she "was watching Measure 58 being overturned," Hill buttonholed Piercy's legislative aide, Morgan Allen, and angrily asked him, "Do you know what kind of amendment this is? This is terrible. I'll have 250 people in this state downstairs in front of the capitol." Allen was shaken at Hill's outburst, but seemed cooperative. According to Hill, Allen replied, "Oh, you are right. That's a horrible thing. Will you help us rewrite this?" Hill immediately agreed. She then called Grimm requesting legal advice. As Hill explained, "whenever I had any legislative or legal problems, like this one that I had to wade through in my very inept way, I would call Shea. And Shea is like, 'O.K. Helen, here is what you do. Here's what you say.' So she was invaluable in that way."[41]

Over the next two weeks, Hill, Wheeler, and two representatives from the Board of Vital Records, Bud Johnson and Katie King, met to revise HB 3194. At the start of the meeting, the representatives from the Board of Vital Records raised nine issues about the bill, several of them closely related to the clause ordering the state to notify birth parents when the adoptee applied for a birth certificate. They asked, "Is the State Registrar responsible for the notification of birth parent/parents?"[42] According to Wheeler, one Vital Records representative said, "There is no way we can do this. This would require that the amendment would go to the Ways and Means [Committee] because there is a fiscal impact and we are not set up to do any of this." And Wheeler replied, "Yes, we didn't expect you to be making contact with birth parents."[43] Hill, of course, was in total agreement. On March 31, the *Oregonian* reported that Piercy intended to "revise [HB 3194] to drop a reference that would have required the state to notify birth parents who were being sought by adoptees."[44]

On April 2, Piercy's office sent Hill a revised bill, minus the notification section and the clause that asked adopted adults to withdraw their requests for their birth certificates if the birth parents did not want contact. Still, much to Hill's and Grimm's consternation, the bill still preserved the original wording in the contact preference form: "I would prefer nondisclosure of identifying information at this time."[45] As Grimm pointed out, the form was called a "contact preference form," so what did "identifying information" have to do with it? Behind her objection lay profound distrust of the state Vital Records bureaucracy and the fear that such language would give its clerks a way "to try and withhold the birth certificate."[46] Hill suggested that the offending phrase be eliminated. Further, she wanted the form to be sealed and attached to the birth certificate. Grimm suggested that the form should be notarized and the entire package handed over to the adopted adult. That way, no clerk would see the form.

Progress on HB 3194 stalled over how the state would protect the privacy of the contact preference form. The disagreements between Piercy's office and Hill were the most difficult of the entire negotiation. Allen, Piercy's legislative aide, dismissed Hill's insistence that the form be notarized because the state registrar or a clerk would be verifying the information, making a notary unnecessary. The state registrar claimed that only an unsealed contact preference form (CPF) could be correctly matched with the adoptee's birth certificate. Hill adamantly stood her ground: "NO GO, we cannot have clerks reading these CPF's meant for the adoptee; that is a situation ripe for abuse." Hill suggested that "the CPF be sealed from the get go and identifying information and notarized signature be placed on the OUTSIDE of the form." But Allen maintained these were mere "details" that could be taken care of by the State Office for Services to Children and Families, which was going to create the form. Hill wrote to Grimm that she was "very nervous about this, [I] don't want to blow this." Grimm agreed. "Some details I agree can be left alone, but not the notarization, and not the sealing so that only the adoptee reads it. It's an invasion of the adoptee's privacy to do anything differently, and ripe for abuse, as you note."[47] But the forces arrayed against her proved to be too strong. Hill eventually had to give in. She later remarked that it was "the only thing I gave up that I really didn't feel good about."[48]

On April 13, Hill wrote to members of Bastard Nation, revealing her and the BN leadership's role in amending Measure 58 and the contents of HB 3194. She apologized for the need for secrecy and asked the members not to "panic and start screaming, which I did and the entire Exec Comm of BN [did] when we first heard of HB 3194," but "hang onto your worthless amended [birth certificates] and just listen." Hill emphasized that the contact preference form was not legally binding. It was voluntary, so the adoptee would get his or her birth certificate whether the birth parent chose contact or not. Moreover, and more important, she reassured them, Measure 58 was intact; not a word of it had been changed. Unconditional access to the birth certificate had not been hindered or threatened in any way. Hill noted other advantages of HB 3194. It would "forestall the far more sickening variety of disastrous amendments which could have befallen M58 in the legislature," as had happened in Delaware, Tennessee, and Illinois. (Here Hill was referring to "contact vetoes," which gave birth mothers the right to veto adopted adults' requests to receive their own original birth certificates.) Instead, Oregonians who opposed Measure 58 and worried about its "fairness" would now feel as if HB 3194 "fixed" the initiative and not bother with it anymore. She predicted "that the passage of this bill will influence our case favorably, and may lead to a summary judgment in our favor by the Judge sometime this summer." She "dare[d] to dream" that HB 3194 would establish a precedent that could be used in other states, leading to a greater sense of "fairness about open records legislation with no abrogation of rights." She urged BN members to write, call, or fax the Oregon House Human Resources Committee members in support of "this excellent bill," which was scheduled for a hearing on April 20 at the Oregon Capitol.[49]

Hill admitted that she was concerned over what Oregon's House Human Resources Committee might do. She confessed that she was "VERRRY worried about amendments or changes to the bill." After all, she noted, this was the same committee that had "essentially gutted Oregon's assisted-suicide Bill" by sending it back to the voters for a second time. But once the hearing was over, Hill found the process "awesome and magic."[50] One reason for her sudden change of opinion was that there was no opposition to HB 3194.[51] Advocates and opponents of Measure 58 all testified before the committee in favor of the bill. Representative Piercy introduced the bill as one "grounded in common sense . . . the result of communication and compromise between two groups that have differing views on the 'open adoption records' issue."[52] Hill assured committee members that she was "very excited about House Bill 3194," which represented the cooperation of adoption agencies and adoption triad members that she had "always dreamed about." To Hill, the bill expanded "the dignity of everyone involved in the post-adoption years, for it is predicated on the assumption that direct correspondence, voluntarily offered by the birthparent, and put directly into the hands of the adoptee, where it belongs will help adult adoptees make even more considerate, careful choices about how to handle the sensitive issues of their own lives."[53]

This time, the Internet lived up to its potential. Bastard Nation inundated the Capitol with dozens of e-mail messages in favor of HB 3194. Hill reported later that "the reps were MOST impressed at all the email. Astounded, really. The chair asked me personally, for him, [to] tell everybody thanks for writing."[54] On April 26, the committee proposed several amendments, which were quickly adopted. Among the most important was the amendment to the clause concerning birth parent contact. The first sentence of the contact preference form remained intact: "I prefer not to be contacted at this time." But the rest of the section was changed. If the birth parent changed his or her mind in the future and wanted contact, the birth parent was now instructed to register with the state's voluntary adoption registry and file an updated medical history.[55] There was no opposition from committee members to the bill or the amendments. They promptly voted 7–0 in favor of it.[56] On April 29, when it came to the House floor, it passed unanimously, 58–0.[57]

A month later, on May 20, the Senate Judiciary Committee held its first and only public hearing on HB 3194 with similar results. Both opponents and advocates of Measure 58—in this case James Wheeler, Lauren Greenbaum, Delores Teller, and Helen Hill—spoke in favor of the bill.[58] After a brief discussion in which no senators raised any objections, the committee voted 6–0 in favor of the bill.[59] The full Senate also passed HB 3194 unanimously, and Governor Kitzhaber signed it into law on July 12, 1999.[60]

The ease with which HB 3194 passed in House and Senate suggested that the legislature had gotten the message from the voters' convincing endorsement of Measure 58. Its passage was also indicative of a significant change in popular opinion that was occurring in Oregon and across the nation. Although HB 3194 was ostensibly about protecting birth parents' privacy, that issue was hardly mentioned in committee or on the House floor. Instead, the few legislators who spoke publicly praised the bill for its support of openness in adoption. State representative Vicki Walker from Eugene urged support for HB 3194 because she believed it was "important to have openness in this process, not secrets and lies." She stressed the joy that a reunion brought to a birth parent and said she thought it "so cruel not to let a birth mother know where her

CONTACT PREFERENCE FORM FOR
BIRTH PARENTS OF ADOPTED CHILDREN

The Oregon Center for Health Statistics needs the following information to find and match your request with your records. (Please print legibly)

Name of child on original birth record: _____

Date of birth: _____ Sex: • Male • Female Hospital: _____

County: _____ City: _____

Mother's name (as shown on birth certificate): _____

Adoption agency involved with adoption (if known): _____

IF THE ORIGINAL BIRTH CERTIFICATE IS RELEASED, WHAT IS YOUR PREFERENCE ABOUT CONTACT WITH THE ADOPTEE?

The Center for Health Statistics cannot accept this Contact Preference Form unless it is fully completed.

I am the: • birth mother • birth father Date: _____

Please check one of the three boxes and provide the required information.

• **I would like to be contacted.** My current name: _____
  Address: _____
  Telephone _____

• **I would prefer to be contacted only through an intermediary.**

• **I prefer not to be contacted at this time.** If I decide later that I would like to be contacted, I will register with an Oregon voluntary adoption registry.* I have completed a Birth Parent Updated Medical History form (Form CF 246R) and have filed it with an Oregon voluntary adoption registry. Attached is a Certificate (Form CF 247R) from an Oregon voluntary adoption registry verifying receipt of the Birth Parent Updated Medical History form. **IF NO CONTACT IS YOUR PREFERENCE YOU MUST:**

  1. Request and complete a Birth Parent Updated Medical History form from an Oregon voluntary adoption registry.* (Form CF 246R)
  2. Request from an Oregon voluntary adoption registry a Certificate of Receipt of Birth Parent Updated Medical History form (Form CF 247R) and attach it to the completed Contact Preference Form and submit it to the Oregon Center for Health Statistics.

For additional information or forms, please contact the adoption agency involved with the adoption or either of the following offices:

Oregon Center for Health Statistics	Permanency and Adoption Services / Registry
Certification Unit	State Office for Services to Children and Families
PO Box 14050	500 Summer Street, NE
Portland OR 97293-0050	Salem, OR 97310-1010
(503/731-4108)	(503/945-6643)

*Voluntary adoption registries may be maintained by the adoption agency involved with your child's adoption. Contact those agencies directly or contact the Oregon Voluntary Adoption Registry maintained by the State Office for Services to Children and Families.
        THIS FORM IS AVAILABLE IN AN ALTERNATE FORMAT UPON REQUEST

45-29(8/99)

HB 3194's contact preference form.

children were." Similarly, Representative Elaine Hopson from Tillamook, an adopted adult herself, viewed HB 3194 as an aid in facilitating reunions, and "any joy we can bring to people's lives, we should do."[61] Most of the people who testified before the committee or sent e-mail messages in favor of HB 3194 reinforced the idea that openness and equality of treatment lay at the heart of the bill.[62] No birth mothers testified at the committee hearing. By and large, the Oregon legislature viewed HB 3194 as a bill that facilitated reunions. This is why it had added a clause in the bill requesting birth parents who changed their minds about contact to register with the state's voluntary adoption registry. But the unacknowledged truth of the matter was that HB 3194 really did not protect the privacy of birth parents. There was nothing in the bill that prevented adopted adults from picking up their birth certificates and searching for their birth parents even if the contact preference form stated that the birth parent wanted no contact. But before the passage of Measure 58 and HB 3194 there was no guarantee of birth parent privacy either. Every day adopted adults contacted their birth parents, either through their own diligent searches or through the services of private detectives.

HB 3194 was a bill for all constituencies: to the 454,122 citizens who voted against Measure 58, it appeared that the Oregon legislature had done something to protect birth parents from the effects of Measure 58; to adoption activists it was acceptable because it did not alter the substance of Measure 58 and was likely to be useful in the upcoming court case; and to the majority of the 609,268 citizens who voted in favor of Measure 58 it symbolically reflected the growing shift in popular attitude toward openness in adoption and against government intrusion in the private lives of citizens in general.

Two weeks after the passage of HB 3194, on May 13 Judge Norblad considered whether the six birth mothers in the *Jane Doe* suit would be allowed to keep their anonymity before the trial. McDermott wanted to conform to standard legal practice and depose each of the women. Hunsaker objected on the grounds that their privacy would be violated. Judge Norblad ruled in favor of Hunsaker, but left open the question of whether he would allow the birth mothers to be interviewed by telephone.[63] During the morning hearing, the judge revealed his previous involvement in adoption reunions. McDermott was stunned to hear the judge say that "as a district attorney [I] advised mothers that they would remain anonymous from their children if they were surrendered for adoption."[64] Norblad had previously alluded to problems with the issue of adoption and offered to recuse himself if counsel thought it appropriate.[65] McDermott wondered if Norblad was "throwing bait out there" to be recused. "I thought he wanted off this one because maybe he was struggling himself as to how objective he could be." McDermott then confronted

Norblad and politely tried to point out the prejudicial nature of the judge's opinion. According to McDermott, Norblad demurred, replying either "I still have an open mind" or "I can be objective." But McDermott was skeptical: what judge would admit he was prejudiced?[66]

McDermott conferred with New York attorney Frederick Greenman and his colleagues in the case, the Oregon state attorney generals.[67] Although members of the state team supported a recusal, they did not want to initiate it: the state and Marion County had a long, discordant history over recusing judges, which had made the issue extremely sensitive.[68] McDermott's acquiring intervenor status was proving its worth. On May 28, McDermott wrote Judge Norblad, cited his work as district attorney with birth mothers, and gingerly stated that "while it is not our intent here to question your judicial objectivity or integrity, your statements have generated great concern among our clients regarding their ability to receive a fair and impartial hearing." McDermott then requested that Norblad "act on your earlier offer to recuse yourself."[69]

Judge Norblad wrote in reply that because of the importance of the case, he would agree to step aside "so there can be no question of impartiality." He also announced that the case would be reassigned to Judge Paul J. Lipscomb. Judge Norblad also sent a copy of his letter to Salem's *Statesman Journal*, which published it. The judge resented the suggestion that he was not "initially open with the Parties as to my involvement in adoptions." Moreover, he thought the request for recusal was too late. He concluded by denouncing McDermott in no uncertain terms: "I consider this request for recusal almost six months after the filing to be disingenuous at best. Therefore, I want an affidavit of prejudice filed and used up so the judge shopping will be limited."[70] This meant that McDermott had to go on the record publicly and request Judge Norblad's recusal. To be accused publicly of "judge shopping" was demeaning.

But for McDermott it was well worth it. As far as he was concerned, the judge's recusal was "the turning point in the case" because he was "convinced Norblad would have ruled against us."[71] On June 17, Judge Norblad announced publicly his recusal from the Measure 58 lawsuit.[72]

8

"The Land of Noodle-Heads"

W hen oral arguments began on a warm Wednesday, July 14, 1999, at 1:30
P.M. Salem's Marion County Circuit Court was surprisingly uncrowded.
Besides the co-counsels and intervenors, there were only a half a dozen Measure 58 supporters and a couple of news reporters.[1] Presiding Judge Paul J. Lipscomb had been on the bench for twelve years before *Jane Does 1–7 v. State
of Oregon* came before him.[2] Though he was soft-spoken in the courtroom,
he rarely minced words. Lipscomb says he tries "to have an honest, open kind
of experience with the individual, and I am not hesitant in expressing my point
of view, but I want to understand yours at the same time."[3] Known for his hard
work and intellectual independence, Lipscomb relished the prospect of a long,
complicated legal case. To him, it was an intellectual challenge, not an occu-
pational hazard to be avoided. Judge Lipscomb had a well-formulated philosophy about oral argument that did not bode well for either party. He believed
that oral argument was "important as a check to make sure the judge . . . has
a good, comprehensive understanding of the arguments on both sides of the
case and makes *absolutely certain* that before you rule against the party they
have had a completely full and fair opportunity to explore with you their arguments and position." But oral arguments were not usually decisive in forming
his decision, if the briefs in a case were decent or good. In his ruling in *Does
1–7 v. State of Oregon,* Lipscomb relied on the briefs because he found them
"at least decent" and the legal issues were not particularly complex.[4]

Franklin Hunsaker was supremely confident: "I just felt there was no way
we could lose," he recalled.[5] His brief in support of the plaintiff's motion for
summary judgment was impressive. Certainly legal precedent was on his side.
In the vast majority of prior rulings, in state lawsuits such as *Application of
Maples* (1978) and at the federal level in *ALMA Soc'y Inc. v. Mellon* (1979),
the courts had ruled against adopted adults when they sought access to their
adoption records.[6] The twenty-one depositions and affidavits in Hunsaker's
brief, together with his thorough research of case law, revealed that between
1957 and 1983, three Oregon statutes expressly stated that adoption records,
including birth certificates, were sealed and could not be opened except on an

Judge Paul J. Lipscomb, the Marion County Circuit Court judge who ruled on Measure 58.

order from a court of competent jurisdiction.[7] After 1983, when these Oregon adoption statutes had been amended to reflect the enactment of the state's voluntary adoption registry, the statutes stated that identifying information about a birth parent could be disclosed only with the mutual consent of the birth parent and the adopted adult.[8] The history of how these Oregon adoption statutes had been interpreted was also on his side. He had depositions from former Oregon judges and physicians, practicing lawyers, and adoption agency officials who had advised birth mothers that they had a reasonable expectation of privacy, should go on with their lives, and need never worry that this information would be disclosed without their consent.[9] He even had an affidavit from Elizabeth Welch, the Chief Judge in Multnomah County Circuit Court, who testified that based on her "substantial experience" with requests from adopted adults to view their records, Measure 58 "would breach a birth mother's reasonable expectations of privacy and confidentiality as to any adoption that took place during the period 1957 through the present . . . where she was promised that the original certificate of birth would be sealed except upon order of a court."[10] Given his legal research, Hunsaker's strategy was to stress the retroactive nature of Measure 58: it wiped out forty years of promises, assurances, and statutes.[11] This legal strategy led him during oral argument to include many emotional appeals to the Jane Doe affidavits in order to show that his clients' lives, and by extension the lives of all birth mothers, would be ruined if Measure 58 went into effect.

Hunsaker opened with what would prove to be a central issue in the case: that Measure 58 impaired the obligation of contracts, in violation of both the Oregon and the U.S. Constitutions. He began with an emotional recounting of the specific experiences of each of the birth mothers.[12] He stressed that the plaintiffs had been promised that their identity and all identifying information would be kept confidential. These birth mothers feared that if Measure 58 became law they would "suffer immediate and irreparable harm, emotional stress, humiliation, and embarrassment."[13] The birth mothers believed they had entered into a contract when they relinquished their children for adoption. Hunsaker asserted that the contracts consisted of "oral promises, numerous promises and assurances of confidentiality and privacy" and "written promises."[14]

Of course, there had to be a party to the contract, or at least some authority under which adoption workers, doctors, and nuns were making these promises to the birth mothers. This is why Hunsaker put so much emphasis on state law. Over and over, he emphasized, it was the state's adoption statutes that "clearly and explicitly create, protect, and enforce the confidentiality and privacy rights of birth parents." Hunsaker brought out two four-foot-square easels for visual emphasis, upon which were written two of Oregon's adoption laws.[15] He discussed Oregon's first sealed adoption records statute, enacted in 1957, which explicitly provided that at the time of an adoption the clerk "shall cause all records, papers, and files relating to the adoption to be sealed in the record of the case and such sealed records, papers, and files shall not be unsealed, opened, or subject to the inspection of any person except upon order of a court of competent jurisdiction."[16] But he also frequently cited Oregon's subsequent 1983 adoption statute (109.430) that established the state's voluntary adoption registry, wherein "The State fully recognizes the right to privacy and confidentiality of birth parents whose children were adopted, the adoptees."[17] This, Hunsaker told the court, was a reaffirmation of the legislature's support for the privacy of birth parents, which always had been of paramount concern to Oregon lawmakers. Hunsaker concluded by emphasizing that each adoption involved a contractual relationship governed by a statute, that Measure 58 impaired the adoption contracts entered into by the plaintiffs because it would nullify the confidentiality obligation, and it did so "retroactively and without exception."[18] Since Oregon's Constitution guaranteed that "no law impairing the obligation of contracts shall ever be passed," Hunsaker declared Measure 58 unconstitutional.[19]

Hunsaker's case ran into trouble early. During Hunsaker's discussion of Oregon's 1983 adoption statute, Judge Lipscomb interrupted him and suggested that perhaps his reliance on that law was not well placed. In the judge's opinion, "109.430 doesn't seem to me to be necessarily inconsistent with Measure 58." Hunsaker "respectfully disagreed." The judge explained that the issue before the Court was not an open records law. The state was simply permitting adopted adults access to their birth certificates. The state still recognized the right to privacy and confidentiality of the birth parents and adoptive parents. With some incredulity, Hunsaker reminded Lipscomb that Measure 58 permitted the adopted adult to obtain identifying information—that is, the name of the birth parent that was on the original birth certificate—when that was exactly the information that the 1957 and 1983 adoption statutes had been— But Judge Lipscomb abruptly cut Hunsaker off. He said, "I think the point is there's only one single person in the entire universe that can get access to any record of any birth parent and that's the child." Hunsaker protested, "But if they have it, Your Honor, then the door is open. I mean that information is no longer confidential, as far as the birth mother is concerned, the birth parents, and the cat's out of the bag." Lipscomb and Hunsaker continued to argue about this issue for another five minutes. Finally, Judge Lipscomb's patience grew thin. He snapped, "My only point is that you're reading into 109.430 an absolute bar to disclosure to anyone and all I'm going to say is, I don't think the words necessarily would support that kind of absolutist reading." Hunsaker was ready to relent, but he could not resist repeating that the 1957 adoption law and others upheld an absolute bar to access adoption records. The judge got the last word, dryly noting that he "was just trying to say that I think you're relying perhaps too strongly on 109.430."[20]

The first defense counsel to respond to Hunsaker was State Assistant Attorney General Katherine Georges. She contended that Measure 58 did not represent a sharp break with the past. It was instead the revival of an old law. Prior to 1957, adult adoptees had a right to access their original birth certificates by simply requesting them from the state registrar. Lipscomb interrupted, saying, "Until 1921 or 1929 they were published annually," a remark that appeared to be both helpful to the defense and to reflect a knowledgeable judge. Georges's purpose in making the point that Measure 58 revived an old law was to reveal that by the plaintiffs' logic every legislative change was in some sense an impairment of birth mothers' contracts and hence unconstitutional.[21]

To show that the Oregon legislature had the right to amend or even repeal Measure 58, if it wanted to, Georges gave as an example House Bill 3194. Granting two premises of Hunsaker's argument—that even if the Court found that a contract existed between birth mothers and the state *and* that a state law substantially impaired that contract—Georges argued that there was still no violation, as long as that law, amended by HB 3194, was a reasonable and necessary law to pass. If it was, then the burden of proof was on the plaintiffs.

"Certainly, if it was reasonable to close these records in 1957, it's equally reasonable to open them in 1998, and it's up to the Legislature and the voters how they are going to balance these competing interests." In the case of Measure 58, the voters had decided to make original birth certificates available to the adopted person when he or she reached the age of twenty-one, and that was entirely reasonable.[22]

But Georges went further, denying the very existence of a contract between birth parents and private individuals. Hunsaker had relied heavily on depositions from adoption attorneys, social workers, and judges; but, Georges pointed out, Oregon law prohibited private adoption contracts. Thus, any "contract" these private citizens had entered into with the birth mothers had been illegal. Georges concluded by asserting that "adoption was a matter of statute, not of contract." Even granting Hunsaker's theory that promises were made to the birth mothers by adoption agencies or lawyers and doctors, Georges argued that Measure 58 did not impair any obligations under those contracts. Measure 58 applied only to the state registrar, and it allowed that office to release only one record—the original birth certificate—to the person whose birth it certified.[23]

Thomas McDermott then addressed the bench. He argued that "almost to a person all of the affidavits they have submitted fail to address this issue of whether there is a contract of adoption." Nor, according to McDermott, had the plaintiffs produced a written contract. This was no surprise, because, he argued, adoption was not a contractual process; it was a statutory one. According to the plaintiff's affidavits, four of the six birth mothers did not think they were involved in a contractual transaction either.[24]

McDermott then abruptly shifted his attack to the failure of the doctors, social workers, and adoption agencies who submitted affidavits to inform the plaintiffs that their children when grown could petition the court to unseal the adoption records. In other words, birth mothers never would have been promised "an eternal anonymity from their own child" because the adoption statute contained the clause "sealed except with a court order." McDermott added that adoption statutes did not put the burden of proof on the petitioner to show critical conditions, such as a life-threatening medical emergency, to release records. He said that "the statute speaks for itself." At this point, Judge Lipscomb asked, "They just have to convince some judge that it's a good idea?" And McDermott replied, "Right. For mental reasons, for physical reasons, for whatever reasons, they just have—right."[25]

Here McDermott was on thin ice for logical, historical, and legal reasons. Logically, if it was so easy and /or common for adoptees to get a judge to open the records by petitioning the court, why was Measure 58 needed in the first place? Moreover, historically and legally, the overwhelming majority of cases that did exist, whether inside or outside of Oregon, demonstrated that it was rare for judges to open adoption records for "good cause."[26] But McDermott was not interested in the historical past or the present. His point was that in the 1957 adoption statute "the *potential* for unsealing the records existed in every single case." The plaintiffs were simply wrong in arguing for a complete promise of confidentiality "when at all times the system recognized the ability of the adoptee to go to court and unseal the records."[27]

Most of Hunsaker's rebuttal was spent defending the impairment-of-contract argument.[28] This may have been a mistake.[29] One exchange certainly revealed Judge Lipscomb's skepticism of Hunsaker's argument about contracts. It occurred during an elaborate hypothetical analogy Judge Lipscomb made concerning changes in the financial provisions of a contract that the government made with parents who adopted a severely disabled individual.[30] When Hunsaker and his law partner, Loren D. Podwill, failed to answer Lipscomb's questions satisfactorily, the judge grudgingly admitted that his analogy was "not 100 percent applicable but I would suggest that that's not a difference." And if that statement was not enough of a warning to Hunsaker, a minute later the judge said, "I just think this contract is a pretty slender reed. Let's move to the next point." But Hunsaker persisted; not two minutes later, he told Judge Lipscomb, "In fact, we believe that the impairment of contract is one of the stronger arguments."[31] This was not a wise statement. But Hunsaker was shocked and surprised at Lipscomb's hostility.[32]

Hunsaker then made a constitutional-rights argument for the privacy and confidentiality of birth mothers. Drawing on the principle first announced in 1965 by Supreme Court Justice William O. Douglas in *Griswold v. Connecticut,* Hunsaker argued that there were certain rights not explicit, but implicit in the "penumbras" of the Constitution: a right of marital privacy found in the Bill of Rights.[33] In 1973, in *Roe v. Wade,* the Supreme Court recognized that the right to privacy applied only to rights declared as "fundamental" or "implicit in the concept of ordered liberty."[34] Using Douglas's idea of "penumbras," Hunsaker referred to Section 133 of Article 1 of the Oregon Constitution, where he said the "the well-recognized principle that natural rights recognized by common law may be constitutionally protected even where not specifically created if they also are recognized by statute." That was the basis of Hunsaker's claim: that birth mothers' rights to privacy were entitled to constitutional protection because these rights were a "category of fundamental liberty" and also because they were embedded in adoption statutes.[35]

Judge Lipscomb was openly skeptical of Hunsaker's argument. He pointed out that at the time Oregon became a state and its constitution was adopted—

and the federal constitution was in force—neither "could have supported a right of privacy in a biological mother giving up her child for adoption because at that time records were public." Lipscomb asked Hunsaker: How is the right of privacy created now? Did the 1957 adoption statute create a right of privacy for birth mothers? Hunsaker replied by analogy. It was the same way that the Supreme Court did not recognize a protected or fundamental liberty interest in matters relating to marriage, procreation, contraception, family relationships, child rearing, and abortion until they became an issue. But when those matters did become issues before the Court, such as contraception in *Griswold* in 1965 and abortion in *Roe v. Wade* in 1973, it recognized a liberty interest protected by penumbras from the fundamental guarantees of the Bill of Rights in the U.S. Constitution. To Hunsaker (as he said to the judge), it seemed self-evident that if there were adoption statutes that mandated that records should be kept confidential they came under this penumbra. "We don't claim that it's expressly covered in the constitution," he said.[36]

Georges hit back hard on Hunsaker's admission that there existed no express right to privacy in the Oregon and federal constitutions. She scornfully noted that instead of "text, history, and case law, we're offered penumbras and emanations . . . it's smoke and mirrors." Even more damaging to Hunsaker's case, however, was Georges's accurate charge that the phrase "natural rights" did not exist in the text of the Oregon constitution. The phrase had been supplied by the legislative counsel as a heading for one of the Constitution's many sections. Georges also disputed Hunsaker's discussion of the Supreme Court's rulings that carved out a liberty interest in matters of procreation and marital privacy—and, by analogy, to sealed adoption records. Adoption records in Oregon, she argued, had been published and accessible to the public from 1864 until 1921, open for adoptees until 1957, and open upon a court order between 1957 and 1998. The adoption statute permitting adoption records to be open upon a court order provided no provision for any notice to the birth parent to be heard or any right to appeal. It followed that the birth parent was not involved in this proceeding. Consequently, birth parents could have "no kind of reasonable expectations of confidentiality or privacy." Georges contended that Measure 58 did not interfere with the right of procreation, marriage, or child rearing. Birth mothers were free to marry or use contraceptives or bear children or relinquish them for adoption. Therefore, she argued, none of the cases that Hunsaker cited, such as *Roe v. Wade*, were applicable.[37]

It was past 4:00 in the afternoon when Hunsaker rose to rebut Georges. He contended that Measure 58 unconstitutionally deprived the plaintiffs of equal protection of the law because *Roe v. Wade* granted another class of women—those who obtained abortions—the privilege of confidentiality and privacy while denying the same privilege to women who relinquished their children for adoption. This, Hunsaker concluded, was discriminatory. Measure 58 had no rational relationship to any legitimate state goal, reasonableness and legitimacy being crucial standards to judge whether a law was discriminatory. Hunsaker asserted that the state's voluntary adoption registry and the open adoption statutes already in place were better ways for adopted adults to get identifying information.[38]

Georges then rose to tackle Hunsaker's equal protection of the law argument head-on. First she fleshed out Hunsaker's argument about the origins of the discrimination between the two classes of persons. The discrimination arose, she told the court, because the plaintiffs claimed the medical records of women who seek abortions were confidential, while the identity of the women who relinquished their children for adoption would be revealed on the birth records under Measure 58. But Georges denied that these were two similarly situated classes of persons. Obviously, women who had abortions did not bear children, so birth records were not relevant to them. Judge Lipscomb helped her along, saying, "And the medical records of birth mothers are not subject to disclosure?" Georges replied, "Correct." She went on to make the point that in regard to medical records everyone was treated equally and that under Measure 58 everyone was treated equally too, so that there was no equal protection violation.[39]

Hunsaker disagreed with Georges's contention that there was a significant difference between mothers who chose abortion and those who chose adoption. Judge Lipscomb pointed out that in *Roe v. Wade* privacy rights for the birth mother extended only until the fetus was six months old; then the balance of privacy rights shifted to the state to protect the interest of the child. "I don't think that *Roe v. Wade* can be stretched beyond birth certainly," said the judge, "and I would say clearly not up to the age of twenty-one where the state is forbidden to prefer the child over the mother." Hunsaker explained that the disparate treatment occurred at birth, not twenty-one years later. If birth mothers made the decision to place their children for adoption they were treated differently than if they had an abortion. It was that disparate treatment that constituted a denial of equal protection under the law. Lipscomb responded by noting that the Court had created three different classes of mothers under *Roe v. Wade*—mothers who had abortions up to the age of three months, mothers who had abortions between three months and six months, and mothers who had abortions after six months—and they were treated differently. To this comment, Hunsaker stated, "Well, your Honor, I don't believe, with all due respect, that that does in fact distinguish a way. I think that the court in *Roe* recognized the privacy interest and I think—" But before he could finish Judge Lipscomb cut him off, saying, "Right." Lipscomb agreed with Hunsaker that *Roe v. Wade* contained a privacy interest, but added this chilling proviso: "but because a privacy interest exists doesn't mean that the State can't interfere with it. If there is another significant important interest—" This time Hunsaker cut Judge Lipscomb off. He denied that in this case there was another important significant interest. The present adoption statutes worked well. There was no need for reform. It was not enough, as the defendants claimed, that the legislature and the people had the power to make laws to open the adoptions records. It must also pass constitutional muster. And with that, Hunsaker rested his case on equal protection.[40]

The hearing had at this point been under way for more than three hours. McDermott rose and said on behalf of the intervenors that he had some brief closing remarks. Judge Lipscomb interjected, "Very brief." But McDermott ignored Lipscomb's admonition and proceeded to reveal some of the passion that motivated his devotion to Measure 58. (It was the only time in the trial when McDermott did not follow his own advice that a lawyer should always listen closely to what the judge says.) Leaving the rarified discourse of case law and legal principles, McDermott launched into the history and sociology of adoption secrecy, explaining that experts in recent years had discovered that secrecy was contrary to the best interests of the child, and citing Betty Jean Lifton's *The Journey of the Adopted Self*. Hunsaker immediately objected to the introduction of something new into the trial record at this stage of the proceedings. Judge Lipscomb sought to put a quick end to this line of pleading from both attorneys by saying, "I'm not going to read the book. I've got plenty else to read here. . . . I don't think the people read your book. Let's move on." But McDermott refused to let the issue go and continued to argue. At this point, Judge Lipscomb was weary; neither side seemed to understand what his role was in the case. He explained that adjudicating the correct, appropriate public policy for Oregon

> was not my job. That's the job that's reserved to the Legislature and if they don't act, then to the people through the initiative power. My decision is not going to be whether Ballot Measure 58 was a good idea or not, whether it's fair or not, it's simply going to be, is it constitutional, which is a much narrower scrutiny. But that's the only authority I have is to determine its constitutionality, not whether it's a good idea, not whether the voters should have approved it, not whether the Legislature should have amended it, just is it constitutional.

The judge then said he hoped to issue his decision as quickly as possible.[41]

The participants walked out of the courtroom with clear, but differing, perceptions of the hearing. Although Hunsaker believed he had been treated fairly by Judge Lipscomb, he left the hearing "quite shaken" and "did not hold out much hope of prevailing" because of the judge's demeanor and disagreement with his arguments.[42] The next day, Helen Hill and Shea Grimm were in high spirits. Grimm announced to Bastard Nation that she had heard from McDermott and he sounded "very upbeat and positive about the outcome." Both women gave detailed capsule accounts of the trial testimony, which emphasized Judge Lipscomb's disagreement with Hunsaker's arguments on the one hand and the defense counsel's "compelling" legal arguments on the other.[43] AP reporter Brad Cain, who was present at the oral hearings, confirmed Hill and Grimm's interpretation of events. He wrote that Judge Lipscomb "seemed skeptical" of Hunsaker's argument that Measure 58 violated a legal contract between birth mothers and the state.[44] None of this dampened Hunsaker's faith that the birth mothers would ultimately triumph. He remained "cautiously optimistic and confident that we would prevail on appeal from any adverse ruling of J[udge] Lipscomb."[45]

Judicial decisions can take weeks to be rendered; but a mere two days later, on July 16, Judge Lipscomb issued his ruling—against the plaintiffs, upholding the constitutionality of Measure 58. It was a stunning verdict. Part of Lipscomb's judicial philosophy was his belief that it was the responsibility of judges to use the press to educate the public about the judiciary's role in lawmaking. Thus Lipscomb, in his three-page ruling, began where he had left off at the end of the hearing. He reiterated that it was not for the judiciary to make public policy. Instead, that task was to be decided by the legislature through the enactment of statutes and by the public through the passage of initiatives and referendums. In his view, Measure 58 was an "attempt to strike a balance between protecting birth parents' rights to privacy and confidentiality and facilitating adopted adults' rights to information of their family of origin." But "although some, and perhaps many may quarrel with where that balance has been struck, this court may not set aside Measure 58 unless it runs afoul of the Oregon or United States Constitutions."[46]

Judge Lipscomb then repudiated every one of the plaintiffs' legal arguments. First, he wrote, there was no permanent and absolute right to privacy or confidentiality for birth mothers in Oregon Revised Statutes (ORS) 109.430, the law establishing Oregon's adoption registry. Instead, the court ruled, the statute was adopted in 1983 by the legislature in the context of broadening, not restricting, access to adoption information. Nor did ORS 109.430 conflict with Measure 58. Thus, "plaintiffs have failed to demonstrate either any contractual right to absolute privacy and confidentiality, or any impermissible impairment of any such rights." Second, neither the Oregon Supreme Court nor the U.S. Supreme Court had ever recognized such a broad penumbra of privacy around intimate personal matters that the plaintiffs claimed Measure 58 violated. Even assuming that birth certificates were an intimate personal matter, Measure 58 provided access to only one person, not the general public. And besides, the history of these records demonstrated that they were originally public in Oregon, indeed published until 1921. Third, the equal protection of the law argument failed because plaintiffs were not members of a previously recognized suspect class and "the balance struck by Measure 58 was not unreasonable in light of the State's responsibility to protect the interests of adoptees as well as those of birth parents." Fourth, Measure 58 did not violate the due process clause of the federal Constitution, nor did it impermissibly impair any previously recognized fundamental personal liberty because it was "rationally related to the government's interest in regulating adoptions."[47]

Judge Lipscomb faxed his opinion to Hunsaker on July 16. Hunsaker, disappointed, was also taken aback by its speed. He speculated that Lipscomb "must have had his mind pretty well made up at the oral argument if it took him only one day after the oral argument to issue his written opinion." Nevertheless, the ruling failed to shake Hunsaker's resolve. Rather, it strengthened his belief that Lipscomb's "written opinion was wrong and ignored or overlooked the facts and some longstanding Oregon statutes." Hunsaker redoubled his efforts "to pursue the case on behalf of my clients to Oregon's appellate courts."[48]

On July 20 Hunsaker, on behalf of the six anonymous birth mothers, filed a motion with Judge Lipscomb to continue the injunction against the law's enactment while he took the case to the Oregon Court of Appeals.[49] Lipscomb denied Hunsaker's request. He also refused a request for a fourteen-day delay so that Hunsaker could ask the higher court to issue a longer stay.[50]

Lipscomb's ruling surprised Hunsaker. He believed strongly that he had demonstrated the merits of the appeal and, at a minimum, Lipscomb should have granted him the fourteen-day stay he requested to make his case to the Court of Appeals. Undeterred, Hunsaker and his team of attorneys raced against the clock to meet the forty-eight-hour deadline and hand-delivered the necessary documents to the Court of Appeals on July 29.[51] The following day, responding to Hunsaker's emergency motion, the Court agreed to keep Measure 58 on hold for two more weeks, until August 12, while it considered whether to grant a longer stay.[52]

Hunsaker was elated.[53] Helen Hill, however, displayed little concern and played down the Court of Appeals' action. Explaining the matter to members of Bastard Nation, she said that the Court's decision was just a technicality—"a jurisdictional glitch. An esoteric point of appellate law." Hill concluded that in all likelihood the injunction would be lifted as soon the Court considered the matter. She rejoiced that at last the case had been taken "out of the emotional arena that is so dangerous to our issue, and placed firmly in the land of noodle-heads (no disrespect meant!), those esoteric lovers of the letter of the law, a panel of judges who are professional experts at disentangling hysterics from the constitution."[54]

On August 12, shortly before noon, the Court of Appeals sided with Hunsaker and issued an order preventing Measure 58 from taking effect for another ninety days, unless it ruled on its constitutionality before then.[55] In other words, the Court would decide within ninety days whether or not to review Judge Lipscomb's ruling. If they decided to hear the case, it would give Hunsaker another chance to strike down Measure 58 as unconstitutional.

Hunsaker, of course, was "delighted and pleased" by the Court of Appeals decision.[56] Hill was "bitter, bummed, and pissed."[57] In a newspaper interview she uncharacteristically struck a pessimistic note: "This waiting," she said, "is just absolutely hell. There are adoptees who are dying to know."[58] Privately, to Bastard Nation, Hill maintained that as a political activist, she remained confident that Measure 58 would eventually triumph, but "as a human being, I'm sick of the stupidity of this affair—we've won at every step, but we have nothing to show for it." She reported that Oregonians shared her despair: they were discouraged, dejected, and fed up.[59] Adoption activist Mary Inselman, in the *Oregonian*, denounced the birth mothers who initiated the lawsuit: "It is not fair that six people can stop this." Adopted adult Jean Walker asked, "Why do they even have people vote on things. This has really taken a toll on me. My (adopted) parents are dead. I have no brothers, no sisters. I'm just kind of alone."[60]

But what were the supporters of Measure 58 to do? Bastard Nation members Damsel Plum and Shea Grimm had the answer. They proposed a public rally to protest the Court of Appeals decision at either or both of Oregon's two key Vital Statistics offices, at Portland or Bend. Plum informed BN members that she and Grimm would "as usual" help write and distribute press releases and get the word to BN's database via e-mail and fax. Plum's e-mail message also informed Hill that "if you would like a name and phone number list from our databases of local open records supporters, we can also get this out to willing volunteers to call people up and ask them to attend." Plum called on BN members to "fight for our right to BASTARDY!!! Onward Bastard soldiers."[61]

Hill's immediate response to Plum reiterated in no uncertain terms the boundaries between her Oregon people and BN: "Just hold it everybody. The people of Oregon need to decide about a protest. If BN wants to protest, you guys come here and do it. I need to talk to folks here in this state before BN goes announcing a protest." She then softened her tone, saying, "please, have a heart. No alert, not yet." The next day, Hill took back her invitation to BN to come into Oregon. If there was popular support for a protest, she would organize it; "If not, I won't." It would be a disastrous public relations event if a protest was held and either it got out of hand or nobody showed up. At this crucial time, caution was paramount for political survival. "You guys in other states can do whatever you like," wrote Hill. "We still do, I'm afraid, need to watch our manners here in Oregon." Hill then hoped she had not "offended" anyone, but closed by saying, "Tough if I have . . . trust me some more."[62] Bastard Nation leaders had little choice but to trust Hill, since to the Oregon public she was the embodiment of Measure 58. No protests against the Court of Appeals ninety-day stay took place.

On September 8, Hunsaker and the six anonymous Jane Does received more good news. The Court of Appeals had decided to review Judge Lipscomb's ruling. It extended the hold on Measure 58 through January 13, 2000, or, as the *Oregonian* more dramatically put it, "into the next century." The reason for the additional delay, presiding Judge Mary J. Deits explained, was that the Court needed the time to read the co-counsels' and intervenors' briefs, hear oral arguments, and take the matter under consideration until it rendered its decision within the time the Court had given itself back on August 13. Deits also announced that on November 22 the Court of Appeals would begin to hear oral arguments.[63]

In the next two and half months, a series of unexpected events took place that in all likelihood helped solidify the public's support for Measure 58 and caused any fence-sitters to join the initiatives' advocates. On September 14, Curtis Endicott, age fifty-one, a Bastard Nation activist who had become a national spokesman for Measure 58, died suddenly in his St. Helens, Oregon, home without ever fulfilling his quest to find his birth parents. Many people, adoptees and non-adoptees alike, must have sympathized with seventy-seven-year-old Mary Inselman, who hoped to find her older sister once she accessed her birth certificate, when she said, "This is terrible. I could be gone tomorrow. At my age, you never know." Delores Teller, president of the Oregon Adoptive Rights Association, used Endicott's death to drive home the point that adult adoptees needed access to their original birth certificates: "For him to die without knowing his medical history, which could have made a difference because he is quite young, and also without knowing his parentage—both of these are just adoption tragedies."[64] To remember Endicott, his adoptive family set up a Curtis Endicott Memorial Fund, with the proceeds to benefit the defense of Measure

58.[65] Thrown into the impossible position of legitimizing his opponents' position by offering condolences or being accused of coldness by ignoring Endicott's death, Hunsaker denied that the plaintiffs "were callous to anyone's feelings. We're doing what we feel we have to do to protect the rights of birth mothers."[66] But his plea rang hollow and sounded defensive.

Endicott's death, which was widely reported throughout Oregon, was followed two weeks later by a legal victory in another state. In *Doe v. Sundquist,* the Tennessee Supreme Court upheld the rights of adoptees to see their birth records. Tennessee's Supreme Court ruled that a 1996 open records law did not violate privacy rights. More ominously for opponents of Measure 58, the Court stated in its conclusion that "there simply has never been an absolute guarantee or even a reasonable expectation by the birth parent or any other party that adoption records were permanently sealed." Although the long and complicated case did not, of course, have any force in Oregon, it raised the same constitutional issues and arguments that Hunsaker would make before the Court of Appeals. William Pierce, president of the National Council for Adoption, who had been a party to the Tennessee case, denounced the ruling as "an absolute assault on privacy principles" and stated that some birth mothers were "absolutely panicked." Thomas McDermott commented that he thought it "a very encouraging decision." Delores Teller believed that the Tennessee ruling "will be a positive influence on the Oregon case."[67]

Immediately after Endicott's death, Helen Hill, who during the election campaign had grown close to Mary Inselman, could not bear to think of Inselman's dying without ever finding her sister.[68] For the next five weeks she worked on a petition to Multnomah County Circuit Court Judge Elizabeth Welch to allow Inselman access to her original birth certificate for "good cause." In the petition, Inselman argued that she should be granted access because "she had been adopted before adoption records were sealed, because her mother probably was not still alive, and because her mother's medical history could be important to her, her children and grandchildren, one of whom has had one kidney transplant and needs another." Inselman's argument convinced the judge, who ordered the Oregon Health Division's vital records section to release the original birth certificate to her. When the seventy-seven-year-old grandmother received the birth certificate, she recalled, "I was stunned. I couldn't believe it." From the birth certificate, Inselman learned her mother's maiden name and confirmed that she had an older sister. The story made the front page of the *Oregonian,* which viewed it as offering "a preview of what thousands of other Oregon adoptees hope to learn under Measure 58."[69]

But the pro–Measure 58 momentum the media was providing came to an abrupt end when, on November 20, two days before the oral hearing, the *Ore-*

gonian published an anonymous letter from a birth mother. The editors explained that the paper ordinarily did not publish anonymous letters, but it was making an exception in this case "for reasons that the editors consider to be valid and extraordinary." It added that a rebuttal from Measure 58's chief petitioner would be forthcoming.

The letter writer began by asserting that throughout the election campaign and thereafter, discussion of Measure 58 had focused on adoptees and birth mothers who wanted to meet each other. The voice of birth mothers like herself, who wanted no contact, had not been heard: "our compelling need for confidentiality has, of necessity, rendered us speechless." She was now telling her personal story with the hope it would help others understand why birth mothers opposed Measure 58. She had become pregnant several decades ago when premarital sex was "frowned upon." After much soul searching, discussions with the father, and futile attempts to secure an illegal abortion, she had agreed that the only viable alternative was to place the baby for adoption. The attorney she had dealt with repeatedly promised her that she would have "life-long confidentiality." He took this assurance so seriously, she said, that he destroyed his own records after the adoption became final. The experience of placing her infant for adoption left deep scars that took years to heal, but after a long struggle, she rebuilt her life and achieved personal and professional success. But "now more than a generation later, this pregnancy again threatens to destroy my life. Allowed no choice and provided no safeguards by Measure 58, I become officially sanctioned quarry to be hunted down by the adult adoptee." She looks into the future and foresees only chaos for her family and herself: having an adult adoptee drop into her life will only serve to disrupt her extended family and upset her elderly mother. The solution to the problem of balancing conflicting needs, she asserted—the right of privacy versus the need to know—is obvious: Oregon's volunteer registry system. It makes information available to both parties who want to meet while respecting the right of privacy of those who do not. It also offers medical information and other nonidentifying information to adoptees who want to know more about themselves. The birth mother concluded with a warning: if her rights were being imperiled successfully, whose would be next?[70]

The next day, the *Oregonian* ran another sympathetic birth mother piece that focused on the disadvantages this group faced in the battle to defeat Measure 58. As staff reporter Bill Graves dramatically put it, "They fight from the shadows in a public war to protect their privacy." The article finally stated some of the facts that should have been mentioned during the election campaign: birth mothers were outnumbered, lacked representation in an organization, and were fearful of their own children. Nancy Simpson, adoption supervisor of the Boy and Girls Aid Society of Oregon, wrote sympathetically, "These women have gone through hell to repress their feelings." "Cindy" was quoted as saying, "It was heart-breaking for all of us." The article stated that Cindy and other birth mothers were so fearful of being discovered that they did not even reveal their real names to each other and communicated only through e-mail. Another birth mother said that as a result of Measure 58 she has had "flashbacks, nightmares, and an inability to sleep."[71]

It was within this superheated emotional context—after the media spotlight on the death of Curtis Endicott; on the plight of elderly, sick adoptees; and the dilemma of birth mothers who wanted to preserve their privacy—that the Court of Appeals convened on Monday, November 22, to hear the case of *Jane Does 1–7 v. State of Oregon.*

9

Victory

The third-floor room that housed the Oregon Court of Appeals in the
Supreme Court building in Salem was packed. Portable chairs had been
added to accommodate the overflow crowd, but still many people spilled out
into the hallway. In attendance, besides law students and spectators, were Helen
Hill and a half dozen Measure 58 advocates, including Barbara Endicott, who
held on her lap throughout the oral argument a large photograph of her late
husband, Curtis Endicott. Below, on the second floor in the Court library a TV-
radio pool had set up cameras and microphones. To Franklin Hunsaker, it
"looked like a media circus."[1] Inside the courtroom all was decorous. Seated
slightly above the spectators and counsel sat the three-judge panel: presiding
Judge Paul J. De Muniz, Judge Virginia Linder, and Judge David V. Brewer.[2]

As Judge De Muniz surveyed the courtroom, he was mindful of the
media's attention on Measure 58 and the importance of the initiative. De
Muniz believed that judges should take their role very seriously and that the
decisions they make "are very important to the citizens; these are not just lawsuits, they are real people." In this particular case, "I envisioned the real agony
that real people were experiencing." De Muniz said he was able to imagine
what it must have been like to relinquish a child for adoption, compartmen-
talize that part of your life, and then all of a sudden have it revived. After
reading the briefs, De Muniz claimed he still had an open mind. For him, oral
argument was not merely an opportunity for the judge to make sure he understood each side's position. Instead, De Muniz viewed oral argument as more
of a contest, where a lawyer "can't win the case, but he can lose it." Because
of the many questions the judges asked, and in the interest of fairness that
each side be heard, Judge De Muniz allowed oral argument to run half an
hour over the scheduled sixty minutes.[3]

The briefs that both sides submitted to the Court of Appeals were practically identical to the ones that they had submitted to the Circuit Court. In
one respect, however, Franklin Hunsaker's brief to the Court of Appeals differed from the one he submitted to Judge Lipscomb. Gone were the arguments
that Measure 58 unconstitutionally deprived birth mothers of equal protec-

Judge Paul J. De Muniz, presiding judge of the Oregon Court of Appeals, who wrote the decision on Measure 58's constitutionality.

tion of the law and violated the constitutional rights of birth mothers to freely exercise their religion.[4] Instead, Hunsaker based his appeal on what he considered his strongest legal arguments: that Measure 58 unconstitutionally impaired the obligation of contracts; that it violated the fundamental right to privacy and confidentiality under both the Oregon and the U.S. Constitutions; and that it violated the substantive due process rights of birth mothers under the U.S. Constitution.[5]

Whereas Judge Lipscomb had listened patiently to the arguments of both sides and broke in only occasionally, the Court of Appeals judges carried on a running dialogue with counsel. In his opening argument concerning Measure 58's unconstitutional impairment of contracts, Hunsaker was frustrated with what appeared to him the inability of one of the judges to follow his argument. When one of the judges[6] said that Hunsaker's statutory contract argument had not been made at the trial court level (that is, before Judge Lipscomb's Circuit Court), he replied, "I'm simply unable to comprehend that argument, where does that come from, because from day one we have asserted that these statutes become part of a contract, part of the promise."[7]

Within fifteen minutes, Judge Linder cut to the heart of the matter and asked Hunsaker "precisely where [does] the contract you're relying on get formed and by whom? Between what parties?" Hunsaker replied that a contract was formed between the birth parents and the adoption agency, if one was involved (and its workers representing the agency); the adoptive parents;

and the state, because the state supervised and oversaw every adoption in Oregon. Linder probed deeper. She asked Hunsaker whether a physician who was attending a mother at birth and making representations about adoption was a party to the contract. Hunsaker said he thought that "at that point" the physician was "acting as an agent." Judge Linder shot back, "An agent of who?" Hunsaker replied: "An agent of the State, or if there is an agency involved, the agency. . . . Particularly if it's based on Oregon law." Linder suggested that an agent of the state had to have express authority to represent the state. Hunsaker disagreed and stated that "any person involved in the adoption process had implied authority because of the fact that the State oversees all adoptions." As Hunsaker continued to speak, Judge Linder interrupted and stated correctly, "My understanding was the law requires an agent to have express authority." Though Linder then moved on to a related subject and let Hunsaker temporarily slip the noose, the plaintiffs' argument was clearly not going well.[8]

There followed a brief discussion of the recent ruling in *Doe v. Sundquist* by the Tennessee Supreme Court, which upheld a constitutional challenge to the legislature's open adoption records law. In order fend off this line of attack, Hunsaker was forced to reverse himself on one of the central arguments he had made before the Circuit Court. He denied that he was challenging Measure 58's constitutionality because it was retroactive. Judge De Muniz returned to the issue of contracts and the ambiguity of the statute. The judge reiterated "that before we can find a contract in the constitutional sense, the statutes need to be unambiguous. And you, in the earlier part of your argument, you kept saying that the statute was ambiguous. Doesn't that cut against you?" Hunsaker believed that when it came to assurances and promises of confidentiality and privacy there was no ambiguity. He replied, "Absolutely not. And that's been our argument from day one." But De Muniz persisted in this line of reasoning. He noted that Oregon case law on contracts needed to be not just a promise of a present status but a promise that future legislatures would be bound not to change or negate the contract. Where, he asked, in the adoption statutes was that future promise? Hunsaker replied that "the future promise is confidentiality" and apologized for sounding "like a broken record." He then explained that he was not arguing that the legislature could not change laws, but that it could not change them if it impaired contracts or violated rights of privacy. What the plaintiffs were claiming was that "the contract is a contract of adoption." Hunsaker's reply never answered Judge De Muniz's original question of where in the adoption statutes was the future promise binding legislatures not ever to change the laws.[9]

The impairment of contracts argument dominated most of Hunsaker's forty-five minutes. After questioning Hunsaker, Judge De Muniz gave him an opportunity to address any issues he wanted to the Court. Hunsaker took the time to talk about privacy, which had not been touched on by the judges. He defined the constitutional right of privacy as "the right to be let alone" and stated that the U.S. Supreme Court called it "the most comprehensive of rights and the right most valued by civilized man."[10] Hunsaker argued that birth mothers' right to be left alone, to maintain their anonymity and confidentiality, was a fundamental right deserving of constitutional protection. He then moved from a legal to an emotional argument that the birth mothers "have a very real fear" of adopted adults' initiating future personal contacts. He then seamlessly moved back to a legal argument citing U.S. and Oregon Supreme Court cases. With that, Hunsaker sat down.[11]

David Schuman, deputy attorney general, second in command in the attorney general's office and an experienced appellate advocate, then stood up and began arguing the case on behalf of the state.[12] Schuman matched Hunsaker's appeal to emotion by one of his own. He noted that Americans love to tell themselves stories that celebrate "every person's freedom to forge a new identity, unconstrained and unencumbered by the misfortunes or accidents or mistakes of the past." But, he added, there was not just one story but two: in addition to the one that made birth mothers heroes for starting new lives there was also another, more tragic one that taught that men and women who cannot know where they came from or from whom they were created and "can never know who they are must live incomplete and crippled." He stated that Oregon voters, who enacted Measure 58, demonstrated they had more sympathy with the second story. According to Schuman, however, the issue before the Court was not whether the voters had made the fair or good choice, or—here he implicitly criticized Hunsaker—the emotionally correct or incorrect choice. Rather, "It is whether this Court must undo the democratic process because the voters made a choice that was constitutionally impermissible." Schuman's answer was the Court must not, because Measure 58 was constitutionally permissible.[13]

For the next thirty minutes, most of the questions that the judges asked Schuman were technical ones, dealing with contract case law at the state and federal level. The judges questioned him over and over again about whether there existed a contract between the state and the birth mother. And over and over again, Schuman denied there was a contract, either explicit or implicit. When pressed by one judge about what it was in the adoption statute that was ambiguous, Schuman replied that the burden of proof was on anybody who would claim that the statute was unamendable. Left unspoken between Schuman and the judge was the legal principle in Oregon case law that a contract had to be unambiguous with an explicit "promise" or "offer" by the state that it could not abrogate or amend. Schuman pointed out that if one looks at the language of Oregon's adoption statutes "there is no evidence whatsoever of the legislature doing that." Similarly, if one looked at the legislative history of those adoption statutes there was not "the slightest hint that the legislature meant these to be one of those . . . rare statutes that are unamendable." The final question the Court asked Schuman on contract law was: "Is that whole argument premised on the theory that the State is not a party to the adoption?" Schuman's reply was affirmative: "It's premised on the theory that the State is not a party to the contract." He had hoped that he demonstrated that the crucial term of the contract—confidentiality—was absent from the contract.[14]

In his closing statement, Schuman addressed Hunsaker's arguments that Measure 58 violated the Fourteenth Amendment's due process protection-of-privacy rights. He went to the very essence of Hunsaker's case by denying that birth certificates were private in the first place because they were available by court order and the court could grant access to them without limitation. More to the point, Schuman observed that the Constitution only protected *fundamental* rights, which were very few. He asserted, "The right to an anonymous adoption was invented by this culture in 1957. It is not a fundamental right." Schuman concluded that a statute was constitutional if it rationally served a legitimate purpose of the state, and Measure 58 rationally served the purpose of helping adopted adults discover who they are. (Ironically, Schuman partly justified finding no violation of privacy rights under the Fourteenth Amendment for Measure 58's constitutionality by employing the ideology of the adoption search groups that Bastard Nation had avoided so strenuously during the election campaign.)[15]

The Court of Appeals decision was announced just thirty-seven days later, on December 29, an unusually quick resolution.[16] The Court unanimously upheld the constitutionality of Measure 58 and lifted the injunction immediately. Judge De Muniz's thirteen-page opinion systematically refuted each of Hunsaker's legal arguments. De Muniz began by putting forth the questions the Court was attempting to answer: First, did the adoption laws of the state create a statutory contract between the state and birth mothers who relinquished their children for adoption? Second, was the guarantee of confidentiality a "material term of that contract"? But De Muniz immediately tempered his framing of the issues: "We recognize, however, the difficulties of characterizing an adoption in traditional contract terms." Children could not be bought and sold, for example, in commercial contractual transactions. Still, despite the difficulties, the Court was willing to characterize an adoption in terms of the "general principles of contract law."

From that point on De Muniz borrowed liberally from the state's brief in deciding whether Measure 58 impaired the obligations of contract of the Oregon Constitution. He found that the two major cases where the Oregon Supreme Court had ruled on governing impairment of the obligations of contract, *Eckles* and *Hughes,* differed from Measure 58 in two major ways.[17] In both these earlier cases, the state's role was "essentially the same [as that of] any contracting party in a commercial transaction between private parties," offering inducements to enter into a commercial transaction with it rather than with another. "By contrast," De Muniz wrote, "the state's role in an adoption is not analogous to the role of an interested private party." Instead, it was merely regulatory, involving the state's oversight of the adoption process for the general welfare of society. The state did not seek any advantage for itself by inducing individuals to agree to adoption on its terms.[18]

In *Eckles* and *Hughes,* the judge noted, there were explicit statutory contracts. They differed from the case at hand because "the state does not directly contract with the birth parents or adoptive parents." Moreover, and most importantly, the adoption statutes did not contain unambiguous expressions of legislative intent to enter into a statutory contract with birth mothers to prevent the disclosure of their identities to their adopted children without their consent. Looking at the history of Oregon adoption statutes, he stated that they had been "amended regularly throughout this century to provide varying degrees of confidentiality at varying times;" that information about birth mothers' identities had always been permitted through court order; and that the legislature had never shown an intent to elevate birth mothers' desire for confidentiality over the legitimate intent of adopted adults to obtain information concerning their birth. It was clear to the Court that the lawmakers' intent in creating Oregon's adoption registry was not to privilege birth mothers, but to balance the conflicting interests of adoption triad members. "In short," De Muniz summed up, "nothing in the text or the context of the adoption statutes on which the plaintiffs rely evinces a legislative intent to enter into a contract with birth mothers to guarantee them that their identities will not be revealed to their adopted children without their consent."[19]

But Hunsaker had also contended that even if there were not explicit statutory guarantees of confidentiality, various social service, medical, and religious authorities employed by private entities had made promises to birth mothers that were binding on the state. Citing various legal precedents, Judge De Muniz adamantly rejected this argument. He failed "to see how the fact that individuals working for private organizations offered opinions about what they believed the law provided could somehow transform them into agents of the state for the purposes of creating binding state contractual obligations." De Muniz contended that the issue ultimately came back to whether the adoption statutes themselves created a binding contractual obligation not to open birth certificates for inspection by adoptees. "If the statutes did not provide for that promise, then state agents were without authority to make any such promise. If the state agents were without authority to make such a promise, then it is a promise that cannot be enforced." He concluded that "the trial court correctly determined that Measure 58 does not impair obligations of contract in violation of Article 1, section 21, of the Oregon Constitution."[20]

De Muniz found that there was simply nothing in the Oregon Constitution that lent any support to the idea that the constitutional framers intended to confer on birth mothers a constitutional right to conceal their identities from their children.[21] He also dismissed Hunsaker's claim that Measure 58 violated fundamental constitutional rights of privacy and confidentiality under the federal Constitution. He indicated that the Court was sympathetic to the plaintiffs' arguments and it understood what an intensely personal decision it was to place a child for adoption. "However," he continued, "we are unable to conclude that a law that permits adult adoptees access to vital records concerning their births has the same sort of constitutional infirmities as the laws that criminalized contraception and abortion that were struck down in *Griswold, Eisenstadt,* and *Roe.*" Individuals who seek to terminate a pregnancy at an early stage may do it unilaterally. A birth mother cannot relinquish a child for adoption unilaterally. At a minimum, according to De Muniz, the decision requires a willing birth mother, willing adoptive parents, and the active oversight and approval of the state. In light of those requirements, De Muniz denied that a birth mother had a fundamental right to give birth to a child and then have someone else assume legal responsibility for that child. "Although adoption is an option that generally is available to women faced with the dilemma of an unwanted pregnancy, we conclude that it is not a fundamental right. Because a birth mother has no fundamental right to have her child adopted, she also can have no correlative fundamental right to have her child adopted under circumstances that guarantee that her identity will not be revealed to the child."[22]

Judge De Muniz concluded the opinion by making an important distinction. He stated that both birth mothers and adoptees may have legitimate interests—the one in keeping secret the circumstances of her giving birth followed by an adoption, and the other in discovering the identity of his or her birth mother. De Muniz added, "Legitimate interests, however, do not necessarily equate with fundamental rights." From a birth mother's point of view it could easily be argued that Measure 58 was bad public policy because it unbalanced the rights of privacy in favor of adoptees, but it was difficult to argue that it was unconstitutional. The Oregon Court of Appeals then lifted the injunction, more than a year after the state's voters had approved the initiative.[23]

The reaction to the Court of Appeals' decision ran the gamut, from joy to despair and from acceptance to rejection. Helen Hill declared, "We're ecstatic. The injunction is lifted, and that means we won the war." A jubilant Delores Teller said, "It's a civil right. It's an undoing of a wrong that happened and shouldn't have happened in 1957." Thomas McDermott exulted that now adopted adults had been given the right to "be masters of their own destinies."[24] The *Oregonian,* which had opposed Measure 58, reversed itself and strongly supported the Appeals Court decision. In an editorial it advised birth mothers that it was time to stop fighting and accept the ruling. "The voters have spoken. The Legislature has acted. The courts have ruled." The adoptees have won. But it also had some advice for adopted adults: "The wishes of the people, and the law, are now clear. So is the responsibility of adoptees to respect the privacy and needs of their birth mothers."[25]

Birth mothers, not surprisingly, had a very different reaction. They feared the Court's decision. "Cindy" stated, "We feel like our lives are being betrayed." "Christina," another birth mother who wanted her identity concealed, believed that the Court's ruling would lead to similar laws elsewhere. At bottom, she said, "there is no respect for the dignity of the birth mother. There is no respect for timing, no respect for what they have gone through." Other birth mothers claimed Measure 58 left them to worry forever more about a knock on the door in the middle of the night.[26]

One day after the December 29 decision, Frank Hunsaker threatened to file an emergency motion with the Court of Appeals asking the judges to put the law back on hold while the birth mothers appealed to the Oregon Supreme Court or at least asked the higher court for a stay.[27] True to his word, Hunsaker succeeded the next day in persuading the Court of Appeals to issue a temporary seven-day further stay of the injunction to halt implementation of Measure 58 so that he could file an emergency appeal to the Oregon Supreme Court to hear the case and impose a more permanent injunction during this period. As a result, Edward Johnson, state registrar, ordered the Bureau of Vital Statistics to stop shipping requests for original birth certificates to adopted adults to the state archives in Salem. Hill was incensed. "We've won every single battle, every step of the way, but they won't let us have this one simple thing: your own birth certificate. Nobody knows what it's like, this emotional roller coaster they've been on."[28] Marley Elizabeth Greiner, executive chair of Bastard Nation, was unsurprised by the course of events and even welcomed it as an opportunity to get a clear ruling in favor of open records. Exaggerating for effect, she asserted, "We have to bury Hunsaker, Pierce, the NCFA, and all of the rest of these guys so deep into the garbage pit that they'll never climb out."[29]

But words were not enough. The Helen Hill who was wary of holding a protest against the Court of Appeals' first injunction against Measure 58 back in August now, within two days of the new injunction, called upon Oregon adopted adults to protest the latest injunction outside Frank Hunsaker's downtown Portland office on January 5. The central target of Hill's wrath was William Pierce and the National Council for Adoption. Hill's motivation for attacking Pierce and the NCFA rather than Hunsaker was that she and Bastard Nation had always viewed Hunsaker as a tool of Pierce, and by focusing on Pierce and the NCFA rather than Hunsaker, she intended to arouse Oregonians' intense dislike of the idea of outsiders interfering with the Oregonian electoral process and costing its taxpayers "hundreds of thousands of dollars" in court costs.[30] Hill later reported to BN members and the leadership that the protest "WENT GREAT." There was from her perspective a very good turnout. There was also, in her view, fantastic media coverage, including "live television coverage from all three major Portland TV stations" as well as all the major Oregon newspapers and the AP.[31]

During the protest, Frank Hunsaker did not make an appearance, and he refused all interviews.[32] He was busy working on the Measure 58 appeal. While the protest was in progress, Hunsaker asked the Oregon Supreme Court to keep Measure 58 on hold. Two days later, on January 7, 2000, he planned to petition the Supreme Court to review the lower court's ruling and decide on Measure 58's constitutionality. Hunsaker's hard work paid off. On January 7, the Oregon Supreme Court ruled to extend the Court of Appeals' seven-day stay indefinitely. If the Supreme Court decided it did not want to hear the case, it would lift the stay immediately. Otherwise, the stay would remain in effect until the Court ruled on the case, which could take a year or more.

Measure 58 advocates published a number of letters expressing anger and frustration with the delays. Betty E. Bergstrom of Southeast Portland wrote a letter to the *Oregonian* attacking the six anonymous birth mothers. The letter was published under the heading "The Few Have Too Much Power." In it, she asked, "What in the world are they afraid of?" She answered: That a child they relinquished for adoption was going "to show up at their front door and force them to reveal a secret they have kept for many years? Tough!" The *Oregonian* also published a letter by Lori Johnson of St. Helens, who protested the Court's "obstruction of justice." After the passage of Measure 58, she said, birth mothers have no rights. "They gave up their rights when they signed the paper to let their children be adopted." She also asked why the taxpayers had to pay for the protracted court proceedings. "The mothers should be paying for this, not us." Another St. Helens citizen, Susan Gotshall, complained in the *Oregonian* of being "angered, hurt and frustrated" every time Measure 58 had been challenged in court. Gotshall asserted that she had rights "just like anybody else, and I have the right to know where I came from, what my medical history is, and just to know the things that are important to me." She accused the six anonymous birth mothers of putting adopted adults through an emotional wringer and begged the six to stop their legal appeals. Bastard Nation's Executive Committee also weighed in, linking Hunsaker's name with the "anti-adoptee National Council for Adoption" and denouncing "the stalling tactics of adoption industry lobbyists . . . while asking Oregon taxpayers to foot the bill for their appeals."[33]

Supporters of the High Court's ruling wrote in response. Barbara Hardy Dugas, a birth mother, replied directly to Betty E. Bergstrom. Dugas assured Bergstrom that the six anonymous birth mothers were only the tip of the iceberg, or rather "only the ones who paid an attorney." There were many more birth mothers outside the courtroom who were unhappy with the idea that their names were being given to adopted adults who planned to contact them. To Dugas, this was similar to "a nasty practice called 'outing' in which people take it upon themselves to publicly announce that somebody else is a homosexual." Birth mothers who chose the right of privacy could similarly be "outed." Dugas concluded by asking: Had it not occurred to Bergstrom that if "we birth mothers wanted to have contact, we would sign up for registries and already be in contact?"[34] Others, like Teresa Bral of North Plains, argued that a birth mother should retain a right to privacy; otherwise the threat of that difficult chapter in her life coming back to haunt her might be an incentive to abort, rather than relinquish, the child. For Bral, it was not a question of birth mothers' rights trumping those of adopted adults. She believed that adoptees should be able to obtain medical history without the birth mother's identity revealed, if she did not want it to be disclosed.[35] Harold Potter of Canby, Ontario, opposed Measure 58 also and recommended a voluntary adoption registry (apparently he was unaware that one already existed in Oregon). But Potter feared that even a registry was filled with pitfalls that threatened the privacy of birth fathers and adoptive parents, who might not be consenting parties. Michael Spiegel, also of Canby, Ontario, attacked the electoral basis of initiative politics by suggesting that only people directly involved in the adoption process should have been allowed to vote on Measure 58 in the first place. But since that had not been done, he sided with the birth mothers: "someone gave the mothers a commitment, and that ought to take precedence over the curiosity of the adoptees."[36]

Lauren Greenbaum, BGAS social worker and one of the chief opponents to Measure 58, also disagreed with those frustrated with Measure 58's implementation. Although she sympathized with adopted adults' need to know, she failed to see "why a compromise is so unfathomable to them." Greenbaum took them to task for venting their anger on the six anonymous birth mothers, who were only fighting for their rights and representing "hundreds, possibly thousands of women who cannot come forward." The fact that there were only six of them was irrelevant. What difference, Greenbaum asked the letter writers, did it make that there was only one Jane Roe, the plaintiff in *Roe v. Wade,* the abortion case? Or that there were only a few black students who fought in court against segregation? "This is how great changes are made—by a few who are brave enough to fight." Greenbaum assured her readers that birth mothers were not fighting to thwart adopted adults. They were fighting "to protect themselves and their information and to provide an opportunity to try again to find a more balanced approach."[37]

Several major local and national newspaper editorials also sided with the birth mothers. Salem's *Statesman Journal* thought the Supreme Court's delay in implementing Measure 58 was appropriate. It understood adopted adults' anger and frustration at the delay, but reasoned the stay was justifiable until the legal issues were resolved. After all, "if the situation was reversed and adoptees faced the closure of their birth records, they would certainly deserve the same right to pursue appeals."[38] In an editorial, *USA Today* supported the Court's ruling and presented the birth mothers' side of the story sympathetically. It asked: "Should the rights of these women be trampled?" and answered, "No." The editorial argued strongly for procedures that would balance the rights of adoptees and birth mothers, such as confidential intermediaries. It concluded that what was wrong with Measure 58 was that the balance was missing and that it broke "the promise of secrecy without considering why it was made in the first place."[39] After mid-January 2000, after fifteen months of constant media discussion, interest in Measure 58 seemed to fade for the next two months, with only a handful of human-interest articles appearing in the *Oregonian.*[40]

On March 21, the Oregon Supreme Court declined to review the Court of Appeals ruling. Its decision was announced to Hunsaker in a three-word sentence: "Review is denied."[41] The Supreme Court gave no explanation for its refusal to review the Court of Appeals ruling upholding Measure 58, nor was it required to do so. The vote was 5–2. Nevertheless, the ruling did not mean that adoptees would gain immediate access to their original birth certificates. The Court agreed to continue to suspend the law for an additional twenty-one days, permitting the birth mothers time to ask the Oregon Supreme Court to reconsider its decision. If the birth mothers petitioned the High Court, the stay would be extended until the Court again decided whether to hear the case.[42]

Measure 58 advocates' reaction to the Supreme Court's ruling was muted.

The morning after the ruling, Thomas McDermott was reported as being overjoyed, but the next day he declared he was "not celebrating until the law was in effect" because he had had too many "ups and downs and disappointments along the way."[43] The *Oregonian* weighed in with an editorial, once again urging the birth mothers to "drop their legal challenge."[44]

Measure 58 opponents also weighed in. Frank Hunsaker said he and his clients were "extremely disappointed and we're very surprised at the court's ruling."[45] The Supreme Court's decision radicalized some birth mothers. The *Oregonian* again broke its policy on anonymous letters and allowed "Mary" to publish one. In it she urged birth mothers, who had been "flooded with overwhelming feelings of disbelief, betrayal, and despair" not to remain in isolation or be passive in the wake of the Supreme Court ruling. She suggested that there were things that could be done "for ourselves and for each other." These included filling out the contact preference form that could be attached to the original birth certificate and calling organizations like the National Council for Adoption for assistance and counsel. Most important, "if you are hurt by the threat or the reality of unwanted contact, you can help others by telling about it." For too long, Mary argued, Measure 58 advocates had manipulated birth mothers' reluctance to speak out into making others think that birth mothers who wished to maintain their privacy did not exist. That had to stop. Mary's was a new, radical voice for birth mothers. She was asking them to come forward and speak publicly if their lives were threatened with being ruined.[46]

The importance of the Oregon Supreme Court's ruling garnered national attention. For the first time, the *New York Times* gave front-page coverage to this "tumultuous legal debate [in Oregon] over the nation's first voter-approved law granting adult adoptees access to long-sealed birth records." The article noted that in light of the sea change in attitudes toward out-of-wedlock pregnancy and open adoption, the entire debate seemed outdated. But, it continued, many birth mothers adamantly wanted no contact with the children they relinquished and feared that their husbands or children would discover their secret. Although everyone agreed that the birth mothers had received promises of secrecy, not everyone was sure that such assurances were legally binding. "That is the crux of the issue here."[47]

The *New York Times* reporter asked me about the future of Measure 58. At the heart of Measure 58's opposition was the fear that an adopted adult would intrude into the privacy of a birth mother and rip apart her family by revealing a secret pregnancy. In short, some feared that opening adoption records would result in social turmoil. The implementation of Measure 58, I told the reporter, would provide a way to test whether these fears were justified. "It appears we are going to have a giant social laboratory," I said. "All of a sudden a lot of people are going to get their birth certificates and then they will search and they'll have reunions with their birth mothers, whether the mothers want them or not. If there's a lot of social turmoil that emerges, I think that's going to strengthen the case for adoption registries. But if this kind of social turmoil fails to come up, then you really have a strong case that there is not a problem, and records should be open." The article also expressed doubt that Hunsaker would appeal to the U.S. Supreme Court, though he said he was considering it. The article concluded that Measure 58 was likely to stand.[48]

While newspaper commentary swirled about, Hunsaker on April 6 asked the Court to grant him an additional three weeks, until May 2, to prepare a petition for reconsideration of the lawsuit.[49] Five days later, the Court agreed to Hunsaker's motion and extended the stay an additional twenty-one days, until May 2.[50] On May 2, Hunsaker filed his petition for reconsideration with the Oregon Supreme Court. It differed significantly in one respect from all his prior briefs in that it raised the issue of the social significance of adoption. Judge Lipscomb had made it clear that he did not believe that social policy was a valid standard by which to judge the constitutionality of a law, and the Oregon Court of Appeals was bound by law to follow Oregon Supreme Court precedents when assessing the constitutionality of a law. But the Oregon Supreme Court was not bound by either standard. On the contrary, as Hunsaker pointed out in his petition, he was at a loss to understand why the Court chose not to review the case in light of the criteria provided in the *Oregon Administrative Procedures* for granting discretionary review. One criterion was "[w]hether many people are affected by the decision in the case" and "[w]hether the consequence is important to the public, even if the issue may not arise often."[51] Hunsaker directed the Court's attention to the fact that 455,000 Oregon voters had voted against Measure 58 and that almost 250,000 birth mothers and their children, spouses, and siblings, along with thirty-six private adoption agencies, could be affected if Measure 58 became law. This was clear evidence to Hunsaker of how important it was for the Court to take the case under review. Moreover, the social significance and overriding public significance of Measure 58 was indicated by the past and continuing coverage in local newspapers like the *Oregonian* and the widespread interest shown by the national broadcast media, as well as the numerous articles, columns, and editorials in the national print media. Hunsaker appealed to the Court's vanity. He called upon it not to fail in its responsibility as a "law-announcing court to the people of Oregon," especially in its role to resolve constitutional issues. If it were to remain silent, Hunsaker concluded, "the public's confidence in this Court and its trust in the laws of this State could be seriously eroded."[52]

On May 15, the Alabama legislature, in a surprising and sweeping overhaul of the Alabama Adoption Code, passed a law opening original birth certificates and court records to any adopted adult who requested them.[53] The following day, the Oregon Supreme Court, by the same 5–2 vote as before, rejected Hunsaker's petition for reconsideration. Again, Hunsaker received a laconic, perfunctory statement: "Reconsideration denied."[54] He told a reporter that he was extremely disappointed, as he "felt it was the court's responsibility to rule on these important constitutional issues." For the Court not to rule was an "abdication of its responsibilities." At bottom, he confessed, "I'm at a loss as to why they didn't" take the case for review.[55] His one consolation was that the two judges that voted for review were family law trial judges with adoption experience. It proved to Hunsaker that any judge who was familiar with the state's adoption system and how it worked would recognize the dire consequences of Measure 58 and would have voted for review. Unfortunately, Hunsaker said, "we couldn't pick up two other votes."[56] The Court had given Hunsaker two more weeks for a possible appeal; if none was forthcoming, the stay would be lifted, and Measure 58 would become law at 5:00 P.M. on May 30. Hunsaker said he was seriously contemplating an appeal to the United States Supreme Court.[57]

While 2,217 Oregon adopted adults who had applied for their birth records had resigned themselves to wait patiently for the stay on Measure 58 to be lifted, Hunsaker filed an emergency motion asking the Oregon Court of Appeals to keep Measure 58 on hold while he prepared an appeal to the U.S. Supreme Court. The Court of Appeals refused to extend the hold on Measure 58. On May 26, he filed an emergency stay request with Justice Sandra Day O'Connor, who handled all procedural matters from the western states in the federal judiciary's Ninth Circuit.[58] Although Hunsaker thought the case "was a perfect vehicle" for review, he realized it would be an uphill battle because the U.S. Supreme Court was highly selective in choosing its cases. In addition, Justice O'Connor favored states rights and would be reluctant to interfere in a case that so clearly had little do with federal laws. Precedent was also against him. The Supreme Court had recently refused to hear Tennessee's *Doe v. Sundquist*.[59] Legal experts were even more pessimistic. Even if Hunsaker got another stay, the consensus was that the chances the highest court of the land would hear the case were practically nil. In the experts' opinion, the case failed to represent an important issue of federal law, and the Court had not even recognized the right of privacy that the birth mothers were advancing as a claim.[60] All of these pessimistic opinions were confirmed when on Monday, May 30, Justice

O'Connor denied Hunsaker's emergency request for a stay of judgment of the Oregon Court of Appeals pending his petition for a writ of certiorari to continue a hold on Measure 58. The final stay ordered by the Oregon Supreme Court expired at 5:00 P.M.[61]

Measure 58 supporters were jubilant. Representing the thoughts of adopted adults all over the state, seventy-two-year-old Helen Hester of Southeast Portland exclaimed, "God bless Sandra Day O'Connor!" Another adopted adult, Michelle Wick, who had been the one hundred seventy-sixth person to file for her birth certificate after Measure 58 passed, said she had "goose bumps thinking about it." Helen Hill declared, "Wow, that's good news. That clears out my whole day. I don't have to stew anymore. . . . It's just, you can't unwind until it's over, and it's a fever pitch, and—oh, man, I'm glad it came through." Thomas McDermott believed it was "a new era for adoption in this state, perhaps in the country. It will ultimately be for everyone's benefit." Jane Nast, president of the American Adoption Congress, could hardly contain her happiness, saying, "This is really good news! I'm so excited. I certainly think this will be the impetus for other states (to open adoptees' birth records) once their legislatures go back into session."[62] The print media failed to mention either Shea Grimm or Bastard Nation. All the credit went to Hill. Adopted adult Gina Stonum of Northeast Portland, for example, one of Hill's Oregon workers, said, "I call her 'The Glue.' There were times when it was so emotional, I didn't think I could go on. People said cruel things. But her energy was so steady." Likewise, Karen Ofenham-Brioso of Troutdale declared, "Helen Hill is my hero. . . . She is a blessing to adoptees, not only in Oregon, but everywhere." McDermott maintained this empyreal metaphor, saying, "Helen is a saint, in my view. She dedicated her time, energy, and more than $100,000 in financial resources for a cause that did not benefit her. She had already found her parents, but she did it so others wouldn't have to struggle as hard."[63]

The law's opponents were stunned. Hunsaker said that his clients were "extremely disappointed, scared, even angry that their rights have been ignored by Oregon's Courts and Oregon's voters." He bitterly observed that birth mothers "ask for compassion and understanding, from adult adoptees who, in their elation over winning this victory, rush to get copies of their birth certificates."[64] The following day, Hunsaker sent to the U.S. Supreme Court by overnight express a second emergency request for a stay, this time to Justice Clarence Thomas. This, McDermott admitted, "unnerved me."[65] Justice Thomas brought the matter before the full Supreme Court, but on June 10 the justices rejected it.[66] It was, as McDermott put it, the "final nail in the coffin." At last, he said, "there's a sense of peace and finality."[67]

More than once in the past—during the initiative petition campaign and in the immediate aftermath of its electoral victory—Measure 58 had seemed about to slip its provincial moorings and gain national prominence. But now, after the U.S. Supreme Court's ruling, it seemed the national media was ready to give the adoption revolution a chance. Media pundits wanted to use Measure 58 as a "social drama" to rehearse the arguments for and against that revolution on a national stage. For a brief moment, Measure 58 would be to the adoption reform movement what Birmingham was to the civil rights movement and the Stonewall riots were to the gay liberation movement: the defining moment of the adoption reform movement, the point at which the movement came of age. Overnight, Measure 58 dominated national broadcast and print media in a way it had never done before. On May 31, for example, Measure 58 was the topic for discussion on CNN's *Today, TalkBack Live,* and *Crossfire,* where birth mother Delores Teller, adopted adult Pam Hasagawa, and Measure 58 attorney Thomas McDermott were the spokespersons for the adoption reform movement and NCFA president William Pierce and birth mother "Christina" argued the opposing side.[68] Both sides continued the battle over birth mothers' right to confidentiality versus adopted adults' civil rights. But this time, rather than going after Oregonian voters, the battle was for the hearts and minds of America, and ultimately the American voter. Momentum, it seemed, was on the side of the adoption reform movement.

CONCLUSION

Within a day after Measure 58 went into effect, nearly 2,400 adoptees had applied to the Oregon Health Division's Center for Health Statistics for their original birth certificates; a month later, at the end of June, the number was up to 3,655, and by November it was 4,962.[1] Some submitted their applications in person, though most mailed or faxed them. Their reasons for wanting their birth certificates varied. Paul Katz, a Portland resident, wished to search for his birth parents, while Terry Serdy, also of Portland, said he was seeking his birth records for medical reasons. "I had wonderful adoptive parents growing up," Serdy said. "This isn't about the search for other parents." Bonnie Widerburg, a spokesperson for the Center for Health Statistics, said the staff hoped to mail all the birth certificates within four to six weeks.[2] Accompanying the Center for Health Statistics' weekly updates of the number of adult adoptees applying for their birth certificates were cautionary admonitions from experienced adoptees and birth mothers that reunions were not easy, given the years of "bottled up feelings of guilt, regret, shame or resentment on both sides." They advised going slowly: the person an adoptee had dreamed of for years inevitably had a real life that would in all likelihood scarcely resemble the adoptee's fantasy.[3] Frank Hunsaker, who in just three days received dozens of calls from distraught birth mothers, also hoped that "adoptees will show some compassion to them, particularly if a birth mother fills out a preference form and says they do not want contact. These are not just names. These are human beings that gave life and made very difficult decisions."[4]

As anticipated, the media focused on reunions. Journalistic accounts of the meetings mentioned none of the complexity that had been predicted. The first publicly recorded reunion occurred on June 26, 2000, when twenty-six-year-old Paul Byan Woods of La Grande found his forty-two-year-old mother, Disa Jeanine Beurman Abbey, in Prospect, a small town in southern Oregon, just a week after receiving his original birth certificate. The reunion was successful, apparently carrying no baggage of feelings of shame and guilt or fantasy. To Woods's e-mail message, Abbey replied, "I have thought of you so often. How good it is to hear you are not only alive but also thriving. . . . Your letter has not upset my life in any way except that I'm overwhelmed in emotions. Good ones."[5] The next day, the *Oregonian* published another successful reunion story, one that seemed almost miraculous: an adoptee, identified only as Kim, reunited with her birth mother within twenty-four hours of acquiring her birth certificate.[6] The article played up the emotion and drama. Kim received her mother's cell phone number from a grandmother, who was happy to hear from her. The story continued:

> Hardly able to hear over the pounding of her heart, Kim dialed the number and caught her mother barbecuing a lamb at a campground on the Molalla River.
>
> " 'Are you sitting down?' was one of the first things she asked me," said Kathy McConaughy of Sandy. "Then she said, 'I was born on December 14, 1969,' and I just started bawling."
>
> The conversation that followed was all confusion, joy, and anxious questions.
>
> "Are you sure you don't hate me?" McConaughy asked at one point.
>
> "Of course not!" Kim said. "I love you! You gave me life!" Talk about meeting sometime turned to talk about meeting right then. Within the hour, Kim was at the barbecue.[7]

During the next couple of months, the *Oregonian* continued to run successful reunion stories on the paper's front page.[8]

But were a handful of happy reunions representative of the hundreds, perhaps thousands, that must have been taking place? What about the emotionally difficult ones? Or the ones that, as Measure 58 opponents predicted, would lead to the breakup of families? Were the media deliberately avoiding these? By the end of June, Thomas McDermott suggested that most adopted adults and birth parents were reuniting quietly because, as Helen Hill put it, "it's a personal and private experience for most people." Frank Hunsaker, who was in contact with a network of birth mothers, admitted, "I have not heard any so-called horror stories."[9] Hunsaker's statement that birth mothers' lives had apparently not been destroyed nor their privacy invaded, as he had repeatedly predicted, seriously undermined the social-damage theory that had been used to attack Measure 58. On its e-mail discussion list, Bastard Nation member Mary Anne Cohen immediately responded to Hunsaker's admission and quipped sarcastically: "Where's our 'social turmoil'????? Guess adoptees having civil rights is just . . . normal."[10]

If we analyze the victory of Measure 58, we find that paradoxes and ironies abound. The common analogy used in the Oregon press for the battle over Measure 58 was David and Goliath, with Helen Hill playing the role of David. Yet this analogy is clearly inappropriate. Looked at from the viewpoint of modern-day initiative campaigns, the fight over Measure 58, financially at least, was waged between two Davids. The total expenses of both adversaries combined—$155,000—were minuscule relative to modern initiative campaigns. But of the two opposing sides, Hill was the financial Goliath. While she and her supporters spent close to $150,000 (her contribution alone being close to $120,000), Measure 58's opponents spent around $6,600. Bastard Nation leaders and Helen Hill never accepted this truth about the campaign. When the *Oregonian* reported this fact accurately after the victory, Marley Greiner wrote an angry letter denouncing the piece. (It was never published.) Hill also refused to accept the financial facts of the campaign or shed the image of herself as the underdog, saying, "It's so funny that they're saying we spent more than them. It's like saying David shot Goliath with a very expensive slingshot." But indeed the whole idea of Hill and her group as David is inappropriate. Hill outspent the opposition 20 to 1 with her liberal use of money for paid signature gatherers, strategic advertising, and rallies. And the supposed Goliath—the opposition—was financially impoverished, or at least unwilling to spend the money necessary to contest the initiative effectively. In the end, Bastard Nation and Helen Hill were Goliath in the Measure 58 campaign.

Still, the question remains, why did Measure 58 hold such a commanding lead in the polls by mid-October and go on to victory? Part of the answer lies in the outstanding leadership of Helen Hill and Shea Grimm. Theirs was a complex and symbiotic relationship. Grimm, the radical political veteran tutored the (as Hill readily acknowledged) politically naïve Hill in how to run an initiative campaign. Grimm, on behalf of Bastard Nation, needed Hill at the front lines directing her "Oregon people" during the daily effort to qualify the initiative for the ballot and the subsequent electoral campaign; Hill needed Grimm's advice at every strategic and tactical stage, from getting the initiative on the ballot to achieving victory at the polling booth. It is difficult to say what the fate of Measure 58 might have been without Grimm's contributions. But there is no question that Measure 58 would never have existed without Helen Hill's vision and energy, and that much of Measure 58's victory is owed to her idealism, pragmatism, and charismatic leadership.

In addition, Bastard Nation had a strong advantage in its widespread and sophisticated use of the media, whether its members were appearing on TV, giving radio interviews, or placing ads on cable TV programs. BN's use of the Internet and its discussion list BEST not only provided the adoption activist group with an identity, but also provided it with a means of communicating that was far in advance of the opposition. The speed with which BN was able to keep up with events and respond to them allowed it to keep ahead of the opposition during the Measure 58 campaign and build esprit de corps among the rank and file. Although BN's tactic of blitzing newspaper editors with e-mail messages was not always effective, sometimes it was; and in general the Internet proved invaluable, especially during the closing days of the campaign, when volunteers were sought for the birth mothers' ad.

Finally, the campaign for Measure 58 was won because of the ideology of Bastard Nation. This ideology was preached by Hill and BN for over a year. It was embedded in the campaign literature that they had so assiduously distributed while getting the initiative qualified; in radio, TV, and newspaper interviews; and in the *Voter's Pamphlet.* BN and Hill had strategically chosen the platform of civil rights for adopted adults and deliberately refrained from emphasizing reunions of long-lost family members or adopted adults' need for medical information or desire to know their genetic history because of the political ineffectiveness of such approaches. Of course, they would not protest when others, even their own attorneys, made these arguments on their behalf, but privately they avoided these rationales for Measure 58. Instead, they invoked three traditional American ideas: the virtue of equality, the evil of discrimination against minorities, and antigovernment prejudice. Measure 58 advocates argued that the system of laws set up by the state discriminated against a minority of the population—adopted adults—by denying them their original birth certificates while granting that civil right to others. State governments, they argued, were clearly responsible for a morally unjust system that lacked compassion and fairness. The remedy was clear: adopted adults must be granted access to their original birth certificates in order to be placed on an equal footing with every other U.S. citizen.[11] In appealing to voters' moral sensibility and their belief in justice, however, the supporters of Measure 58 violated a cardinal rule of modern initiative campaigns. Experts have noted that professional initiative firms have been most successful when they deliberately frame issues to appeal to voters' self-interest, such as California's Proposition 13, which reduces taxes by granting property tax relief.[12] Measure 58 offered Oregon voters nothing tangible in return for their vote except the satisfaction of righting an apparent wrong perpetrated by the state upon a minority. This ideological appeal for equality and its concomitant attack on government intrusion into citizens' private lives proved powerfully attractive to Oregonians, whose libertarian political actions are often mistaken for liberalism.

What does the future hold for the adoption reform movement? The members of Bastard Nation exulted in their victory but were of several minds concerning what it portended. No one really believed that it signaled a coming revolution and the immediate opening of adoption records nationwide. But some members, like David C. Ansardi, one of the leaders of an Alabama-based group for open records, believed it was nothing short of miraculous that two states, Oregon (in 1998) and Alabama (in 2000), had passed unconditional-access laws. "Ask any of us," he said, "who were around when BN first formed whether we thought that by June of 2000 we would have two states in the plus column," and the answer would certainly be "no." He went on to use popcorn as a metaphor for the future of the movement: "the first few kernels will pop sporadically, but then the rest will all go in a flurry. The precedents are being set now, and other states will be watching the newly open states to see what happens."[13] Others, like Steven J. Drahozal, pointed out that Oregon and Alabama were "only 4 percent of the states. Hardly a landslide."[14] But all BN members were eager to capitalize on Measure 58's victory and, in Cynthia Bertrand Holub's words, "to reap the fruits we have sown in Oregon."[15] They realized, however, that additional victories would "take time, money, and patience."[16]

To that end, Holub informed the BN e-mail discussion list in June 2000 that she was forming a membership-building campaign in an attempt to double the membership by the end of the year.[17] BN also kicked off a fund-raising drive to launch the organization into a "new era of Adoption Rights." The appeal for money noted that the one question the media, BN supporters, the members, and the organization's leaders immediately raised after the victory was "Who's next?" Adoption activists across the nation who contacted Bastard Nation wanted to know how to institute adoptee-rights initiatives in their state.

After due consideration, BN leaders came to the remarkable conclusion that, for a number of reasons, Oregon's Measure 58 campaign was unique and could not be duplicated elsewhere. For one thing, the initiative campaign had depended on a single large donor, Helen Hill, for most of its financing, a situation unlikely to be repeated. In addition, they felt, the victory owed much to the fact that the opposition was completely taken by surprise, which would certainly never occur again. Finally, the opposition remained disorganized until the very last month of the campaign, allowing the initiative's supporters to run Measure 58 on a small budget. Next time, Bastard Nation and its affiliates would not have these advantages. "Our opponents will not be caught off-guard again," the organization noted. "They are waiting anxiously for our next move." It was thus imperative for BN supporters to contribute money in support of adoptee-rights ballot measures and legislative efforts nationwide.[18]

This analysis was only partially correct. What was truly unique about the Measure 58 electoral campaign was something Bastard Nation never noticed: that the opposition, from the Boys and Girls Aid Society of Oregon (BGAS), Concerned Adoption Professionals (CAP), Catholic Charities (CC), and the Coalition of Oregon Adoption Agencies (Coalition), was not monolithic. More important, it was ideologically closer to BN than was the National

Council for Adoption (NCFA). BGAS executive director Michael Balter, Coalition leader James Wheeler, and adoption workers such as Lauren Greenbaum, Nancy Simpson, and CC's Paula Lang opposed Measure 58, but all refused to work with NCFA's president, William Pierce, and all supported the compromise legislation HB 3194. Finally, Bastard Nation leaders failed to acknowledge, at least in its fund-raising ads, that their grassroots initiative campaign was smarter and more sophisticated in the way it was run than that of the opposition. Still, they were probably right in predicting that if in the future a professional initiative company, with legions of paid signature gathers and bottomless financial pockets, opposed them, the outcome would be far different from their triumph in Oregon. Or would it?

In many ways, Measure 58 was a model piece of legislation. For the first time, adopted adults gained access to their original birth certificates through the ballot initiative process, while an amendment allowed birth parents to indicate whether they wanted contact and to provide health information. Significantly, the resulting bill, HB 3194, was passed by the state legislature with the support of both adoption activists and their opponents. But in the past three years, no other state initiative campaign has emerged, and BN has had only one victory (in Alabama) and many legislative defeats (in California, New Hampshire, Missouri, Washington, New Jersey, Georgia, and Louisiana).[19] The possibilities for killing state legislation are endless, due in part to whims of powerful committee chairs,[20] but also to BN's principled, but ultimately self-defeating, insistence on unconditional open records legislation. Bills so designed will always draw fierce opposition and can too easily be killed or amended to death in committee.

Laws such as Measure 58 can cut the Gordian knot among adoption activists, their opponents, and legislators, even if it is not an ideal solution for perfectionists on either side. But to achieve this goal nationwide, Bastard Nation and its supporters must free themselves of ideological blinders and recognize that adoption agencies do not constitute a single, monolithic "adoption industry." They must also recognize that, either out of altruism or self-interest, the majority of adoption agencies support openness in adoption, including open records. Adoption-rights activists need to recruit these agencies as their allies in legislative battles. The National Council for Adoption, though it can still stir up trouble by lobbying a single, influential state legislator, will become increasingly isolated. After mending fences with more moderate adoption reform groups like the American Adoption Congress and bringing on board adoption agencies friendly to open records, Bastard Nation could play a constructive role by introducing laws like Measure 58 in as many states as possible. Opposition arguments, whether based on constitutional or birth mother's privacy rights, could be easily countered. The constitutional issues are fully laid out in the defendants' briefs in *Doe 1–7 v. State of Oregon* and Judge De Muniz's opinion, and the birth mothers' privacy issues in HB 3194 (though support for privacy issues could be made stronger by providing exemptions for rape and incest victims like "Cindy"). Those fearing "social turmoil" could easily be refuted by the fact of the lack of any such disturbances to date in Oregon under Measure 58, as well as in other open records states, such as Kansas and Alaska.

A coalition of adoption activists, adoption agencies, and social workers would have other advantages. It would clearly demonstrate to state lawmakers the collapse of the traditional "us versus them" dichotomy that has dominated the battles over sealed records for the past three decades. It would not only confirm that a new age is dawning, but also that this new age makes it imperative to give adult adoptees access to their original birth certificates. It would be a clarion call that in the world of adoption it is time to look with fresh eyes at an old institution.

APPENDIX: TEXT OF HB 3194

Chapter 604
AN ACT   HB 3194
Relating to adoption rights; amending chapter 2, Oregon Laws 1999.
Be It Enacted by the People of the State of Oregon:

SECTION 1. Chapter 2. Oregon Laws 1999 (Ballot Measure 58, 1998), amended to read:

(1) Upon receipt of a written application to the state registrar, any adopted person 21 years of age and older born in the state of Oregon shall be issued a certified copy of his/her unaltered, original and unamended certificate of birth in the custody of the state registrar, with procedures, filing fees, and waiting periods identical to those imposed upon nonadopted citizens of the State of Oregon pursuant to ORS [432.120] 432.121 and 432.146. Contains no exceptions.

(2) A birth parent may at any time request from the State Registrar of the Center for Health Statistics or from a voluntary adoption registry a Contact Preference Form that shall accompany a birth certificate issued under subsection (1) of this section. The Contact Preference Form shall provide the following information to be completed at the option of the birth parent:

(a) I would like to be contacted;
(b) I would prefer to be contacted only through an intermediary; or
(c) I prefer not to be contacted at this time. If I decide later that I would like to be contacted, I will register with the voluntary adoption registry. I have completed an updated medical history and have filed it with the voluntary adoption registry. Attached is a certificate from the voluntary adoption registry verifying receipt of the updated medical history.

(3) The certificate from the voluntary adoption registry verifying receipt of an updated medical history under subsection (2) of this section shall be in a form prescribed by the State Office for Services to Children and Families and shall be supplied upon request of the birth parent by the voluntary adoption registry.

(4) When the State Registrar of the Center for Health Statistics receives a completed Contact Preference Form from a birth parent, the state registrar shall match the Contact Preference Form with the adopted person's sealed file. The Contact Preference Form shall be placed in the adopted person's sealed file when a match is made.

(5) A completed Contact Preference Form shall be confidential and shall be placed in a secure file until a match with the adopted person's sealed file is made and the Contact Preference Form is placed in the adopted person's file.

(6) Only those persons who are authorized to process applications made under subsection (1) of this section may process Contact Preference Forms.

Approved by the Governor July 12, 1999
Filed in the Office of Secretary of State July 12, 1999

NOTES

Introduction

1. In a survey of 1,554 Americans, six out of ten reported having a personal experience with adoption, meaning that they themselves, a family member, or a close friend was adopted, had adopted a child, or had placed a child for adoption. See Evan B. Donaldson Adoption Institute, *Benchmark Adoption Survey: Report on the Findings* (New York: Evan B. Donaldson Institute, 1997).

2. Rose M. Kreider, *Adopted Children and Stepchildren: 2000 Census.* 2000 Special Reports, CENSR-6 (Washington, D.C.: U.S. Census Bureau, 2003), 3.

3. Paul J. Placek, "National Adoption Data," in National Council for Adoption, *Adoption Factbook 3* (Waite Park, Minn.: Park Press, 1999), 30, 34. Unless otherwise indicated, the term "adoption" in this book refers to unrelated adoptions.

4. U.S. State Department, "Immigrant Visas Issued to Orphans Coming to the U.S. 2002." <http://travel.state.gov/orphan_numbers.html> (accessed April 24, 2003). (Note: dates in parentheses throughout refer to dates the Website was accessed.)

5. Alan Gallay, *The Indian Slave Trade: The Rise of the English Empire in the American South, 1670–1717* (New Haven: Yale University Press, 2002), xiii.

1. The Problem

1. The Maples case was unusual in that she was given her adoption decree, which under normal circumstances would not have been done because the form contains identifying information—the names of the biological parents. But on the decree that Maples was given these names were blacked out. See Gregory R. Smith, "In Re the Application of Annetta Louise Maples: The Adoptee's Right to Know," *Saint Louis University Law Journal* 23: 4 (1979): 733, n. 14.

2. *Application of Maples,* 563 S.W.2d 760 (Mo. 1978); Smith, "Maples," 731–733.

3. See, for example, *Mills v. Atlantic City Department of Vital Statistics,* 148 N.J. Super. 302, 372 A.2d 646 (1977); *In re Linda F.M.,* 148 N.J. Super., 310, 372, A.2d at 650 (1977); *In re Maxtone-Graham,* 92 Misc. 2d 224, 399 N.Y.S.2d 857 (Sur. Ct. 1977); *In re Spinks,* 32 N.C. App. 422, 232 S.E.2d 479 (1977); *In re Sage,* 21 Wash. App. 803, 586 P.2d 1201 (1979); *Alma Society v. Mellon,* 601 F.2d 1225 (2d Cir.), *cert. denied,* 100 S. Ct. 531 (1979); *In re Application of*

George, 625 S.W.2d 151 (Mo. App. 1981); *Bradey v. Children's Bureau,* 274 S.E.2d 418, 422 (S.C. 1981); and *In re Roger B.,* 84 Ill.2d 323, 418 N.E.2d 751 (1981).

4. Elton B. Klibanoff, "Genealogical Information in Adoption: The Adoptee's Quest and the Law," *Family Law Quarterly* 11:2 (1977): 186–187; E. Wayne Carp, *Family Matters: Secrecy and Disclosure in the History of Adoption* (Cambridge, Mass.: Harvard University Press, 1998), chap. 2.

5. Carp, *Family Matters,* chap. 2, esp. 40–41. See also Elizabeth J. Samuels, "The Idea of Adoption: An Inquiry into the History of Adult Adoptee Access to Birth Records," *Rutgers Law Review* 53 (Winter 2001): 367–375.

6. *General Laws of Oregon,* Title IV, and 60–72, pp. 692–693 (Deady, 1845–1864).

7. *Doe 1–7 v. State of Oregon,* Oregon Court of Appeals, "Redacted Joint Respondents' Brief Pursuant to Court Order Sealing Deposition Testimony," Oct. 16, 1999, 9.

8. *Oregon Laws* 1919, chap. 405, clause 6 (Olson).

9. *Doe 1–7 v. State of Oregon,* "Redacted Joint Respondents' Brief Pursuant to Court Order Sealing Deposition Testimony," 9. The authors of the "Respondents' Brief" claim that name changes "remained available to the public until 1939," but they were apparently unaware of the 1919 statute, and they provide no evidence for their assertion.

10. Carp, *Family Matters,* 71–86.

11. Ibid., 52–53.

12. Sheldon L. Howard and Henry B. Hemenway, "Birth Records of Illegitimates and of Adopted Children," *American Journal of Public Health* 21 (June 1931): 645. Model statutes, which do not have the force of law, are usually proposed by the National Conference of Commissioners of Uniform State Laws. The commissioners are a group of law school deans, professors, judges, and practicing lawyers appointed by state governors. The finished product is then presented to the states as a prototype, which each state is then free to adopt in whole, in part, or not at all, as their particular needs and interests dictate. Christine Adamec and William L. Pierce, eds., *The Encyclopedia of Adoption* (New York: Facts on File, 1991), s.v. "Model State Adoption Act."

13. Quotations in ibid., 644, 643, 644.

14. Quotations in ibid., 646, 646–647, 647.

15. Agnes K. Hanna to Clarissa Lehman, October 18, 1941, U.S. Department of Labor, Children's Bureau, Reports, File 4-2-1-2-4, Central File 1941–1944, Box 85. For adopted adults' requests for birth certificates, see Maud Morelock to Mrs. Grace L. Knox, May 29, 1942, ibid.

16. *Oregon Laws* 1941, chap. 130, sect. 21.

17. Helen C. Huffman, "The Importance of Birth Records," in *National Conference of Social Work, Proceedings* (New York: Columbia University Press, 1949), 357; Carp, *Family Matters,* 100.

18. *Oregon Laws* 1919, chap. 405, clause 6 (Olson).

19. The difference between Oregon's 1919 and 1939 statutes was considerable. The earlier one was limited by the judge's discretion and to three types of children; Oregon's 1939 law did not give the judge any discretion, was applicable to all children, and sealed "the journal, index, and fee book." Still, these records remained subject to inspection only with a court order. *Oregon Laws* 1939, chap. 321.

20. Morton L. Leavy, *Law of Adoption Simplified* (New York: Oceana, 1948), 18.

21. *Oregon Revised Statutes* 691.110 chap. 412, section 3. The 1957 statute was very similar to the 1939 one; it simply amended this conflict in the law. *Doe 1–7 v. State of Oregon,* "Respondents' Brief," 10.

22. Samuels, "Idea of Adoption," 385.

23. Carp, *Family Matters,* 41.

24. Carp, *Family Matters,* 111–112.

25. Child Welfare League of America, "Regarding Adoptions," *Special Bulletin* (March 1937): 5. Given the climate of severely negative opinion in America regarding illegitimacy, unwed mothers wanted as few people to know about their status as possible—which meant preventing everyone but close family members from being aware of their pregnancy. Yet it is clear from the forms that they were forced to sign, agreeing not to search for the children they relinquished, that not all single mothers wanted to sever ties with their children forever. The Children's Home Society of Washington before the 1950s provided birth mothers with nonidentifying information while the child was a minor, but when the child gained his or her majority, it cooperated with reuniting birth mothers with their children.

26. Child Welfare League of America, "Minimum Standards in Adoption," Nov. 5, 1938, Child Welfare League of America Records, Box 15, folder 5, Social Welfare History Archives, University of Minnesota, Minneapolis.

27. Child Welfare League of America, *Standards for Adoption Service* (New York: Child Welfare League of America, 1958), 14.

28. Carp, *Family Matters,* 115–116.

29. Ibid., 82–83.

30. See Florence Clothier, "Some Aspects of the Problem of Adoption," *American Journal of Orthopsychiatry* 9 (1939): 612–614; Florence Clothier, "The Psychology of the Adopted Child," *Mental Hygiene* 27 (April 1943): 228–230; Viola W. Bernard, "Application of Psychoanalytic Concepts to Adoption Agency Practice," in Marcel Heiman and M. Ralph Kaufman, eds., *Psychoanalysis and Social Work* (New York: International Universities Press, 1953), 207.

31. Carp, *Family Matters,* 118–119.

32. Ibid., 110.

33. U.S. Department of Labor, Children's Bureau, *The Confidential Nature of Birth Records,* Pub. 332 (Washington, D.C.: Government Printing Office, 1949), 7.

34. *Oregon Laws* 1957, chap. 193.

35. Hearings on S.B. 240 before the Senate Committee on State and Federal Affairs, 49th Oregon Legislative Assembly (March 22, 1957), Oregon State Archives, Salem.

36. Kathleen O'Brien, "Access to the Past: Opening Oregon's Sealed Adoption Records," manuscript, 11, n. 22 (in possession of the author).

37. Samuels, "Idea of Adoption," 378–379.

38. Carp, *Family Matters*, 139–142.

39. Ruthena Hill Kittson [Jean Paton], *Orphan Voyage* (New York: Vantage Press, 1968), 23.

40. Jean Paton, *The Adopted Break Silence* (Philadelphia: Life History Study Center, 1954).

41. Paton quoted in Jean White, "Adoptee Lib vs. Sealed Records," *Los Angeles Times*, Oct. 12, 1975, sec. 5, p. 16.

42. Carp, *Family Matters*, chap. 4.

43. See Michael J. Crozier, Samuel P. Huntington, and Joji Watanuki, *The Crisis of Democracy: Report on the Governability of Democracies to the Trilateral Commission* (New York: New York University Press, 1975); David Chalmers, *And the Crooked Places Made Straight: The Struggle for Social Change in the 1960s* (Baltimore: Johns Hopkins University Press, 1991); Edward P. Morgan, *The Sixties Experience: Hard Lessons about Modern America* (Philadelphia: Temple University Press, 1991); Stewart Burns, *Social Movements of the 1960s: Searching for Democracy* (Boston: Twayne, 1990); David Steigerwald, *The Sixties and the End of Modern America* (New York: St. Martin's Press, 1995); and David Farber, *The Age of Great Dreams: America in the 1960s* (New York: Hill and Wang, 1994).

44. Douglas T. Miller, *On Our Own: America in the Sixties* (Lexington, Mass.: D. C. Heath, 1996), 206; Farber, *Age of Great Dreams;* James T. Patterson, *Grand Expectations: The United States, 1945–1974* (New York: Oxford University Press, 1996), 568. See also Morgan, *The Sixties Experience;* Burns, *Social Movements of the 1960s;* Steigerwald, *The Sixties.*

45. Florence Fisher, *The Search for Anna Fisher* (New York: Fawcett Crest, 1973), 154.

46. Enid Nemy, "Adopted Children Who Wonder, 'What Was Mother Like?'" *New York Times,* July 25, 1972, sec. 1, p. 22; Fisher, *Search for Anna Fisher,* 203.

47. Nemy, "Adopted Children Who Wonder." See also Lynn Lilliston, "Who Am I? Adoptees Seek Right to Know," *Los Angeles Times,* July 22, 1973, sec. 10, p. 15.

48. *Time,* June 24, 1974, p. 81; Hal Aigner, *Faint Trails: A Guide to Adult Adoptee–Birth Parent Reunification Searches* (Greenbrae, Calif.: Paradigm Press, 1987), 67.

49. Florence Fisher, "Our Time Is Now!!" *Alma Searchlight* (1976): 2.

50. Leslie Allan, "Confirming the Constitutionality of Sealing Adoption Records," *Brooklyn Law Review* 46 (1980): 723.

51. Debra D. Poulin, "The Open Adoption Records Movement: Constitutional Cases and Legislative Compromise," *Journal of Family Law* 26 (1987–1988): 406.

52. Ibid., 406–407; Marshall A. Levin, "The Adoption Trilemma: The Adult

Adoptee's Emerging Search for His Ancestral Identity," *University of Baltimore Law Review* 8:3 (1979): 509–510.

53. Allan, "Constitutionality of Sealing Adoption Records," 731; Poulin, "Open Adoption Records Movement," 398.

54. *ALMA Soc'y, Inc. v. Mellon*, 601 F.2d 1225 (2d Cir.) *cert denied*, 100 S. Ct. 531 (1979) at 1232.

55. Ibid., at 1237–1239.

56. Ibid., at 1233–1236.

57. Ibid., at 1235.

58. Jean Paton to Associates, May 20, 1982; Jean Paton to Penny Partridge, July 8, 1981; Jean Paton to ACC Board Members et al., all Canada—AAC, 1980–1993, Papers of Jean Paton (in possession of the author). For confirmation of the AAC's turning to credentialed professionals, see Kate Burke to Jean Paton, Nov. 19, 1988, CA—Burke, Kate, Papers of Jean Paton.

59. Carp, *Family Matters*, 144–145.

60. Ibid., 148.

61. Annette Baran, Reuben Pannor, and Arthur D. Sorosky, "Adoptive Parents and the Sealed Record Controversy," *Social Casework* 55 (November 1974): 531–536; Arthur D. Sorosky, Annette Baran, and Reuben Pannor, "The Reunion of Adoptees and Birth Relatives," *Journal of Youth and Adolescence* 3 (1974): 195–206; Reuben Pannor, Arthur D. Sorosky, and Annette Baran, "Opening the Sealed Record in Adoption—The Human Need for Continuity," *Journal of Jewish Communal Service* 51 (1974): 188–196; Annette Baran, Arthur D. Sorosky, and Reuben Pannor, "The Dilemma of Our Adoptees," *Psychology Today* 9 (1975): 38, 42, 96, 98; Carp, *Family Matters*, 148–149.

62. Baran, Sorosky, and Pannor, "Dilemma," 42.

63. Baran, Pannor, and Sorosky, "Adoptive Parents," 532.

64. Pannor, Sorosky, and Baran, "Opening the Sealed Record," 193.

65. Sorosky, Baran, and Pannor, "Reunion of Adoptees and Birth Relatives," 204.

66. Pannor, Sorosky, and Baran, "Opening the Sealed Record," 193; Carp, *Family Matters*, 154–155.

67. Pannor, Sorosky, and Baran, "Opening the Sealed Record," 193.

68. Ibid., 194; Sorosky, Baran, and Pannor, "Reunion of Adoptees and Birth Relatives," 204.

69. Arthur D. Sorosky, Annette Baran, and Reuben Pannor, "Identity Conflicts in Adoptees," *American Journal of Orthopsychiatry* 45 (1975): 19.

70. Arthur D. Sorosky, Annette Baran, and Reuben Pannor, "Adoption and the Adolescent: An Overview," in Sherman C. Feinstein and Peter L. Giovacchini, eds., *Adolescent Psychiatry*, vol. 5: *Annals of the American Society for Adolescent Psychiatry* (New York: Jason Aronson, 1977): 59–62.

71. Arthur D. Sorosky, Annette Baran, and Reuben Pannor, *The Adoption Triangle: The Effects of the Sealed Record on Adoptees, Birth Parents, and Adoptive Parents* (New York: Anchor Press/Doubleday, 1978).

72. Sorosky, Baran, and Pannor, "Reunion of Adoptees and Birth Relatives,"
199; Pannor, Sorosky, and Baran, "Opening the Sealed Record," 191, 192.

73. No reliable statistics were used in "Adoptive Parents." The authors made
a vague reference to "the large number" of letters they received and generalized
that "two-thirds" believed such-and-such or "the majority of adoptees" responded thusly. There were also statistically meaningless references such as
"twelve letters were received" (Sorosky, Baran, and Pannor, "Adoptive Parents,"
534–535). By December 1975, when the *Psychology Today* article appeared, the
number of reunions in the sample had risen to fifty (Baran, Sorosky, and Pannor,
"Dilemma," 38).

74. See Edmund V. Mech, "Adoption: A Policy Perspective," in Bettye M. Cald-
well and Henry N. Ricciuti, eds., *Review of Child Development Research*
(Chicago: University of Chicago Press, 1973), vol. 3: 480–489, esp. 484, 486.
Four additional studies conducted in the 1980s support these positive evaluations
of adoptions. See the fine discussion in Alfred Kadushin and Judith A. Martin,
Child Welfare Services, 4th ed. (New York: Macmillan, 1988), 613–622.

75. Serious criticism of Sorosky and his associates did not begin until 1986,
and then it was only a single article. See Patrick A. Curtis, "The Dialectics of Open
versus Closed Adoptions of Infants," *Child Welfare* 65 (September–October
1986): 439.

76. Biographical details from Betty Jean Lifton, *Twice Born: Memoirs of an
Adopted Daughter* (New York: McGraw Hill, 1975). Robert Jay Lifton made his
own contributions to the adoption search movement, both as an expert witness
in a 1974 court case dealing with identity conflicts in adopted persons and as an
advocate of opening sealed adoption records. See Edwin Kiester, Jr., "Should We
Unlock the Adoption Files?" *Today's Health* 52 (August 1974): 59; Robert Jay
Lifton, "Foreword," in Mary Kathleen Benet, *The Politics of Adoption* (New
York: Free Press, 1976), 1–7.

77. Betty Jean Lifton, "The Search," *New York Times Magazine,* Jan. 25, 1976,
pp. 15–19; quotations on 15, 18.

78. Betty Jean Lifton, "So That Adoptees Do Not Have to Vent Their Rage,"
New York Times, Sept. 19, 1977, sec. 1, p. 34.

79. David Kirschner, " 'Son of Sam' and the Adopted Child Syndrome," *Adelphi University Society for Psychoanalysis and Psychotherapy Newsletter,* June
1978: 7; David Kirschner, "The Adopted Child Syndrome: Considerations for
Psychotherapy," *Psychotherapy in Private Practice* 8:3 (1990): 93–100. In 1992,
Kirschner abandoned his scientific methodology and published a paper that with-
out a random or representative sample implicated all adoptees in the adopted child
syndrome and made no mention of the atypicality of his subjects. See David
Kirschner, "Understanding Adoptees Who Kill: Dissociation, Patricide, and the
Psychodynamics of Adoption," *International Journal of Offender Therapy and
Comparative Criminology* 36 (1992): 323–333.

80. Betty Jean Lifton, "How the Adoption System Ignites a Fire," *New York*

Times, March 1, 1986, sec. 1, p. 27. Lifton habitually makes assertions without clinical or theoretical evidence. See, for example, E. Wayne Carp, "Adoption, Blood Kinship, Stigma, and the Adoption Reform Movement: A Historical Perspective," *Law & Society Review* 36:1 (October 2002): 450.

81. Nancy Newton Verrier, *The Primal Wound: Understanding the Adopted Child* (Baltimore, Md.: Gateway Press, 1993), 16. The book's popularity is suggested by the fact that it was in its sixth printing in 2003. Ann Hughes, personal e-mail, Aug. 13, 2003.

82. Ibid.

83. Marcie A. Griffin, "The Adult Adoptee: The Biological Alien," *Adoption Therapist* 2 (Fall 1991): 8–9; Robert Childs, "The Orphaned Element of the Adoptive Experience," *Adoption Therapist* 4 (Spring 1993): 1–4.

84. Annette Baran and Reuben Pannor, "It's Time for Sweeping Change," *Decree* (Summer 1990): 5; Annette Baran, Reuben Pannor, and Arthur D. Sorosky, "Open Adoption," *Social Work* 21 (March 1976): 97–100; Annette Baran and Reuben Pannor, "Open Adoption," in David M. Brodzinsky and Marshall D. Schechter, eds., *The Psychology of Adoption* (New York: Oxford University Press, 1990), 317–331.

85. Carp, *Family Matters,* 175–176; Melissa Arndt, "Severed Roots: The Sealed Adoption Records Controversy," *Northern Illinois University Law Review* 6:1 (1986): 103.

86. *In re Anonymous,* 92 Misc. 2d 224, 399 N.Y.S.2d 857 (Sur. Ct. Queens County 1977); *In re Carol S.,* 172 N.Y.L.J. 31 (Sup. Ct.); *In re C.A.B.,* 384 A.2d 679 (D.C. Ct. App. 1978).

87. *Chattman v. Bennett,* 57 A.D.2d 618, 393 N.Y.2d 768 (1977). The *Chattman* court, while allowing adopted adults to inspect medical records, specifically held that names of biological parents, if mentioned, be deleted from the medical record. See Kathryn J. Giddings, "The Current Status of the Right of Adult Adoptees to Know the Identity of Their Natural Parents," *Washington University Law Quarterly* 58:3 (1980): 684, n. 43.

88. *Spillman v. Parker,* 332 So. 2d 573, 576 (La. App. 1976); Giddings, "Adult Adoptees," 678, n. 6.

89. Katarina Wegar, *Adoption, Identity, and Kinship: The Debate over Sealed Birth Records* (New Haven: Yale University Press, 1997), 33. For a critique of Wegar, see Carp, "Adoption, Blood Kinship, Stigma, and the Adoption Reform Movement."

90. Anne Crane, "Unsealing Adoption Records: The Right to Know versus the Right to Privacy," *1986 Annual Survey of American Law* (1986): 660–665; Patricia Gallaghar Lupack, "Sealed Records in Adoptions: The Need for Legislative Reform," *Catholic Lawyer* 21 (Summer 1975): 214–216; Carol Gloor, "Breaking the Seal: Constitutional and Statutory Approaches to Adult Adoptees' Right to Identity," *Northwestern University Law Review* 75:2 (1980): 316–344; Giddings, "Adult Adoptees," 685.

91. Child Welfare League of America, *Standards of Excellence: CWLA Standards of Excellence for Adoption Services,* rev. ed. (Washington, D.C.: Child Welfare League of America, 2000), 31–32.

92. *Oregon Revised Statutes* 109.425 to 109.507. Without consent, however, a person still must obtain a court order to inspect adoption records (ibid., 109.440, 109.445).

93. *Oregon Revised Statutes* 109.430.

94. For a list of the states, see Joan H. Hollinger, ed., "Aftermath of Adoption: Legal and Social Consequences," *Adoption Law and Practice,* 2000 Supplement, vol. 2 (New York: Matthew Bender, 2000), 51, Appendix 13-A, 73–75.

95. Naomi Cahn and Jana Singer, "Adoption, Identity, and the Constitution: The Case for Opening Closed Records," *University of Pennsylvania Journal of Constitutional Law* 2 (1999): 165–166; Jason Kuhns, "The Sealed Adoption Records Controversy: Breaking Down the Walls of Secrecy," *Golden Gate University Law Review"* 24:1 (Spring 1994): 282–283; Antoinette Martin, "Adoptees Debate Intermediary's Role," *New York Times,* October 10, 1995, sec. 3, pp. C1, C4.

2. New Kid on the Block

1. Marley Elizabeth Greiner, "Take the Power," Feb. 2, 1996, <alt.adoption> (Nov. 30, 1998). According to Greiner, she was not thinking of "Queer Nation" when coining the phrase "Bastard Nation." Instead, Greiner had in mind Michael Moore's TV program, *Television Nation.* Marley Greiner, personal e-mail, Aug. 11, 2002.

2. For a history of Usenet, see Michael Hauben and Ronda Hauben, *Netizens: On the History and Impact of Usenet and the Internet* (Los Alamos, Calif.: IEEE Computer Society Press, 1997). For a critical look at Usenet communication, see Richard Davis, *The Web of Politics: The Internet's Impact on the American Political System* (New York: Oxford University Press, 1999), chap. 6.

3. Marley Greiner, personal e-mail, Dec. 7, 2000.

4. Marley Elizabeth Greiner, "Letter from the Executive Chair," *Bastard Quarterly* 1:2 (1997): 4.

5. "Mission Statement," ibid., back cover.

6. "Founding Foundlings," <http://www.bastards.org/members/found.htm> (Dec. 1, 2000).

7. Katherine Mieszkowski, "Culture Shock: Bastards Unite!" *San Francisco Bay Guardian,* Aug. 12, 1998, 3, <http://www.sfbg.com/SFLife/shocked/28.html> (Aug. 12, 1998).

8. Damsel Plum, personal e-mail, Nov. 30, 2000.

9. Randy Shaw, *Reclaiming America: Nike, Clean Air, and the New National Activism* (Berkeley: University of California Press, 1999), 284.

10. Lainie Petersen, personal e-mail, Aug. 16, 2001; Greiner, "Letter from the Executive Chair," 4–5.

11. Damsel Plum, personal e-mail, Dec. 1, 2000.

12. Dana Boggs, "Adoptee Humor," *Bastard Quarterly* 1:1 (1997): 5.

13. Helen Hill, "Bastard Recipes," *Bastard Quarterly* 1:2 (1997): 6.

14. Gavi Person, "Bastard Cheers," ibid., 12.

15. Both quotations can be found in "Mission Statement," ibid., back cover.

16. Damsel Plum, "The Psychology of Self-Defeatism in Adoption Reform," ibid., 1.

17. Ibid.

18. Shaw, *Reclaiming America*, 284.

19. Damsel Plum, personal e-mail, Dec. 7, 2000.

20. "Opening the Door to Open Records," <http://www.bastards.org/activism/orlift.htm> (Dec. 8, 2000).

21. Deb Schwartz, "Bastard Nation Organizes Nationwide Open Records Events for *Secrets and Lies*," *Bastard Quarterly* 1:1 (1997): 6–7, quotation on 6; Shaw, *Reclaiming America*, 285.

22. Ron Morgan, "BN Hits the Oscars," *Bastard Quarterly* 1:3 (1997): 4–5, 8–10.

23. Greiner, "Letter from the Executive Chair," 4–5.

24. "Shea's Search Series: The Definitive Guide to Self-Empowered Adoptee Search," <http://www.bastards.org/search/series.html> (Dec. 9, 2000). In addition, an innovative BN program, TIES (Terminal Illness Emergency Search), was founded in November 1996 by the BN Executive Committee and Denise Castellucci of Voices of Adoption. It unites terminally ill adoptees with their birth families for free. "T.I.E.S. Homepage: Welcome to T.I.E.S.," <http://www.ties-search.org/home.htm> (Dec. 1, 2000); "T.I.E.S. Terminal Illness Emergency Search: PROGRAM HISTORY," <http://www.ties-search.org/history.htm> (Dec. 1, 2000).

25. Bastard Nation, "Introduction: What Is Bastard Nation," *The Basic Bastard* (Des Moines, Wash.: Bastard Nation), 3.

26. Kate Burke, "The Case for Open Adoption Records," *Decree* 13:1 (1996): 1. In advertising its 1996 annual conference, the AAC announced proudly that the meeting would have both Nancy Verrier, author of *The Primal Wound*, and "the controversial and notorious folks from Bastard Nation." Mary Anne Cohen, "Join Your Partners," *Decree* 13:3 (1996): 15–16.

27. "Report Card to the Membership," *Decree* 13:1 (1996): 21.

28. For a description of the conference workshops, see Mary Ann Cohen, "Annual Conference Offers Something for Everyone," *Decree* 12:24 (1995): 14.

29. Bastard Nation, "Birth of a Bastard Nation Conference," Program for Chicago Conference (n.p., 1997).

30. (Berkeley: University of California Press, 1996).

31. Bastard Nation, "Birth of a Bastard Nation Conference."

3. A Tale of Two Bastards

1. Unless otherwise noted, all biographical information and quotations on the life of Helen Hill are from Helen Hill, interview by author, tape recording, Nehalem, Ore. (hereafter cited as Hill, interview), Dec. 13, 2000. My account differs slightly from Randall Sullivan, "The Bastard Chronicles, Part One: Helen Hill's Crusade," *Rolling Stone*, Feb. 15, 2001, 53–62.

2. Hill quoted in Sullivan, "Bastard Chronicles," 55.

3. Hill quoted in the *Tillamook (Ore.) Preview*, Oct. 15, 1997, 4.

4. Salvador Hill had been adopted at the age of two from an Oklahoma Indian reservation. The news devastated him. Helen Hill, telephone conversation with the author, Jan. 2, 2001.

5. Sullivan, "Bastard Chronicles," 55.

6. Hill's husband was later arrested for bank robbery and sentenced to fifteen years in a federal penitentiary. Sullivan, "Bastard Chronicles," 56.

7. Hill quoted in ibid.

8. *Tillamook (Ore.) Preview*, Oct. 15, 1997, 4–5; quotations on 4.

9. Ibid., 4.

10. Sullivan, "Bastard Chronicles, Part One," 56.

11. Betty Jean Lifton, *Journey of the Adopted Self: A Quest for Wholeness* (New York: Basic Books, 1994).

12. Ibid., 11.

13. Ibid., 65–66.

14. Ibid., chap. 10.

15. Helen Hill, "Secrets of the Universe," *Bastard Quarterly* 1:3 (1997): 12–13, quotation on 13.

16. Sullivan, "Bastard Chronicles, Part One," 59. Cf. Sam Howe Verhovek, "An Adoptee Rights Hero Who Knows All the Arguments," *New York Times*, June 3, 2000, A7.

17. Delores Teller, personal e-mail, Dec. 27, 2000.

18. Randy Shaw, *The Activist's Handbook: A Primer for the 1990s and Beyond* (Berkeley: University of California Press, 1996); David D. Schmidt, *Citizen Lawmakers: The Ballot Initiative Revolution* (Philadelphia: Temple University Press, 1989), 3. Political scientist Thomas Cronin explains that "the *initiative* allows voters to propose a legislative measure (statutory initiative) or a constitutional amendment (constitutional initiative) by filing a petition bearing a required number of valid citizen signatures." Thomas Cronin, *Direct Democracy: The Politics of Initiative, Referendum, and Recall* (Cambridge, Mass.: Harvard University Press, 1989), 2.

19. Damsel Plum, personal e-mail, Aug. 24, 2000.

20. Shaw quoted in Sullivan, "Bastard Chronicles, Part One," 61.

21. Shea Grimm, personal e-mail, Sept. 26, 2001. I have honored Grimm's request that I not reveal specific dates in her life, such as her birth, date of marriage, school graduation, and so forth.

22. Shea Grimm, personal e-mail, Sept. 29, 2001.

23. Shea Grimm, personal e-mail, March 12, 2002.

24. Shea Grimm, personal e-mail, Sept. 26 and 29, 2001.

25. Shea Grimm, personal e-mail, Sept. 26, 2001.

26. Shea Grimm, personal e-mail, March 12, 2002.

27. Shea Grimm, personal e-mail, March 12, 2002, Sept. 29, 2001.

28. Shea Grimm quoted in Rene Sanchez, "Oregon Unseals a Painful Adoption Issue," *Washington Post,* Nov. 26, 1998, A1. This is a unique public interview given by Grimm. Note also that it is only after the victory of Measure 58 that Grimm allowed herself the luxury of stepping out from behind the curtain of anonymity in which she characteristically wrapped herself.

29. Shea Grimm, personal e-mail, Sept. 26, 2001.

30. Shea Grimm, personal e-mail, Sept. 26 and 29, 2001.

31. Shea Grimm, personal e-mail, Sept. 29, 2001.

32. Shea Grimm, "Adoption Reform and the Internet," *Decree* 13:4 (1996): 19–20, quotation on 20.

33. Shea Grimm, personal e-mail, Sept. 29, 2001.

34. Ibid. One such assignment got Grimm involved in a Washington state legislative committee assigned to overhaul the law on the confidentiality of adoption records. This committee recommended a disclosure veto bill, which in a confidential intermediary system would have permitted adopted adults to refuse contact or to release information to their family of origin. The experience soured Grimm on disclosure vetoes. A modified version of the bill was eventually enacted into law in 1996.

35. All quotations from Shea Grimm, personal e-mail, Sept. 29, 2001.

36. Shea Grimm, "Why Contact Vetoes Are Not an Acceptable Compromise," *Bastard Quarterly* 1:1 (1997): 2–3, quotations on 2.

37. Shea Grimm to Helen Hill, personal e-mail, Aug. 4, 1997 (copy in possession of the author). Grimm's animosity toward Teller was reinforced the following year when, according to Grimm, Teller and the Oregon Adoptive Rights Association lobbied the Oregon legislative committee for an open records bill with a disclosure veto rather than an unconditional access records bill. Shea Grimm, personal e-mail, June 24, 2001.

38. To date, there exist two short historical accounts of Measure 58, and both ignore Shea Grimm's crucial role in the event: Sullivan, "Bastard Chronicles, Part One"; and Richard J. Ellis, *Democratic Delusions: The Initiative Process in America* (Lawrence: University Press of Kansas, 2002), 5–16.

4. Qualifying the Initiative

1. Philip L. Dubious and Floyd Fennel, *Lawmaking by Initiative: Issues, Options and Comparisons* (New York: Agathon Press, 1998), 17; Robert Horvat,

"The Oregon Initiative Process: A Critical Appraisal," *Oregon Law Review* 65:1 (1986): 172. The historiography of the Populists is enormous. An excellent overview, with an extensive bibliography, is Gene Clanton, *Populism: The Humane Preference in America, 1890–1900* (Boston: Twayne, 1991).

2. The first ballot initiative (Direct Primary Law) permitted selection of U.S. senators by the people rather than state legislatures; the second (Local County Option) allowed the people of a town or a district of a county, by a majority vote, to prohibit the sale of liquor. See Allen H. Eaton, *The Oregon System: The Story of Direct Legislation in Oregon* (Chicago: A. C. McClurg & Co., 1912), 54–55.

3. Richard J. Ellis, *Democratic Delusions: The Initiative Process in America* (Lawrence: University Press of Kansas, 2002), 32.

4. Ibid., 79.

5. David D. Schmidt, *Ballot Initiatives: History, Research, and Analysis of Recent Initiative and Referendum Campaigns* (Washington, D.C.: Initiative News Service, 1983), 8–9.

6. Ellis, *Democratic Delusions*, 32.

7. Joseph F. Zimmerman, *The Initiative: Citizen Law-Making* (Westport, Conn.: Praeger, 1989), 5–6.

8. Both Howe and the *Hampton's Magazine* editor are quoted in Ellis, *Democratic Delusions*, 33.

9. Eaton, *Oregon System*, 51–52, 123.

10. Ellis, *Democratic Delusions*, 33.

11. Eaton, *Oregon System*, 6.

12. Ibid., chap. 14.

13. Sam Howe Verhovek, "A Ballot Full of Voter Initiatives Becomes an Issue Itself in Oregon," *New York Times*, Oct. 25, 2000, A1.

14. David D. Schmidt, *Citizen Lawmakers: The Ballot Initiative Revolution* (Philadelphia: Temple University Press, 1989) 261. California holds the record for most initiatives voted on in one year: 48 in 1914. See Joseph G. Lapalombara and Charles B. Hagan, "Direct Legislation: An Appraisal and a Suggestion," *American Political Science Review* 45:2 (1951): 400, n. 23.

15. Barbara S. Gamble, "Putting Civil Rights to a Popular Vote," *American Journal of Political Science* 41:1 (1997): 253–254.

16. Lisa Oakley and Thomas H. Neale, *Citizen Initiative Proposals Appearing on State Ballots, 1976–1992* (Washington, D.C.: Congressional Research Service, Library of Congress, 1995), 73. The Oregon Court of Appeals subsequently found that Measure 8 violated the Oregon constitution. See Hans A. Linde, "When Initiative Lawmaking Is Not 'Republican Government': The Campaign against Homosexuality," *Oregon Law Review* 72 (1993): 36, n. 71.

17. Richard Ellis, personal e-mail, April 19, 2002.

18. Ellis, *Democratic Delusions*, 90.

19. Helen Hill to Shea Grimm, personal e-mail, July 28, 1998 (copy in possession of the author); Shea Grimm, personal e-mail, Feb. 8, 1998.

20. Unless otherwise noted, all references to and quotations from Helen Hill are from Helen Hill, interview by author, tape recording, Nehalem, Ore. (hereafter cited as Hill, interview), Dec. 13, 2000.

21. David S. Broder, *Democracy Derailed: Initiative Campaigns and the Power of Money* (New York: Harcourt, 2000), 69, 72.

22. Quote in ibid., 84.

23. Randall Sullivan, "The Bastard Chronicles, Part One: Helen Hill's Crusade," *Rolling Stone*, Feb. 15, 2001, 89.

24. Because hundreds of initiatives are filed with the Oregon secretary of state's office during the precertification period but a quarter or fewer actually are certified, the secretary of state assigns every initiative a temporary, internal control number. It is only when an initiative officially is certified for the ballot that it is given a permanent number. Thus, Initiative 46 was what the initiative was known as before it was certified for the November ballot; Measure 58 was its name after it was certified.

The vagaries of the numbering took even Helen Hill and her Open '98 Committee by surprise. In February 1998, they were startled to discover that 46 would not be the initiative's number during the November election. They quickly resolved "to dump the number immediately, and use a name only when referring to the campaign." They also realized that they needed a new slogan on everything, i.e., stationery, T-shirts, and bumper stickers. See "Minutes," Measure 46 Meeting, Feb. 19, 1998, typescript (in possession of the author); Helen Hill, "BEST: Measure 58 FIFTY EIGHT," June 20, 1998, <best@lakenet.org> (June 20, 1998).

25. Clear initiative titles are especially important; many initiatives have gone down to defeat due to convoluted or confusing language. See Roger Gafke and David Leuthod, "The Effect on Voters of Misleading, Confusing, and Difficult Ballot Titles," *Public Opinion Quarterly* 43:3 (1979): 394–401. Oregon statutes mandate that the attorney general write initiative titles. State of Oregon, *1998 State Initiative and Referendum Manual* (Salem: Elections Division, 1998), 4, hereafter cited as *1998 State Initiative Manual*.

26. Shea Grimm, "RE:BEST: authorship of M58," Jan. 11, 1999, <best@lake net.org> (Jan. 11, 1999). Hill would deny Grimm any meaningful authorship of Measure 58 (see chap. 7, note 29). In light of Hill's convoluted wording of the ballot title, it is hard to imagine that Measure 58 could have been composed by Hill alone.

27. This was specifically Grimm's suggestion. See Helen Hill, "BEST: Oregon," July 1, 1998," <best@lakenet.org> (Jan. 7, 2001).

28. Hill, interview. In addition to conferring with Grimm, Hill made an appointment with Joel Sachs, Nehalem's city attorney, and had him review the initiative. Sachs suggested substituting the phrase "his/her" for "their," advice that Hill followed. Helen Hill, personal e-mail, Jan. 9, 2001.

29. State of Oregon, *1998 General Election Voters' Pamphlet*, "Measure 58," 54; hereafter cited as *Voters' Pamphlet*.

30. Shea Grimm, personal e-mail, March 27, 2001.

31. The draft title ballot can be found in Helen Hill, personal e-mail, Jan. 10, 2001.

32. *Oregon Revised Statutes* 250.065.

33. Warren Deras, interview by author, tape recording, Portland, Ore., Jan. 17, 2001, hereafter cited as Deras, interview.

34. "State of Oregon, Statement of Organization: Designation of Political Committee and Appointment of Treasurer and Directors," Aug. 7, 1997. In addition to the document forming a political committee, Hill was legally obligated to submit a statement of sponsorship signed by twenty-five registered voters, an explanation of how the petition circulators would be paid, and the complete text of the initiative. *1998 State Initiative and Referendum Manual* (Salem, Ore.: Elections Division, Secretary of State, 1998), 3.

35. Helen Hill Siegel to Hardy Myers, Aug. 20, 1997 (copy in possession of the author) (Hill was still using her married name); Shea Grimm to Damsel Plum, personal e-mail, Aug. 20, 1998 (copy in the possession of the author).

36. Ellis, *Democratic Delusions,* 149.

37. Siegel to Myers, Aug. 20, 1997. Hill and Grimm worked together on drafting the letter.

38. *1998 State Initiative Manual,* 4. Any registered voter may also comment in writing. Ibid.

39. Catherine M. Dexter to Elections Division, facsimile message, Aug. 27, 1997 (copy in possession of Warren Deras).

40. All biographical information and quotations in this paragraph and the next are from Deras, interview, and Warren C. Deras, curriculum vitae, n.d. (copy in possession of the author).

41. Deras, interview.

42. Warren C. Deras, letter to the author, Feb. 13, 2001. None of the legislation Deras crafted was enacted by the Oregon legislature.

43. Deras, interview.

44. Warren C. Deras to [Donna] Birkey, letter, Aug. 28, 1997 (copy in possession of the author).

45. Philip Schradle to Colleen Sealock, facsimile message, Sept. 10, 1997 (copy in possession of the author).

46. For the increasing use of this tactic and extended commentary, see Ellis, *Democratic Delusions,* 149–157, 91–92.

47. Deras, interview.

48. To qualify an initiative for placement on the Oregon ballot, the Oregon Constitution requires a number of voter signatures equal to 6 percent of the total cast for all candidates for governor at the previous election. (*Oregon Constitution,* Article IV, §1[2][b]).

49. *1998 State Initiative Manual,* 3.

50. Caroline J. Tolbert, Daniel H. Lowenstein, and Todd Donovan, "Election

Law and Rules for Using Initiatives," in Caroline J. Tolbert, Daniel H. Lowenstein, and Todd Donovan, eds., *Citizens as Legislators: Direct Democracy in the United States* (Columbus: Ohio State University Press, 1998), 35; Ellis, *Democratic Delusions,* 57–58.

51. Ellis, *Democratic Delusions,* 56.

52. Kennedy quoted in ibid., 57.

53. Discussed in ibid., 58. See also Charles Pierce, "Signing for Fun and Profit: The Business of Gathering Petition Signatures," *California Journal* (November 1992): 545–548.

54. Tolbert, Lowenstein, and Donovan, "Election Law and Rules for Using Initiatives," 35.

55. Cronin, *Direct Democracy,* 62–63; David B. Magleby, *Direct Legislation: Voting on Ballot Propositions in the United States* (Baltimore: Johns Hopkins University Press, 1984), 62–63.

56. For Oregon's efforts to restrict the use of professional petition circulators, see note 67 below.

57. Initiative 46 meeting, minutes, Feb. 5, Feb. 19, and Feb. 26, 1998 (copies in possession of the author).

58. Patty Wentz, "Barking for Justice," *Willamette Week,* Dec. 23, 1997, 8.

59. Initiative 46 meeting, minutes, Feb. 5, Feb. 19, and Feb. 26, 1998.

60. Delores Teller to "Karen," personal e-mail, Jan. 17, 1998 (copy in possession of the author).

61. Hill, interview, Dec. 13, 2000.

62. Hill quoted in Broder, *Democracy Derailed,* 168.

63. Helen Hill to Shea Grimm, personal e-mail, Dec. 2, 1997 (copy in possession of the author).

64. Hill quoted in Broder, *Democracy Derailed,* 168. Hill's pragmatism was in accord with reality. Research shows that the success rate in qualifying an initiative for the ballot by use of paid petitioners is extremely high (for those with unlimited money to spend), while for those groups who use volunteers only, the success rate is small. Ellis, *Democratic Delusions,* 50–53.

65. Hill, interview, Dec. 13, 2000.

66. Ultimately, Hill spent close to $120,000 of her own money on the Measure 58 campaign. After the victory of Measure 58, Hill immediately pulled her money out of the stock market and put it back into municipal bonds (Hill, interview).

67. Like Hill, many state legislatures were hostile to the idea of professional signature gatherers because of their frequently corrupt practices and their challenge to the lawmakers' prerogative. As early as 1935 in Oregon and 1941 in Colorado, paid petitioners were outlawed. Ellis, *Democratic Delusions,* 47–49. But in 1988 the Supreme Court ruled that such bans were unconstitutional, declaring that the use of paid circulators in initiative qualification drives was protected by the First Amendment: *Meyer v. Grant,* 486 U.S. 414 (1988). For cogent criticism of the Court's decision, see Tolbert, Lowenstein, and Donovan, "Election Law

and Rules for Using Initiatives," 35–37. More recent state efforts, such as Colorado's legislation in 1994 to require paid circulators "to wear name badges, be registered voters, or file detailed financial reports" met a similar fate: Broder, *Democracy Derailed,* 67. Despite the Supreme Court's ruling, the Oregon legislature had passed a law requiring paid petition circulators to be registered voters, and at the time of the Initiative 46 drive, a lawsuit challenging that requirement was pending. Patty Wentz, "Out of Circulation," *Willamette Week,* Dec. 10, 1997, 12–13.

68. Unless otherwise stated, all quotations and biographical information are from Donna Harris, interview by author, tape recording, Dec. 12, 2000, Portland, Ore., hereafter cited as Harris, interview.

69. Harris qualified the City of Portland term limits initiative and the referendum against the legislature's light rail project. She also qualified the property tax initiative and the union dues initiative. The charter schools initiative and term limits for Oregon initiative did not make the ballot. Harris, interview.

70. Ibid.; Ellis, *Democratic Delusions,* 8.

71. Hill, interview, Dec. 13, 2000; Harris, interview.

72. *1998 State Initiative Manual,* 9.

73. *ORS* 250.105.

74. Talena Ray to Helen Hill, letter, May 22, 1998 (copy in possession of the author); Craig Harris, "Adoption Petitioners to File," *Salem (Ore.) Statesman Journal,* May 22, 1998.

75. Patty Wentz, "And the Winner Is," *Willamette Week,* May 20, 1998, 14.

76. Helen Hill to Fred F. Greenman, personal e-mail, April 4, 1998 (copy in possession of the author).

77. John Caher, "Rediscovered Father Seeks Adoption Reform," *New York Law Journal,* Aug. 14, 2001.

78. All quotations from Frederick F. Greenman to Helen Hill, letter, April 27, 1998 (copy in possession of the author). Even before the initiative qualified for the ballot, Greenman made good on his promise to help Hill, sending her copies of correspondence that he had provided to a New Jersey senate committee in support of a bill granting adopted adults access to their birth certificates. Greenman to Helen Hill, letter, June 3, 1998 (copy in possession of the author). Hill thanked him for "the important materials you have sent." Hill to Greenman, letter, n.d. (copy in possession of the author). Cf. Sullivan, "Bastard Chronicles, Part One," 61.

79. The petition contained only 68,707 valid signatures, or 79.9 percent of the 85,992 signatures submitted. Office of the Secretary of State, "Signature Verification Results Announced for Second Sampling of Initiative Petition #46," news release, June 19, 1998 (copy in possession of the author).

80. Talena Ray to Helen Hill, letter, July 2, 1998 (copy in possession of the author).

81. Helen Hill, "BEST: Oregon," July 2, 1998, <best@lakenet.org> (Jan. 7, 2001).

82. Helen Hill, press release, "Adoptee Rights Initiative Speeds to Ballot," July 9, 1998 (copy in possession of the author).

5. The Rise of the Opposition

1. Opposition to opening adoption records sprang up at the very beginning of the 1970s adoption search movement. In the wake of the publication of *The Search for Anna Fisher* (1973), the Adoptive Parents Committee, 1,000 members strong, denounced Florence Fisher's search. Leaders of the organization called the Adoptees' Liberty Movement Association's goal of opening adoption records "an invasion of privacy on the part of the child into the lives of the biological parents who may not want to be identified." Enid Nemy, "Adopted Children Who Wonder, 'What Was Mother Like?'" *New York Times,* July 25, 1972, sec. 1, p. 22. In 1974, Ralph D. Maxfield, who had been adopted as a child, founded the Association for the Protection of the Adoptive Triangle, a nonprofit informational organization dedicated to preventing open adoption records activists from "gaining their 'rights' at the expense of the 'rights' of everyone else." He and his group's 3,000 members argued that permitting adoptees access to their adoption records threatened "the very existence of the institution of adoption by destroying the factor of confidentiality." R. D. Maxfield to Joseph Reid, Oct. 1, 1975, Child Welfare League of America Records, Supplement, Box TT, Social Welfare History Archives, University of Minnesota, Minneapolis). These small, poorly financed, ad hoc citizen groups attracted little media attention, however, and had no real political influence.

2. Its name was originally the National Committee for Adoption. To avoid confusion, I will refer to the organization by its current name.

3. National Council for Adoption (hereafter NCFA), *Adoption Factbook 3* (Waite Park, Minn.: Park Press Quality Printing, 1999), 20–21; E. Wayne Carp, *Family Matters: Secrecy and Disclosure in the History of Adoption* (Cambridge, Mass.: Harvard University Press, 1998), 145, 186–187; NCFA, "Minutes of the Organizational Meeting of the *National Committee for Adoption,*" July 14, 1980 (copy in possession of the author). I am indebted to Fred Greenman for providing me with a copy of this last document and explaining to me the complicated ways the Federal Registry works.

4. William L. Pierce, "Meet the Fellows," n.d., <http://www.discovery.org/fellows/BillPierce/index.html> (April 25, 2002); quotation from William L. Pierce, personal e-mail, April 26, 2002.

5. NCFA, "1980–81 Goals of the National Committee for Adoption, Inc." I am indebted to Fred Greenman for providing me with a copy of this document. The NCFA's first goal was to "work for elimination of non-agency adoption to insure better protection for infants." Today, NCFA lobbies for tax credits for adoption, supports basic research on children orphaned by HIV/AIDS, defends

adoption in the media, works for reforms in foster care, and attempts to block any effort to open adoption records. NCFA, *Adoption Factbook 3*, 20–21.

6. Pierce's rhetorical style—questioning the mental stability of adoption activists—made him notorious and brought out visceral attacks from triad members. See Judith Modell, "Natural Bonds, Legal Boundaries: Modes of Persuasion in Adoption Rhetoric," in Marianne Novy, ed., *Imagining Adoption: Essays on Literature and Culture* (Ann Arbor: University of Michigan Press, 2001), 215–216.

7. Helen Hill to Shea Grimm, personal e-mail, July 28, 1997 (copy in possession of the author).

8. William L. Pierce, "President's Briefing," Feb. 11, 1998 (copy in possession of William L. Pierce).

9. William L. Pierce, "NCFA Board of Directors," June 16, 1998 (copy in possession of William L. Pierce). Pierce reported in June that there was an "unscheduled conference call" on the Oregon initiative with eight members of the board. No details were recorded. William L. Pierce to Bertha M. Holt, letter, June 25, 1998 (copy in possession of William L. Pierce).

10. Warren Deras, interview by author, tape recording, Portland, Ore., Jan. 17, 2001, hereafter cited as Deras, interview.

11. The committee was composed of two proponents, two opponents, and a fifth member chosen by the other four, who typically became the tiebreaker. If the four members of the committee could not agree on a fifth person, the secretary of state appointed him or her (*ORS* 251. 205). The five committee members chosen were Helen Hill and Shea Grimm for the initiative, adoption attorneys Catherine Dexter and Jim Wheeler against it, and Michael Schrunk, a Multnomah County district attorney. "Ballot Measure 58 Contact Information, Committee," Aug. 5, 1998 (copy in possession of the author).

12. Warren Deras, "Problems with Measure 58 Explanatory Statement," n.d. (copy in possession of the author).

13. Catherine Dexter to Warren Deras, "Measure 58 Explanatory Statement," facsimile message, Aug. 5, 1998 (copy in possession of the author).

14. *Oregon Revised Statutes* 251.215.

15. Warren Deras to Everyone at Right to Life, facsimile message, Aug. 5, 1998 (copy in possession of the author).

16. Dennis Keenan, Doug Alles, Paula Rose Lang to Robert Castagna, memorandum, July 15, 1998 (copy in possession of the author); Castagna to Deras, facsimile message, Aug. 5, 1998 (copy in possession of the author).

17. Deras, interview.

18. Warren C. Deras, "Petition to Review Explanatory Statement," Aug. 6, 1998, 1–9, quotations on 3, 8 (copy in possession of the author).

19. Helen Hill, "BEST: Radio Show," June 4, 1998, <best@lakenet.org> (June 4, 1998). See also Helen Hill, "Re: BEST: Radio Show," June 5, 1998, <best@lakenet.org> (June 5, 1998).

20. Helen Hill, "BEST: Measure 58 FIFTY EIGHT," June 20, 1998, <best@lakenet. org> (June 20, 1998).

21. Shea Grimm to BN ExecComm "(Fwd) We're being sued," Aug. 11, 1998 (copy in possession of the author). Grimm had second thoughts after the explanatory statement oral hearing of August 18: "I originally thought he must be some sort of NCFA operative, but I am now wondering if he isn't just a sad adoptive parent who believes this measure will knock down the house of cards that makes him a parent." Shea Grimm, "Oregon Supreme Court hearing today," Aug. 18, 1998, <best@lakenet.org> (Aug. 18, 1998).

22. The respondents in Deras's petition were the Members, Citizens Explanatory Statement Committee for Measure 58. Catherine Dexter, Jim Wheeler, and Michael Schrunk declined to file a memorandum in opposition to Deras's petition. Shea Grimm to Helen Hill, "WARREN," personal e-mail, Aug. 13, 1998 (copy in possession of the author).

23. Hill, however, agreed with Deras about the distinction between original and amended birth certificates: Hill declared that original birth certificates contained accurate birth parent information and amended birth certificates contained accurate adoptive parent information. Helen Hill, "Memorandum in Opposition to Petition to Review Explanatory Statement," Aug. 23, 1998 (copy in possession of the author).

24. Shea Grimm, "Memorandum in Opposition to Petition to Review Explanatory Statement," Aug. 13, 1998 (copy in possession of the author). Internal evidence (date-stamp on Grimm's "Memorandum") suggests that both memoranda were submitted on the date of the oral argument, Aug. 18, 1998.

25. *Oregon Revised Statutes* 251-185.

26. Warren C. Deras to Evelyn Lamb, letter, Aug. 11, 1998 (copy in possession of the author).

27. Deras, interview. Deras held the conventional view that citizens were rational actors who would read and understand the *Voters' Pamphlet* thoroughly before entering the voter polling booth. See, for example, Robert Horvat, "The Oregon Initiative Process: A Critical Appraisal," *Oregon Law Review* 65:1 (1986): 179. Political scientists, however, have been challenging these notions since the early 1950s. See, for example, Joseph G. Lapalombara, *The Initiative and Referendum in Oregon, 1938–1948* (Corvallis: Oregon State College Press, 1950), 119; David B. Magleby, *Direct Legislation: Voting on Ballot Propositions in the United States* (Baltimore: Johns Hopkins Press, 1984), 136–138.

28. Michael H. Balter, interview by author, tape recording, Portland, Ore., March 29, 2001, hereafter cited as Balter, interview; Patricia M. Collmeyer, "From 'Operation Brown Baby' to 'Opportunity': The Placement of Children of Color at the Boys and Girls Aid Society of Oregon," *Child Welfare* 74:1 (January–February 1995): 242–263.

29. Balter, interview. Balter's reorganization of the BGAS reversed the structure

of authority from top down to bottom up. Thus, from a traditionally hierarchical model of authority, running from the board of directors to Balter and then to the social workers, Balter introduced a more participatory model, where decisions were made first at the level of the social workers and then were brought before Balter and from him to the board of directors. The group found itself unable to resolve many of the most divisive ballot measures that came up prior to Measure 58, including initiatives concerning sexual orientation, abortion rights, and legislation that remanded juveniles to adult courts. As a result, these issues were never brought up to the board of directors. Ibid.

30. Ibid.

31. All quotations from Lauren Greenbaum and Lynne Schroeder, "Summary of the Issues around Ballot Measure #46," n.d. (copy in possession of the author).

32. Balter, interview.

33. Ibid.

34. A list of coalition members can be found at <http://www.oregonadoption agencies.org/members.html> (July 26, 2002).

35. Balter, interview.

36. Lauren Greenbaum, interview by author, tape recording, Beaverton, Ore., March 10, 2001, hereafter cited as Greenbaum, interview.

37. Deras, interview.

38. Ibid.; Nancy Simpson, interview by author, tape recording, Portland, Ore., Feb. 23, 2001, hereafter cited as Simpson, interview.

39. Balter, interview.

40. Simpson, interview.

41. Deras, interview.

42. Warren Deras, "Political Committee and Appointment of Treasurer and Directors," Aug. 24, 1998 (copy in possession of the author).

43. Judith VanDuzer to Warren Deras, facsimile message, Aug. 25, 1998 (copy in possession of the author).

44. 327 *Oregon Reports,* 472 (1998): 472–478. In his dissent, Judge Robert D. Durham argued that the court had no constitutional authority to hear the case, that, in effect, by ruling on the issue, the Supreme Court was usurping the legislative power, and ultimately the power of the electorate. 327 *Oregon Reports,* 472 (1998): 479–483.

45. 327 *Oregon Reports,* 472 (1998): 478.

46. Deras, interview.

47. Shea Grimm to Patty Wentz, personal e-mail, Aug. 27, 1998 (copy in possession of the author). The actual quote from the Court's decision reads: "We have considered petitioner's other contentions, but do not find them well taken." 327 *Oregon Reports,* 472 (1998): 478.

48. Deras, interview.

49. Betty H. Zisk, *Money, Media, and the Grassroots: State Ballot Issues and the Electoral Process* (Newbury Park, Calif.: Sage, 1987), 102; Thomas E. Cronin,

Direct Democracy: The Politics of Initiative, Referendum, and Recall (Cambridge, Mass., and London: Harvard University Press, 1989), 109.

50. Patty Wentz, "Dr. No Strikes Again," *Willamette Week,* Sept. 2, 1998, 13.

51. Deras, interview.

52. Simpson, interview.

53. Deras, interview.

54. Simpson, interview.

55. Deras, interview. See also Warren C. Deras, "Statement of Individual/Independent Expenditures," General Election, 1st Pre-election Report, Aug. 24–Sept. 24, 1998; Warren C. Deras, "Statement of Individual/Independent Expenditures," General Election, 2nd Pre-election Report, Sept. 25–Oct. 23, 1998. Secretary of State, Elections Division, Salem, Ore.

56. Deras, interview.

57. Tom Adam, *Grass Roots: How Ordinary People Are Changing America* (New York: Carol Publishing Group, 1991), 9–10, quotation on 9.

58. Deras, interview.

59. See for example, Dick Hughes to Concerned Adoption Professionals, letter, Sept. 10, 1998 (copy in possession of the author).

60. Deras, interview.

61. Included in the packet sent to Hughes, in addition to Deras's "Summary of Arguments against Measure 58," were a copy of CAP's arguments against Measure 58 from the *1998 Voters' Pamphlet* and an essay Deras had written on confidentiality in Oregon adoptions. Warren Deras to Dick Hughes, facsimile message, Sept. 15, 1998 (copy in possession of the author).

62. Warren C. Deras, "Summary of Arguments against Measure 58," n.d. (copy in possession of the author).

63. Oregon Newspaper Association, "Oregon Newspapers," Aug. 27, 1998 (copy in possession of the author). Deras would later update the opposition arguments and add to CAP's informational packet anti–Measure 58 editorials such as the ones appearing in the *Oregonian* on Sept. 23 and the *Eugene Register Guard* on Oct. 7, 1998.

64. Greenbaum to Deras, facsimile message, Sept. 24, 1998 (copy in possession of the author).

65. Ibid.

66. Ibid. The "Position Paper" had been originally suggested to them by Michael Balter, who had been meeting regularly with Simpson and Greenbaum and who, according to Simpson, "had an idea of how naïve we were." Balter told them that they needed a document that contained a statement of belief, a statement of the BGAS's history around the issue of confidentiality in adoption, and a statement on why they were opposing Measure 58. Balter thought that such a document would help clarify for BGAS personnel in CAP what they really believed and could also be used for publication purposes and for talking points on TV or radio. Simpson wrote the first draft, Greenbaum the second, and it was passed

around to their BGAS colleagues for revision before Deras received it. Simpson, interview; Balter, interview; Greenbaum, interview.

67. Nancy Simpson and Lauren Greenbaum, "A Position Paper by Concerned Adoption Professionals," Sept. 24, 1998 (copy in possession of the author), quotations on 2, 4.

68. For example, the end of the "Position Paper" contains the deferential request "We hope that you will vote no on this insufficient measure until a more fair initiative is presented." Ibid., 5.

69. *Tenn. Code Ann.*, Clause 36-1-125–132 (1996). Although Tennessee's open adoption records law was passed in 1995, there were two legal challenges to it that unsuccessfully challenged its constitutionality. The law finally went into effect in 1997. See M. Christina Rueff, "A Comparison of Tennessee's Open Records Law with Relevant Laws in Other English-Speaking Countries," *Brandeis Law Journal* 37:3 (1998–1999): 453–468, esp. 455–457.

70. Simpson and Greenbaum, "Position Paper," 4.

71. Nancy Simpson et al., "Summary of Arguments against Ballot Measure 58," Sept. 29, 1998 (copy in possession of the author).

72. Deras, interview.

73. Deras to Greenbaum and Simpson, facsimile message, Sept. 17, 1998 (copy in possession of the author).

74. *Town Hall,* Oct. 4, 1998, Channel 2, KATU-TV, Portland, Ore., videocassette recording. I am indebted to "Cindy" for providing me with a copy of this program.

75. It is impossible to know how many CAP informational packets Deras sent out after September 24 with Greenbaum and Simpson's "Position Paper." Deras generously provided me with the last packet and it did contain their "Position Paper." The front page of that same packet, however, contained Deras's "Summary of Arguments against Measure 58." Internal examination suggests that that particular packet could not have been sent out any earlier than October 6.

76. Educational activities were strictly segregated from purely political activities. The latter were not paid for by BGAS. Balter, interview.

77. Ibid.; Boys and Girls Aid Society of Oregon (BGAS), "Statement of Individual/Independent Expenditures," General Election, 2nd Pre-election Report, Oct. 1–Oct. 25, 1998; BGAS, "Statement of Individual/Independent Expenditures," General Election, Post-election Report, Oct. 26–Nov. 23, 1998, Secretary of State, Elections Division, Salem, Ore.

78. Greenbaum, interview.

79. See below, chap. 6, note 24. Patty Wentz, "Bastard," *Willamette Week,* Sept. 16, 1998, 28.

80. Greenbaum, interview.

81. Simpson, interview.

82. Quotations from Greenbaum, interview. See also Balter, interview. A pre-1999 search by the Usenet newsgroups search engine DejaNews of the word "birthwhore" (or "birth whore") reveals that in the period 1996–1997 there were 229 e-mail messages with that term, many of which were written by Bastard

Nation members. I am indebted to "Cindy" for hard copy of twenty-five of these messages. Both Greenbaum and Balter were incorrect in identifying the messages as appearing on BN's "chat room," since BN did not (and as of this writing still does not) have one. The 229 messages appeared on the unmoderated newsgroup <alt.adoption>. In Bastard Nation's defense, however, among themselves and in their publications members never used the term "birth whore" during the Measure 58 campaign. Nor did this term ever appear in *Bastard Quarterly,* the organization's journal, or on BEST, where, in the privacy of its members-only e-mail discussion list, such opinions, if they were common, would be rife. Moreover, virulent anti–birth mother beliefs had no place in an organization where birth mothers—including Linda Corbin, Jane Edwards, Teri Leber, and Mary Anne Cohen, for example—were both members and respected leaders.

83. Greenbaum, interview. Bastard Nation lost the T-shirt argument.

84. Simpson, interview. None of the people I interviewed singled out Helen Hill for condemnation. Their anger seems to have been directed at unnamed Bastard Nation members. Deras, interview; Simpson, interview; Greenbaum, interview.

85. The following Oregon newspapers opposed Measure 58 in their editorials: *Portland Oregonian* (Sept. 23, 1998); *Grant's Pass Daily Courier* (Sept. 26, 1998); *Bend Bulletin* (Sept. 30, 1998); *Eugene Register-Guard* (Oct. 7, 1998); *Corvallis Gazette-Times* (Oct. 13, 1998); *Tillamook Headlight-Herald* (Oct. 20, 1998).

86. National Conference of Commissioners on Uniform State Laws, *Uniform Adoption Act (1994)* (Chicago: National Conference of Commissioners on Uniform State Laws, 1994), 117.

87. Editorial, "Oregon Must Keep Its Word," *Oregonian,* Sept. 23, 1998, B10.

88. Editorial, "Changing the Rules on Adoption," *Boston Globe,* Oct. 5, 1998, A14.

89. Mona Charen, "What 'Measure 58' Would Do," *Jewish World Review,* Oct. 28, 1998.

90. ACLU of Oregon, *Voters Guide to Ballot Measures,* Oct. 8, 1998, <http://www.aclu-or.org/voters.htm#Measure58> (Sept. 25, 2000).

91. Ecumenical Ministries of Oregon, *Voters' Guide,* "58 Requires Issuing Copy of Original Birth Certificate to Adoptees" [n.p., n.d.] (copy in possession of the author).

92. Helen Hill to Shea Grimm, personal e-mail, Aug. 5, 1998 (copy in possession of the author).

93. Deras, letter to the editor, *Oregonian,* Oct. 14, 1998, B10.

94. Namba, letter to the editor, *Oregonian,* Oct. 16, 1998, B8.

95. Greenbaum, letter to the editor, *Oregonian,* Oct. 19, 1998, C8.

96. *1998 Voters' Pamphlet,* 35–40 (arguments in favor), 40–41 (arguments in opposition).

97. Ibid., 40.

98. Ibid., 41.

99. Ibid.

100. Nevertheless, Deras remained optimistic. Warren Deras to Matthew Parrott/ Bill Pierce, facsimile message, Oct. 13, 1998 (copy in possession of the author).

101. Warren C. Deras, untitled, n.d. Deras wrote a three-page untitled letter to the Oregon newspaper editorial boards in which he outlined the positions of the supporters and opponents of Measure 58 (copy in possession of the author).

102. *Town Hall,* Oct. 4, 1998, Channel 2, KATU-TV, videocassette recording.

103. William Pierce, personal e-mail, March 6, 2001; Simpson, interview; William Pierce to Warren Deras, facsimile message, Oct. 1, 1998 (copy in possession of the author).

104. William Pierce to Warren Deras, facsimile message, Oct. 1, 1998 (copy in possession of the author).

105. Pierce to Deras, facsimile message, Oct. 7, 1998 (copy in possession of the author).

106. Deras, interview.

107. Pierce to Deras, facsimile message, Oct. 17, 1998 (copy in possession of the author).

108. Simpson, interview.

109. Deras, "Measure 58 Brochure," n.d. (copy in possession of the author).

110. Warren Deras to Matthew Parrott/Bill Pierce, Oct. 13, 1998 (copy in possession of the author). Pierce was enthusiastic about Deras's brochure (Deras, interview).

111. Deras, interview.

112. Simpson, interview; Balter, interview; Greenbaum, interview.

113. Nancy P. Simpson, "More Balanced Approach Needed," *Oregonian,* Oct. 28, 1998, B11.

114. "Cindy," personal e-mail, June 24, 2001.

115. "Cindy" quoted in Margie Boulé, "Measure Could Rip Privacy in Dire Way," *Oregonian,* Oct. 25, 1998, L1.

116. Margie Boulé, "Adoption-Rights Measure Lacks Crucial Safeguard for Rape," *Oregonian,* Oct. 29, 1998, E1.

117. Margie Boulé to "Cindy," personal e-mail, Nov. 2, 1998 (copy in possession of the author).

118. *Today Show,* Oct. 26, 1998, ABC Channel 2, KATU-TV, Portland, Ore., videocassette recording.

119. Ibid. Helen Hill also appeared paired against Hunsaker.

120. Amalie Young, "Bid to Ease Birth-Parent Searches under Fire," *Seattle Times,* Oct. 25, 1998.

6. The Bastards Strike Back

1. Randall Sullivan, "The Bastard Chronicles, Part Two: The Birth Mother's Story," *Rolling Stone,* Mar. 1, 2001, pp. 42–48, 61, esp. 46.

2. Delores Teller, interview by author, tape recording, Beaverton, Ore., Nov. 27, 2000, hereafter cited as Teller, interview.

3. Teller, interview; Teller to Mark Alter, July 15, 1998, (copy in possession of the author); Teller to Alaskan State Vital Statistics Department, memorandum, n.d.; Teller to Kansas Department of Vital Statistics, memorandum, n.d. (copies in possession of the author).

4. Teller, interview; Teller to Oregon Department of Human Resources, letter, Aug. 26, 1998 (copy in possession of the author).

5. Teller, interview.

6. Patty Wentz, "State Secrets," *Willamette Week,* Oct. 15, 1997, 15.

7. Teller, interview. Teller to Paula Lang, letter, July 15, 1998 (copy in possession of the author). In this letter, Teller identifies the Pope's quote as coming from the "United Nations Convention of the Rights of the Child," articles 2, 4, 7, and 8. Although the phrases can be found scattered in the various articles Teller cites, the quotation does not exist as Teller recorded it. Apparently, the Pope never uttered that particular quotation. UNICEF, "Convention on the Rights of the Child," Nov. 20, 1989, <http://www.unicef.org/crc/> (May 28, 2001).

8. Lang was an experienced licensed clinical social worker, having worked at Advantist's Medical Center for twelve years before coming in July 1997 to Catholic Charities. Paula Lang and Douglas S. Alles, interview by author, tape recording, Portland, Ore., April 20, 2001, hereafter cited as Lang and Alles, interview.

9. Delores Teller, "Open Records: The People Decide," *Adoptive Families* 31:5 (September–October 1998): 26–27, quotation on 27; Teller, interview.

10. Lang and Alles, interview.

11. Ibid.

12. Quotation from memorandum, Dennis Keenan, Doug Alles, and Paula Rose Lang to Robert Castagna, July 15, 1998 (emphasis in the original) (copy in possession of the author); Lang and Alles, interview.

13. Teller, interview; Teller to Robert Roy, letter, July 15, 1998; Teller to American Civil Liberties Union, letter, Sept. 10, 1998 (copies in possession of the author).

14. Donna Harris, interview by author, tape recording, Portland, Ore., Dec. 12, 2000, hereafter cited as Harris, interview; *Oregon Revised Statutes* 251.255.

15. Harris, interview.

16. *1998 Voters' Pamphlet,* vol. 1, 40.

17. Shea Grimm to ExecComm, personal e-mail, Aug. 7, 1998 (copy in possession of the author).

18. Donna Martz, personal e-mail, Dec. 16, 2000; *1998 Voters' Pamphlet,* 36–39.

19. Shea Grimm to ExecComm, personal e-mail, Aug. 16, 1998; Shea Grimm to Judy Kennett, personal e-mail, Aug. 21, 1998; Shea Grimm to Ian Hagemann, personal e-mail, Aug. 21, 1998; Shea Grimm to ExecComm, personal e-mail, Aug. 21, 1998 (copies in possession of the author). When the arguments appeared in the *Voters' Pamphlet* one was identified as written by Bastard Nation, the other by the group Washington State Open '98 (*1998 Voters' Pamphlet,* 37).

20. *Oregon Revised Statutes* 251-185.

21. Helen Hill, "Financial Public Disclosure Statement, Open '98 Political Committee," Sept.–Oct. 5, 1998, 3. For price increases, see Harris, interview.

22. Harris, interview.

23. See <http://www.wweek.com/html/circulation.html> (Nov. 20, 2000).

24. As a graduate student at the University of Oregon's School of Journalism and Communication, Wentz had written a favorable essay about Bastard Nation. See Patty Wentz, "Bastard Nation," *Influx 1997 Online,* 1997, <http://influx.u oregon.edu/> (Oct. 1, 2000).

25. Wentz, "Bastard," *Willamette Week,* Sept. 16, 1998, 21.

26. Ibid.

27. Bastard Nation, "Contact Oregon Newspapers," [July 3–Aug. 19, 1998], <http://www.plumsite.com/oregon/newspapers.html> (Aug. 20, 1998).

28. Bastard Nation, "Frequently Asked Questions," [July 3–Aug. 19, 1998], <http://www.plumsite.com/oregon/faq.html> (Aug. 20, 1998).

29. Helen Hill, "BEST: Answer to Oregonian editorial," Sept. 23, 1998, <best@lakenet.org> (Sept. 23, 1998).

30. Shea Grimm, "BEST: Measure 58 Oregon editorial," Sept. 23, 1998, <best@lakenet.org> (Sept. 23, 1998).

31. Damsel Plum, "URGENT: Letters to Oregonian needed ASAP," Sept. 24, 1998, <best@lakenet.org> (Sept. 24, 1998).

32. Patricia Florin, letter to the editor, "The Need to Know Origins," *Oregonian,* Sept. 29, 1998, B11. Though BN's use of e-mail in the campaign for Measure 58 was pioneering, Randy Shaw vastly exaggerates, if he is not wholly mistaken, when he asserts that "Bastard Nation's reliance on mobilizing through e-mail alerts . . . is creating a sea change in American attitudes toward adoption." Randy Shaw, *Reclaiming America: Nike, Clean Air, and the New National Activism* (Berkeley: University of California Press, 1999), 285. The revolution in American adoption attitudes and practices is a product of complex demographic, social, and political changes that have been going on in the United States for over thirty years. See E. Wayne Carp, *Family Matters: Secrecy and Disclosure in the History of Adoption* (Cambridge, Mass.: Harvard University Press, 1998); and Adam Pertman, *Adoption Nation: How the Adoption Revolution Is Transforming America* (New York: Basic Books, 2000).

33. Florin, "Need to Know Origins."

34. Helen Hill, "BEST: Good News from the Oregonian," Sept. 29, 1998, <best@lakenet.org> (Sept. 29, 1998).

35. Russell Sadler, "Where's Mommy?" *Medford Mail Tribune,* Oct. 4, 1998, 13A.

36. J. Nichols, "BEST: OMG," Oct. 4, 1998, <best@lakenet.org> (Oct. 4, 1998).

37. Helen Hill, "Emergency Response Needed!" Oct. 4, 1998, <best@lake net.org> (Oct. 4, 1998).

38. Julie M. Dennis, "More from Sadler," Oct. 6, 1998; David C. Ansardi,

"BEST: FW: Regarding Russell Sadler's Commentary: 'Where's Mommy,' " Oct. 4, 1998; C. K. Bertrand Holub, "BEST: Reply to Russell Sadler's 'Where's Mommy,' " Oct. 5, 1998; Mary Anne Manning Cohen, "BEST: Russell Sadler and Measure 58," Oct. 6, 1998; Thomas Clement, "BEST: Reply to Russell Sadler's 'Where's Mommy?' " Oct. 6, 1998; Marley Greiner, "My Letter to Medford," Oct. 6, 1998; all <best@lakenet.org> (Nov. 6, 1998).

39. Ansardi, "BEST: FW: Regarding Russell Sadler's Commentary."

40. Clement, "BEST: Reply to Russell Sadler's 'Where's Mommy?' "

41. Cohen, "BEST: Russell Sadler and Measure 58."

42. Similarly, the *Eugene Register-Guard* waited two weeks before it published any letters to the editor and then it neglected to publish any Bastard Nation letters to the editor in response to its editorial of October 7 advising a "no" vote on Measure 58. Editorial, "Respect Adoption Privacy: Measure 58 Breaks Promise of Confidentiality," *Eugene Register-Guard*, Oct. 7, 1998, 12A. Like the *Medford Mail Tribune*, the letters it did publish were local, in this case coming from Eugene. (See letters, *Eugene Register-Guard*, Oct. 20, 1998, 10A; Oct. 22, 1998, 14A).

43. Hill, interview, Dec. 13, 2000.

44. Editorial, "No Vote Urged on Measure 58," *Bend (Ore.) Bulletin*, Sept. 20, 1998, E2.

45. Ben Raines, letter to the editor, Sept. 30, 1998; Pamela J. Zaebst, letter to the editor, Oct. 6, 1998, A6; C. K. Bertrand Holub, letter to the editor, Oct. 5, 1998, A6; all in *Bend (Ore.) Bulletin*.

46. ACLU of Oregon, *Voters Guide to Ballot Measures*, Oct. 8, 1998, <http://www.aclu-or.org/voters.htm#Measure58> (Sept. 25, 2000).

47. Mary Anne Cohen, "BEST: Measure 58," Oct. 9, 1998, best@lakenet.org> (Nov. 6, 1998).

48. Ibid.

49. Shea Grimm, "Measure 58," Oct. 8, 1998, <best@lakenet.org> (Nov. 6, 1998).

50. Damsel Plum, "BEST: OR ACLU—You're doing great!" Oct. 9, 1998, <best@lakenet.org> (Nov. 6, 1998).

51. Damsel Plum, "AAC Officially Endorses Measure 58," Oct. 5, 1998, <best@lakenet.org> (Nov. 6, 1998).

52. Julie M. Dennis, "BEST: Eugene Register-Guard speaks out against M58," Oct. 8, 1998, <best@lakenet.org> (Nov. 6, 1998).

53. Shea Grimm, "Re: BEST: Eugene Register-Guard speaks out against M58," Oct. 8, 1998, <best@lakenet.org> (Nov. 6, 1998).

54. Cynthia Holub, "BEST: Re: we're doing great," Oct. 9, 1998, <best@lakenet.org> (Nov. 6, 1998); Helen Hill, "BEST: we're doing great," Oct. 9, 1998, <best@lakenet.org> (Nov. 6, 1998).

55. August Philippo, "BEST: What if?" Oct. 7, 1998; Helen Hill, "BEST: what if?" Oct. 8, 1998; both <best@lakenet.org> (Nov. 6, 1998).

56. Damsel Plum, "BEST: what if?" Oct. 9, 1998, <best@lakenet.org> (Nov. 6, 1998).

57. Cecile Lambie, letter to the editor, *Oregonian,* Sept. 30, 1998, B11; Gloria Price, letter to the editor, ibid.; Curtis H. Endicott, letter to the editor, *Oregonian,* Oct. 3, 1998, C7; John Frey, letter to the editor, *Oregonian,* Oct. 4, 1998, G5.

58. Adam Pertman, "Oregon Voters Could Open Door to Adoptees' Past," *Boston Globe,* Oct. 2, 1998, A1. The article was reprinted in the *San Jose (Calif.) Mercury News,* Oct. 5, 1998, A3.

59. Damsel Plum, "Boston Globe article—PLEASE ACT," Oct. 2, 1998, <best@ lakenet.org> (Nov. 6, 1998).

60. Heinz's was one of the better pieces of reporting on the issue and gave both sides a chance to air their viewpoints. Spencer Heinz, "Ballot Measure Stirs Fears, Hopes as Adoptees Seek Birth Certificates," *Oregonian,* Oct. 2, 1998, A18.

61. Shea Grimm to ExecComm, "Town Meeting," personal e-mail, Oct. 2, 1998, (copy in possession of the author).

62. Helen Hill, "BEST: an endorsement at last," Oct. 12, 1998, <best@lakenet. org> (Nov. 6, 1998). The *Statesman Journal* endorsement of Measure 58 contained the proviso that the legislature should add amendments "to address the concerns of adoption professions and some birth parents." Editorial, "Adoption measure merits passage, but officials will need to amend it," *Salem Statesman Journal,* Oct. 10, 1998. On closer reading, Hill had second thoughts about her public enthusiasm over the editorial, which suggested that "lawmakers should require county clerks to inform birth parents when an adult adoptee has requested his or her original birth certificate." As she did on almost every issue, Hill consulted Grimm for advice. Grimm was not happy with any "legislative changes to the Measure," but in light of all the hostile newspaper editorials before this one, she advised Bastard Nation members that in replying they should "heavily focus on praising the newspaper and reiterating the YES vote, with maybe very gentle rebukes for the county clerk crap." Shea Grimm to bnlead@lists.com, personal e-mail, Oct. 12, 1998 (copy in possession of the author).

63. Shea Grimm to bnlead@lists.com, personal e-mail, Oct. 13, 1998, (copy in possession of the author).

64. Editorial, "Perceived Problem," *Willamette Week,* Oct. 14, 1998, <http://www.plumsite.com/oregon/wweek-981014.html> (Sept. 25, 2000). In addition to the *Salem Statesman Journal* and *Willamette Week,* only one other paper endorsed Measure 58. Early in the campaign, Hasso Herring, editor of the *Albany Democrat-Herald,* did so, citing adoptees' need of medical information, personal history, and justice. Hasso Herring, "Opinion: Birth Certificates Are a Matter of Justice," *Albany Democrat-Herald,* July 31, 1998, <http://www.plumsite.com/ oregon/albanydh-980731.html> (Aug. 20, 2000). However, the paper also ran a vituperative letter to the editor from Quinton Hamel, an adoptive parent, which vitiated the editorial's measured position and sparked a heated battle over the merits of the initiative. Quinton Hamel, "Birth-Record Initiative Could Do Much Damage," *Albany Democrat-Herald,* Aug. 5, 1998, http://www.plumsite.com/ oregon/quintonhamel.html, (Sept. 25, 2000). Patty Wentz, "Birth of a Notion," *Williamette Week,* Aug. 26, 1998, 21.

65. Shea Grimm, "BEST: Week Endorsement," Oct. 14, 1998, <best@lakenet. org> (Nov. 6, 1998).

66. Shea Grimm to Ron Morgan, personal e-mail, Oct. 27, 1998 (copy in possession of the author).

67. Grimm's dislike of Delores Teller bordered on a personal vendetta, albeit one shared by many BN members. As early as August 1997, Grimm warned Hill about "Delores what's-her-name, that OARA birthmother," who was responsible earlier that year for killing an open records bill in the Oregon legislature and pushing for compromise legislation. Shea Grimm to Helen Hill, personal e-mail, Aug. 4, 1997 (copy in possession of the author). Grimm remembered Teller's triad status more clearly than her last name. Similarly, Grimm was adamantly opposed to Hill's including birth mothers, like Linda Corbin, on her '98 Open Committee. (See text at note 71 below.)

68. Shea Grimm to Helen Hill, personal e-mail, Dec. 24, 1997 (copy in possession of the author).

69. Margie Boulé, "Measure Could Rip Privacy in Dire Way," *Oregonian*, Oct. 25, 1998, L1; Margie Boulé, "Adoption-Rights Measure Lacks Crucial Safeguard for Rape," *Oregonian*, Oct. 29, 1998, E1.

70. Hill, interview, Dec. 13, 2000.

71. Ibid.

72. Ibid.

73. Shea Grimm to Helen Hill, personal e-mail, Oct. 26, 1998 (copy in possession of the author).

74. Jane Edwards, personal e-mail, July 3, July 4, 2001. Hill and Edwards were both unaware that this was the same idea Delores Teller had suggested to Damsel Plum and Grimm back in September. Teller to Damsel Plum and Shea Grimm, personal e-mail, Sept. 19, 1998 (copy in possession of the author).

75. Hill, interview, Dec. 13, 2000. Hill first contacted BN's Damsel Plum and "once again, Damsel Plum with her incredible computer skills" put out the call for birth mothers on the Oregon network (ibid.).

76. Teller, interview.

77. Hill, interview, Dec. 13, 2000.

78. *Oregonian*, Nov. 1, 1998, E6.

79. Hill, interview, Dec. 13, 2000; Ckbh, "BEST: Report from the troops in OR," Nov. 3, 1998, <best@lakenet.org> (Nov. 9, 1998).

80. Ckbh, "BEST: Report from the troops in OR."

81. David C. Ansardi, "BEST: Everybody BREATHE!" Nov. 3, 1998, <best@ lakenet.org> (Nov. 9, 1998).

82. David C. Ansardi, "BEST: RE: Oregon," Nov. 4, 1998, <best@lakenet.org> (Nov. 9, 1998).

83. CellRack, "BEST: Oregon Ramblings," Nov. 5, 1998, <best@lakenet.org> (Nov. 9, 1998).

84. Hill quoted in Kate Taylor, "Adoptees Gain Access to Their Birth Records," *Oregonian*, Nov. 4, 1998, B4.

85. Hill quoted in ibid.

86. Damsel Plum, "Historic Adoption Initiative Restores Adoptee Rights in Oregon," Nov. 11, 1998, <best@lakenet.org> (Dec. 16, 1998).

87. Ibid.

88. Hill quoted in Spencer Heinz, "Birth Certificate Effort May Spread," *Oregonian*, Nov. 5, 1998, B5.

89. Lshipley, "Re: BEST: The Victory," Nov. 6, 1998, <best@lakenet.org> (Dec. 11, 1998).

7. The Legislature Weighs In

1. Shea Grimm to <best@lakenet.org>, personal e-mail, Nov. 4, 1998 (copy in possession of the author). Had Hill or Grimm chosen to make Measure 58 a constitutional initiative rather than a statutory one, the legislature would have been unable to amend it. Richard Ellis highlights this error as an illustration of how amateurish Helen Hill's campaign was. Hill admitted that she was a political novice and did not know the differences between the two types of initiatives. See Richard J. Ellis, *Democratic Delusions: The Initiative Process in America* (Lawrence: University Press of Kansas, 2001), 9. However, Ellis never spoke with the politically astute Shea Grimm and seems unaware of Hill and Grimm's close partnership in writing Measure 58. From the outset, Grimm was aware of the constitutional amendment option and had pragmatically rejected it because it required one-third more signatures—8 percent versus 6 percent—to qualify for the November ballot. She also felt that amending the constitution by initiative would have ensnared the campaign in unnecessary political battles that Measure 58 advocates preferred not to fight. Finally, BN leadership was fairly confident that the legislature would not alter significantly an initiative that had been passed by a large majority of the people. Shea Grimm, personal e-mail, April 22, 2002.

2. All quotations from Thomas E. McDermott, interview by author, tape recording, Portland, Ore., Sept. 5, 2000, hereafter cited as McDermott, interview; *Town Hall*, Oct. 4, 1998, Channel 2, KATU-TV, videocassette recording. Grimm, personal e-mail, Sept. 25, 2001.

3. Shea Grimm to ExecComm and Helen Hill, personal e-mail, Nov. 5, 1998 (copy in possession of the author).

4. Ibid.

5. Ibid.; Shea Grimm to ExecComm and Helen Hill, personal e-mail, Nov. 8, 1998 (copy in possession of the author).

6. Shea Grimm to ExecComm and Helen Hill, personal e-mail, Nov. 8, 1998 (copy in possession of the author).

7. Kate Taylor, "Adoptees Gain Access to Their Birth Records," *Oregonian*, Nov. 4, 1998, B3.

8. Greenbaum quoted in Spencer Heinz, "Birth Certificate Effort May Spread," *Oregonian*, Nov. 5, 1998, B5.

9. Nancy Simpson and Lauren Greenbaum, "For Friday Bulletin: November 6, 1998," (copy in possession of the author); Carol Chumney, "Tennessee's New Adoption Contact Veto Is Cold Comfort to Birth Parents," *University of Memphis Law Review* 27 (1997): 852.

10. Pierce quoted in Cheryl Wetzstein, "Oregon Adoptees May Get Records, but Ballot Victory Hasn't Settled Issue," *Washington Times,* Nov. 12, 1998, A4.

11. See below, chap. 9.

12. I. Franklin Hunsaker, interview by author, tape recording, Portland, Ore., Sept. 5, 2000, hereafter cited as Hunsaker, interview.

13. Ibid.

14. Spencer Heinz, "Suit, Show of Support Loom on Adoption Rights," *Oregonian,* Nov. 28, 1998, A1. The Measure 58 lawsuit was heard in Marion County because Salem is the capital of Oregon and the home of the state government. By statute, all suits against the state are heard in Marion County.

15. Hunsaker quoted in Spencer Heinz, "Plan to Open Birth Certificates to Adoptees Is Stalled," *Oregonian,* Dec. 2, 1998, A1. On December 18 three other birth mothers joined the lawsuit. Spencer Heinz, "Three More Birth Mothers Join Measure 58 Suit," *Oregonian,* Dec. 18, 1998, B12.

16. Kate Taylor, "Adoption Case Judge Focuses on Law," *Oregonian,* Dec. 5, 1998, D1, D6, quotation on D1. The "Darth Vader" sobriquet came from his "commanding presence, black robe and low, raspy voice" (ibid.).

17. Katherine Georges, Oregon's assistant attorney general, who was going to defend the state against the lawsuit, explained the delay in terms of the need to allow both parties adequate time to present fully their cases to the judge, who could then decide whether the measure was valid. Heinz, "Plan to Open Birth Certificates to Adoptees Is Stalled," A1.

18. Ibid.

19. Another angry bastard, "BEST: Oregon Lawsuit—Isn't It MOOT," Dec. 2, 1998, <best@lakenet.org> (Dec. 16, 1998).

20. Shea Grimm, "Re: BEST: Re: BN Goal?" Dec. 2, 1998, <best@lakenet.org> (Dec. 16, 1998).

21. Ron Morgan to Albert Wei and Cynthia Bertrand Holub, "BEST: Re: Dec. 3 in Trenton," Dec. 2, 1998, <best@lakenet.org> (Dec. 16, 1998).

22. Cynthia Bertrand Holub, "BEST: Re: BN Goal?" Dec. 2, 1998, <best@lakenet.org> (Dec. 16, 1998).

23. See for example, Al Wei, "BEST: Re: Dec. 3 in Trenton," and Deni, "BEST: Re: Dec. 3 in Trenton," both Dec. 3, 1998, <best@lakenet.org> (Dec. 16, 1998).

24. Spencer Heinz, "Adoptees Wait for Vital Link," *Oregonian,* Dec. 4, 1998, C1. Nationwide, the event was a bust. See the reports that Damsel Plum posted on <rushlead@plumsite.com> and <best@lakenet.org>.

25. McDermott, interview.

26. Spencer Heinz, "Parties Seek Role on Court on Adoptee Law," *Oregonian,* Dec. 10, 1998, B14.

27. McDermott, interview.

28. Helen Hill, "Report on the Preliminary Hearing, 19 January 1999," March 8, 1999, <http://www.plumsite.com/oregon/preliminary_hearing.html> (Aug. 20, 2000).

29. With the prospect of appearing in Judge Norblad's Salem chambers to give oral arguments, Hill grew tense, knowing how important it would be to succeed. One day during this period, she was startled to read on BEST, Bastard Nation's e-mail list, that Measure 58 succeeded because of a division of labor: Grimm was responsible for writing the initiative, Hill had run the campaign. Hill immediately replied to the BEST list and stated that her "validity will be compromised in court next week if it is widely held that I am not the author of the law." Somehow forgetting about all the consultations and revisions with Grimm, Hill declared, "the truth is, I did write the proposed law. I asked Shea to read it over and she suggested adding the phrase citing the Oregon Revised Statute numbers and the wording 'pursuant to.' All other words were mine, and carefully researched." Helen Hill, "BEST: authorship of M58," Jan. 11, 1999, <best@lakenet.org> (Feb. 10, 1999). Within an hour, Grimm was denying the accuracy of Hill's claim to sole authorship. She stated that "in fact, I wrote the first draft of M58, which we bandied back and forth before the final version." Grimm also stated correctly that authorship of the initiative would not be an issue in the circuit court. Rather, Hill's status as intervenor would be determined by her status as chief petitioner, not as the author of Measure 58. Shea Grimm, "Re: BEST: authorship of M58," Jan. 11, 1999, <best@lakenet.org> (Feb. 10, 1999). In the next and final exchange, Grimm stated, "I wrote the bulk of Measure 58. I don't consider it important, but I'm not going to lie about it either, and I won't be lied about." She made an effort at reconciliation by praising Hill: "Helen deserves continued kudos for her work on the Measure. . . . We all do so many things, that there should be no need for us to attempt to take credit for other people's efforts within the open records movement. What she DID do was worth months of praise on its own." Shea Grimm, "Re: BEST: authorship of M58," Jan. 13, 1999, <best@lakenet.org> (Jan. 13, 1999). But these words fell on deaf ears. Hill only heard that she was being denied sole authorship of Measure 58. "All of a sudden, they'd cut my knees off," she recalled. "They're in public saying I never wrote this law." Helen Hill, interview by author, tape recording, Nehalem, Ore., (hereafter cited as Hill, interview), Aug. 28, 2001. Shortly thereafter, with no mention of the conflict, Hill rejoined Bastard Nation.

30. David E. Rovella, "Two Dads, Two Responses," *National Law Journal,* March 13, 2000, A1, A10–A11; Janie Har, "Courtroom Foes Take Adoption Law to Heart," *Oregonian,* March 5, 2000, A1.

31. Spencer Heinz, "Judge to Let Adoption Law Backers Participate in Suit," *Oregonian,* Jan. 23, 1999, D8.

32. This and the next paragraph are based on James Wheeler, interview by author, tape recording, West Linn, Ore., Sept. 27, 2001, hereafter cited as Wheeler, interview.

33. Ibid.

34. Ibid.

35. A copy of the draft of HB 3194 can be found in Shea Grimm to Executive Committee, personal e-mail, March 24, 1999. I am indebted to Shea Grimm for sharing this rare document with me.

36. Wheeler, interview. Wheeler cannot remember if he talked directly to the legislative counsel or if Piercy's legislative aide did (ibid.). If Piercy's office did relay Wheeler's information to the legislative counsel, the miscommunication is readily explained. Patty Wentz reported to Grimm that Representative Piercy's legislative aide, Morgan Allen, admitted that he and Piercy had not tracked the bill very carefully. In essence, Allen said, he did not know what was in the bill. Wentz upbraided him ("I told him to read the damn thing"), and was happy to report to Grimm that Piercy's office was in agreement with Bastard Nation's ideas. See Shea Grimm to Patty Wentz, personal e-mail, March 25, 1999 (copy in possession of the author).

37. Wheeler, interview. Two years later, Hill, who had worked closely with Wheeler on HB 3194, stated, "I don't think there was much evil intent because it was so easy to get the bill revised." Hill, interview, Aug. 28, 2001.

38. Shea Grimm to Thomas McDermott, facsimile message, March 24, 1999 (copy in possession of the author).

39. Shea Grimm to Patty Wentz, personal e-mail, March 24, 1999 (copy in possession of the author).

40. Shea Grimm to Executive Committee, personal e-mail, March 24, 1999 (copy in possession of the author).

41. All quotations and content from Hill, interview, Aug. 28, 2001.

42. [Board of Vital Records], "Issues for Consideration on HB 3194, adoption rights 'measure 58' amendment bill," n.d. (copy in possession of the author).

43. Wheeler, interview.

44. Spencer Heinz, "Bill Would Allow Birth Parents to Ask Not to Be Contacted," *Oregonian*, March 31, 1999, B6.

45. Shea Grimm to Patty Wentz, personal e-mail, March 24, 1999 (copy in possession of the author).

46. Shea Grimm to Executive Committee, personal e-mail, April 2, 1999 (copy in possession of the author).

47. All quotations from Grimm to Hill, personal e-mail, April 6, 1999, (copy in possession of the author).

48. Hill, interview, Aug. 28, 2001.

49. Helen Hill, "BEST: Oregon's HB 3194," April 13, 1999, <best@lakenet.org> (June 17, 2000). Grimm echoed Hill and stated that HB 3194 was "a big victory for us, guys." Shea Grimm, "Re: BEST: Oregon's HB 3194," April 13, 1999, <best@lakenet.org> (June 17, 2000).

50. Helen Hill, "BEST: HB3194," April 21, 1999, <best@lakenet.org> (June 17, 2000).

51. Oregon House of Representatives, House Human Resources Committee Minutes, Tape 63, side A, Oregon State Archives, Salem.

52. Kitty Piercy, Testimony in favor of House Bill 3194 with dash-1 amendments, April 20, 1999, Oregon House of Representatives, House Human Resources Committee, Oregon State Archives, Salem.

53. "Written testimony in support submitted by Helen Hill," April 20, 1999, Oregon House of Representatives, House Human Resources Committee, Exhibit F, Oregon State Archives, Salem.

54. Helen Hill, "BEST: HB3194," April 21, 1999, <best@lakenet.org> (June 17, 2000).

55. "Proposed Amendments to House Bill 3194" (Submitted by Rep. Piercy), April 20, 1999, Exhibit D, Oregon House of Representatives, House Human Resources Committee, Oregon State Archives, Salem.

56. The closest thing to a snag occurred when some committee members posed technical questions to State Registrar Edward Johnson about which department—his or the State Office for Services for Children and Families—would be responsible for administering the contact preference form. Oregon House of Representatives, House Human Resources Committee, Oregon State Archives, Salem.

57. Lisa Grace Lednicer, "Lawmaker's Own Story Helps Push Adoption Bill," *Oregonian,* April 30, 1999, D1.

58. Written testimony in support of 3194-A, submitted by James Wheeler (Exhibit D), Lauren Greenbaum (Exhibit I), Helen Hill (Exhibit G), and Bastard Nation member Mark Fyer (Exhibit H), April 20, 1999, Oregon Senate, Senate Judiciary Committee, Oregon State Archives, Salem.

59. Oregon Senate, Senate Judiciary Committee Minutes, Tape 191, side A, Oregon State Archives, Salem.

60. *Oregon Revised Statutes,* 1999, chap. 604, § 1. See the Appendix for the text of approved HB 3194.

61. Walker and Hopson quoted in Lednicer, "Lawmaker's Own Story."

62. Even Lauren Greenbaum and James Wheeler did not argue that HB 3194 should pass because it protected the privacy of birth parents. Instead, they endorsed the bill, in the words of Greenbaum, because "it allows [birth parents] to make their wishes regarding contact known to the children they placed for adoption." Written testimony in support of 3194-A, Submitted by Lauren Greenbaum, Exhibit I, James Wheeler, Exhibit D, April 20, 1999, Oregon Senate, Senate Judiciary Committee, Oregon State Archives, Salem.

63. Spencer Heinz, "Lawyers Wrestle with Confidentiality in Adoption Suit," *Oregonian,* May 13, 1999, D6.

64. Thomas E. McDermott to Albin W. Norblad, May 28, 1999, Marion County Circuit Court, August 1999, *Does 1, 2, 4, 5, 6, and 7 v. State of Oregon and Intervenors, Appellants' Abstract of Record,* A-172.

65. McDermott, interview. These discussions took place in Judge Norblad's chambers and were off the record. McDermott was working from memory and notes.

66. Ibid.

67. Frederick Greenman, interview by author, tape recording, New York, N.Y., Oct. 13, 2000.

68. McDermott, interview.

69. McDermott to Norblad, May 28, 1999, Marion County Circuit Court, August 1999, *Does 1–7 v. State of Oregon, Appellants' Abstract of Record*, A-172.

70. Albin W. Norblad to Franklin Hunsaker, Katherine Georges, and Thomas McDermott, June 9, 1999, Marion County Circuit Court, August 1999, *Appellants' Abstract of Record*, A-174–175. McDermott filed the formal "Motion for Change of Judge" on July 14. See *Does 1–7 v. State of Oregon, Appellants' Abstract of Record*, A-171.

71. McDermott, interview.

72. Kate Taylor, "Judge Withdraws from Oregon Adoption Records Case," *Oregonian*, June 17, 1999, B5.

8. *"The Land of Noodle-Heads"*

1. I. Franklin Hunsaker, personal e-mail, Nov. 13, 2001.

2. Paul J. Lipscomb, résumé, n.d. (copy in possession of the author).

3. Paul J. Lipscomb, interview by author, tape recording, Salem, Ore., Dec. 4, 2001, hereafter cited as Lipscomb, interview.

4. Ibid.

5. I. Franklin Hunsaker, interview by author, tape recording, side A, Portland, Ore., Sept. 5, 2001, hereafter cited as Hunsaker, interview.

6. See chap. 1 above.

7. *Jane Does 1, 2, 4, 5, 6, 7 v. The State of Oregon*, "Plaintiff's Memorandum in Support of Motion for Summary Judgement Challenging the Constitutionality of Ballot Measure No. 58," 5, 22–26.

8. *Oregon Revised Statutes* 7.211 and 109.430. Hunsaker would frequently have recourse to this argument in the oral hearings. See, for example, *Jane Does 1, 2, 3, 4, 5, 6 and 7 v. The State of Oregon* (Case No.: 98C20424), *Transcript of Proceedings*, July 14, 1999, 31–39, hereafter cited as *Transcript of Proceedings*. See also I. Franklin Hunsaker, "Oregon's Ballot Measure 58: A Grossly Unfair and State-Sanctioned Betrayal of Birth Mothers," *Family Court Review* 39:1 (2001): 77.

9. *Jane Does 1, 2, 4, 5, 6, 7 vs. The State of Oregon (Case No.: 98C20424), Appellants' Abstract of Record*, A-75–A-100, hereafter cited as *Appellants' Abstract of Record*.

10. Elizabeth Welch, affidavit, June 2, 1998, ibid., A-167–A-168.

11. Hunsaker, "Oregon's Ballot Measure 58," 78.

12. By the time of the oral argument, there were only six birth mothers. In March 1999, one of the seven original birth mothers requested to be dismissed from the suit.

13. *Transcript of Proceedings*, 24–29, quotation on 29.

14. Ibid., 30.

15. Helen Hill, "BEST: Trial commentary LONG," July 15, 1999, <best@lakenet.org> (July 9, 2000).

16. *Transcript of Proceedings,* 31–32. This is a direct quotation from *Oregon Revised Statutes,* 1957, chap. 412 §3 (7.211).

17. *Oregon Revised Statutes,* 109.430.

18. *Transcript of Proceedings,* 46, 36.

19. Oregon Constitution, Art. I, sect. 21. The Oregon Constitution can be found in the *Oregon Bluebook,* 2001–2002, 1999 ed. (Salem: Government Printing Office, 2001), 384. Hunsaker did not discuss in much detail Measure 58's impairment of the contract clause of the U.S. Constitution, except to say that the analysis was "essentially the same" as the one made to Oregon's Constitution. See *Transcript of Proceedings,* 47–48.

20. *Transcript of Proceedings,* 41–44; quotations on 41, 42, 43–44, 44.

21. Ibid., 50.

22. Ibid., 51, 60; quotation on 60.

23. Ibid., 49–56; quotation on 55. Finally, Georges returned to *Oregon Revised Statutes* 109.430, the 1983 adoption registry statute, and accused Hunsaker of not putting up on his display easel "the actual full text of that measure and it's frequently the case in this case what plaintiff leaves out is as important as what they insert." Ibid., 58. Georges was specifically referring to three sentences of the statute, one of which stated, "The State also further recognizes that some birth parents have a strong desire to obtain identifying information about their biological children who were adopted while other birth parents have no such desire." Georges noted correctly that the statute said nothing about the right of birth mothers to remain anonymous from their birth children. In fact, as Georges correctly pointed out, the statute merely set up a voluntary adoption registry. As for Hunsaker's quotation of the last sentence of the statute, it merely recognized the privacy interests of *all* triad members. Ibid., 57–58, quotations on 57. It did not privilege birth mothers.

24. Ibid., 61–63.

25. Ibid., 63–65, quotations on 65.

26. See chap. 1 above.

27. *Transcript of Proceedings,* 66 (author's emphasis).

28. During the rebuttal, besides reiterating that adoption statutes were contracts, Hunsaker took "offense at Ms. Georges saying we've somehow tried to hide statutes. The statutes are all set out in their entirety in our memorandum [legal brief]. We haven't tried to hide anything." But Georges was referring to Hunsaker's easel presentation in the courtroom, not his brief. Later, he explained that it was only space limitations that prevented him from displaying the entire passage on the easel. *Transcript of Proceedings,* 67–73.

29. McDermott thought so. He believed that lawyers must be alert to "a signal from the court and if you know something is not working, then you should move on." But "Frank kept hammering contract, contract, and the judge finally got, I think, a little tired of it." McDermott, interview.

30. *Transcript of Proceedings,* 74–75.

31. Ibid., 75, 76, 78. In the *Transcript of Proceedings,* "reed" is spelled "read."

32. I. Franklin Hunsaker, personal e-mail, Nov. 26, 2001.

33. *Griswold v. Connecticut* 381 U.S. 479 (1965), Douglas at 485; Lawrence Tribe, *American Constitutional Law,* 2d ed. (New York: Foundation Press, 1988), 775–776, 1309.

34. *Roe v. Wade,* 410 U.S. 113, 152 (1973).

35. *Transcript of Proceedings,* 82–83, quotation on 83.

36. Ibid., 84–85, quotations on 84.

37. Ibid., 88, 89–90, 92–94. For the Oregon Constitution, see *Oregon Bluebook,* 384. When Georges had finished, McDermott spoke, returning to the Jane Doe affidavits and using them, as he had done before, as virtual hostile defense witnesses. *Transcript of Proceedings,* 96–97.

38. *Transcript of Proceedings,* 100–102.

39. Ibid., 105. Roy Pulvers, McDermott's law partner, had begun the defense's rebuttal by denying Hunsaker's claim that Measure 58 "was not a rational exercise of legitimate state authority." He then rhetorically challenged Hunsaker to produce one case stating "that something violates Article I, Section 20 or the Fourteenth Amendment because it's outside the scope of the Legislature's authority to enact such a law." Ibid., 103. In responding, Hunsaker vehemently denied Pulvers's major points. Ibid., 106–107.

40. Ibid., 108, 109–110. Hunsaker brought up one final issue. He claimed that Measure 58 violated the constitutional rights of the plaintiffs to exercise their religion and rights of conscience. He charged that Measure 58 forced a mother to choose between abortion or adoption. By doing so, it would put undue pressure on a woman to have an abortion, which might conflict with her religious beliefs, thus violating the rights guaranteed by the Oregon Constitution. (Ibid., 113, 121.) For Pulvers's response, see ibid., 117.

41. Ibid., 123, 124–126, 127.

42. I. Franklin Hunsaker, personal e-mail, Nov. 26, 2001.

43. Shea Grimm, "BEST: More on the Trial," July 15, 1999, <best@lakenet.org> (July 9, 2000).

44. Brad Cain's AP story is reproduced in Albert Wei, "BEST: AP article-repost w/complete article, sorry," July 15, 1999, <best@lakenet.org> (July 9, 2000).

45. I. Franklin Hunsaker, personal e-mail, Nov. 26, 2001.

46. *Appellants' Abstract of Record,* A-177–A-179.

47. Ibid. Finally, Lipscomb found that Measure 58 did not unconstitutionally interfere with the plaintiffs' right to freely exercise their religion because it was a "religiously neutral law of general applicability, and therefore, did not violate any protections afforded to religious beliefs and practices by the Oregon and U.S. Constitutions." Ibid.

48. I. Franklin Hunsaker, personal e-mail, Nov. 26, 2001. No doubt Judge Lipscomb informed McDermott in a similar manner. On the day of the ruling, Grimm e-mailed members of Bastard Nation an Associated Press story containing news

of Lipscomb's decision. Shea Grimm, "BEST: The Decision," July 16, 1999, <best@lakenet.org> (July 9, 2000). Helen Hill learned about it from a radio reporter. Patty Wentz, "Open Sesame," *Willamette Week,* July 21, 1999. The *Oregonian* carried a more detailed story the following morning. Bill Graves and Romel Hernandez, "State Adoption-Rights Law Back on Track," *Oregonian,* July 17, 1999, A1.

49. "Motion for Stay of Judgment," July 20, 1999, *Appellants' Abstract of Record,* A-180. On July 23, the defendants and intervenors opposed the plaintiffs' motion. On July 26, plaintiffs filed a reply to the opposing memos. Ibid.

50. Bill Graves, "Mothers Lose Battle to Keep Adoption Law Inactive until Appeal," *Oregonian,* July 28, 1999, C1. On July 28, Lipscomb filed an order denying plaintiff's motion for stay of judgement. *Appellants' Abstract of Record,* A-180.

51. I. Franklin Hunsaker, personal e-mail, Nov. 26, 2001. The legal documents were delivered by a courier service, which telephoned Hunsaker when they were filed with the Court "in order to ensure that filing and also service on opposing counsel" (ibid.). "Notice of Appeal," July 29, 1999, *Appellants' Abstract of Record,* A-181.

52. "Order on Motion for Stay," July 30, 1999, *Appellants' Abstract of Record,* A-181. Bill Graves, "Appeals Court Places Hold on Adoption Law," *Oregonian,* July 31, 1999, D6.

53. I. Franklin Hunsaker, personal e-mail, Nov. 26, 2001.

54. Helen Hill, "Re: BEST: Unfortunate News," July 30, 1999, <best@lakenet. org> (July 9, 2000).

55. "Order Giving Leave under ORS 19.270(4); Granting Stay; and Expediting Appeal," *Appellants' Abstract of Record,* A-184.

56. Hunsaker quoted in Bill Graves, "Court Keeps Adoption Law in Limbo," *Oregonian,* Aug. 14, 1999, D1.

57. Henry Stanley [Helen Hill], "Re: BEST: Re: M58 on N.P.R.," Aug. 13, 1999, <best@lakenet.org> (July 9, 2000).

58. Julie Dennis, "BEST: Oregon Law on Hold for 90 days," Aug. 13, 1999, <best@lakenet.org> (July 9, 2000). Dennis posted an AP newspaper article.

59. Henry Stanley [Helen Hill], "Re: BEST: Re: M58 on N.P. R."

60. Inselman and Walker quoted in Graves, "Court Keeps Adoption Law in Limbo." Surprisingly, Thomas McDermott did not denounce the Court's stay. Graves reported McDermott as saying that the court's "ruling was a reasonable compromise between protecting the mothers and taking swift action for anxious adoptees." Ibid.

61. Plum's message is found in the reply of Henry Stanley [Helen Hill], "BEST: Re: Oregon—Next Stop," Aug. 13, 1999, <best@lakenet.org> (July 9, 2000).

62. Ibid.

63. Bill Graves, "Adoption Law Faces Further Delays," *Oregonian,* Sept. 8, 1999, B6.

64. Inselman and Teller quoted in Bill Graves, "Advocate for Adoptees Dies at Age 51," *Oregonian,* Sept. 14, 1999, B1.

65. Helen Hill, Press Release, "Adoptee Rights Spokesman Dies Waiting for Measure to Take Effect," September 13, 1999, <http://www.plumsite.com/oregon/ M58Curtis.html> (Oct. 28, 2000).

66. Hunsaker quoted in Graves, "Advocate for Adoptees Dies at Age 51."

67. All quotations from Bill Graves, "Tennessee Court Supports Access to Birth Records," *Oregonian,* Sept. 29, 1999, B1.

68. Helen Hill, "BEST: Oregonian article today," Oct. 30, 1999, <best@lakenet. org> (July 1, 2001).

69. All quotations from Bill Graves, "Birth Records Unlocks Past for Adoptee," *Oregonian,* Oct. 19, 1999, A1. Helen Hill was ambivalent about the way the media played on the emotion of its readers. Prompting Hill's self-questioning was another front-page story in the *Oregonian* that described in detail the serious medical problems of Bob Whalley, an adoptee who planned to submit an affidavit and a blank court order designed by Hill. Accompanying the piece was a photograph of the white-haired Whalley with an oxygen tube running up his nose. Janie Har, "Case Raises Hopes for Adoptees," *Oregonian,* Oct. 30, 1999, A1. The major problem for Hill was that the press was totally ignoring the issue of adoptee civil rights and was turning Measure 58 into a search-and-reunion issue. Hill, "BEST: Oregonian article today," Oct. 30, 1999, <best@lakenet.org> (July 1, 2001). But at the same time, Hill appreciated the pragmatic benefits to the cause that these emotional adoptee articles provided. She was sure that the accumulation of events—the death of Curtis Endicott, her personal intervention in successfully obtaining Mary Inselman's original birth certificate, and the "flood" of stories about older and sick adoptees unable to receive medical information about their condition—were affecting public opinion in favor of Measure 58. As she put it: "I think what is registering with Joe Oregon and Joe Appellate Court Judge is 'gosh, this is even more unfair than I even thought.' " Hill, "BEST: Oregonian article today."

70. Letter to the editor, *Oregonian,* Nov. 20, 1999, D11. Helen Hill's response was published on Nov. 23, 1999.

71. Bill Graves, "Birth Mothers Fight for Their Privacy with Empty Arms," *Oregonian,* Nov. 21, 1999, D1.

9. Victory

1. I. Franklin Hunsaker, personal e-mail, Nov. 13, 1999; Bill Graves, "State: Secret Adoptions Were Never Promised," *Oregonian,* Nov. 23, 1999, A1; Ron Morgan, "BEST: (Fwd) Oregon Update," Nov. 23, 1999, <best@lakenet.org> (July 11, 2000).

2. Chief Justice Mary Deats had asked Judge De Muniz to assemble and preside

over the special three-judge panel. Paul J. De Muniz, interview with author, tape recording, March 21, 2001, Salem, Ore., hereafter cited as De Muniz, interview.

3. Ibid.

4. Compare *Jane Does 1, 2, 4, 5, 6, 7 v. State of Oregon,* "Plaintiff's Memorandum in Support of Motion for Summary Judgement" to *Jane Does 1, 2, 4, 5, 6 and 7 v. State of Oregon,* "Appellants' Opening Brief" (Marion County Circuit Court, Salem, Ore.).

5. *Jane Does 1–7 v. State of Oregon,* "Appellants Opening Brief" (Appeal from the Judgement of Circuit Court for Marion County).

6. "Oregon Court of Appeals Oral Argument, November 22, 1999," *Jane Does 1–7 v. State of Oregon,* hereafter cited as Court of Appeals Oral Argument Transcript. The transcript does not usually identify the individual judges by name; it uses the generic "Court." However, occasionally the transcript does identify specific judges, and I have taken advantage of those rare instances in the text.

7. Ibid., 6.

8. Ibid., 10–11.

9. Ibid., 22–24, quotations on 22, 23.

10. Ibid., 25. The phrases were from Justice Louis Brandeis's famous 1928 dissent in *Olmstead v. United States* and were not, as Hunsaker mistakenly suggested, the opinion of the Supreme Court. (*Olmstead v. United States,* 277 U.S. 438, 278). The phrase "the right to be let alone" was first used in 1879 by influential jurist Thomas Cooley. Janna Malamud Smith, *Private Matters: In Defense of the Personal Life* (Reading, Mass.: Addison-Wesley, 1997), 233–234.

11. Court of Appeals Oral Argument Transcript, 25–26.

12. Ron Morgan, "BEST: (Fwd) Oregon Update."

13. Court of Appeals Oral Argument Transcript, 26, 27.

14. Ibid., 30–36, 44, quotations on 34, 44. The judges also asked Schuman hypothetical questions about confidentiality and Hunsaker's methodology of using affidavits from retired judges and lawyers. Ibid., 36–38.

15. Ibid., 44–46, quotation on 46. In the final five minutes, Thomas McDermott spoke on behalf of the intervenors in the case. He called for an immediate lifting of the injunction that had delayed Measure 58's implementation, if the Court found in favor of the state.

16. Acting on his belief in the importance of the case, Judge De Muniz threw all his energy into writing the decision. He also thought it important that the case be unanimous and consequently wrote it "as tightly and strongly as possible because we have ten judges on the Court and any one judge can affect that opinion." De Muniz, interview.

17. *Eckles v. State of Oregon,* 306 Or. 380, 390, 760 P.2d 846 (1988), *appeal dismissed* 490 U.S. 1032 (1989); *Hughes v. State of Oregon,* 314 Or. 1, 13, 838 P.2d 1018 (1992).

18. *Does 1, 2, 3, 4, 5, 6, and 7 v. STATE,* 993 P.2d 822 (Or.App. 1999), quotations at 829.

19. Ibid., quotation at 833.

20. Ibid. The Court found the analysis of constitutional protection against federal impairment of contract parallel to the Oregon analysis.

21. The relevant constitutional article and sections spoke the language of the Declaration of Independence, emphasizing such traditional American values as liberty, equality, and popular sovereignty. Ibid., 833–834.

22. Ibid., 834–836, quotations on 836.

23. Ibid., 836.

24. Hill, Teller, and McDermott quoted in Bill Graves, "Adoptees Gain Access," *Oregonian*, Dec. 30, 1999, A1. Edward Johnson, state registrar of the Center for Health Statistics, announced that the Oregon vital records office would begin immediately to process the 1,468 requests it had already received from adult adoptees seeking their birth certificates. Ibid.

25. Editorial, "Bring Peace to Adoptees," *Oregonian*, Dec. 30, 1999, C8.

26. "Cindy" and "Christina" quoted in Graves, "Adoptees Gain Access."

27. Ibid.

28. Hill quoted in Janie Har and Bill Graves, "Court Keeps Adoption Records Sealed, After All, for Seven Days," *Oregonian*, Dec. 31, 1999, A1.

29. Marley Greiner, "BEST: (Fwd) Oregon Update," Nov. 23, 1999, <best@lake net.org> (Dec. 30, 1999).

30. Helen Hill, press release, "BEST: IMPORTANT PROTEST," Jan. 2, 2000, <best@lakenet.org> (Jan. 4, 2000). Quotation from Helen Hill, "STOP THE STALL," Jan. 3, 2000, <best@lakenet.org> (Jan. 4, 2000).

31. Helen Hill, "Portland Protest," Jan. 7, 2000, <best@lakenet.org> (July 11, 2000). Hill estimated that about fifty people turned out; she was disappointed that the evening newscasts reported only twenty. Hill, "STOP THE STALL."

32. Hill, "Portland Protest."

33. Letters to the editor by Betty E. Bergstrom; Lori Johnson; Susan Gotshall; and Cynthia Bertrand Holub and Ron Morgan (the last two from BN's Executive Committee), *Oregonian*, Jan. 9, 2000, G4.

34. Barbara Hardy Dugas, letter to the editor, *Oregonian*, Jan. 12, 2000, B10.

35. Teresa Bral, letter to the editor, *Oregonian*, Jan. 9, 2000, G4.

36. Harold F. Potter and Michael Spiegel, letters to the editor, *Oregonian*, Jan. 13, 2000, C2.

37. Lauren Greenbaum, letter to the editor, *Oregonian*, Jan. 15, 2000, C2.

38. Editorial, "Delay in Adoption Law Appropriate Decision," *Salem Statesman Journal*, Jan. 10, 2000.

39. Editorial, "Push to Open Adoption Record Invades Birth Parents' Privacy," *USA Today*, Jan. 10, 2000, 18A.

40. Bill Graves, "A Tangle of Heartstrings," *Oregonian*, Jan. 30, 2000, L1; Janie Har, "Courtroom Foes Take Adoption Law to Heart," *Oregonian*, March 5, 2000, A1; Bill Graves, "State Court Still Silent on Review of Adoption Law," *Oregonian*, March 13, 2000, E12.

41. Bill Graves and Janie Har, "Court OKs State Adoption Law," *Oregonian*, March 21, 2000, A1; Hunsaker, interview; Janie Har and Steven Carter, "Court Upholds State Adoption Rights Law," *Oregonian*, March 22, 2000, A1.

42. Graves and Har, "Court OKs State Adoption Law"; Hunsaker, interview; Har and Carter, "Court Upholds State Adoption Rights Law." Legal experts were dubious about the chances that the High Court would reverse itself if Hunsaker petitioned for reconsideration. Former Supreme Court Justice Jacob Tanzer thought that the presence of two dissenting votes suggested that there was a thorough airing of the issue by both sides, making a grant of reconsideration even more unlikely. In any case, Tanzer said, petitions for reconsideration were rarely granted. Tanzer quoted in Har and Carter, "Court Upholds State Adoption Rights Law."

43. Graves and Har, "Court OKs State Adoption Law"; McDermott quoted in Har and Carter, "Court Upholds State Adoption Rights Law."

44. Editorial, "Now It's a Family Matter," *Oregonian*, March 22, 2000, C8.

45. Har and Carter, "Court Upholds State Adoption Rights Law."

46. "Mary," letter to the editor, *Oregonian*, March 28, 2000, E15.

47. Sam Howe Verhovek, "Oregon Law Heightens Debate over Opening Adoption Records," *New York Times*, April 5, 2000, A1.

48. Ibid.

49. There followed the usual verbal sparring between the two legal adversaries. After Hunsaker argued for more time on the basis that since the Court had handed down its adverse ruling he had been tied up with pressing legal obligations and a short family vacation, Thomas McDermott opposed Hunsaker's motion because, he said, "the fact that Mr. Hunsaker has been busy with other matters, in my view, is not sufficient to justify further delay." Hunsaker responded, "We're not doing this to intentionally delay. It's a good-faith motion to get time to enable to us to explain to the Supreme Court why they ought to reconsider their decision denying review." McDermott and Hunsaker quoted in Bill Graves, "Adoptees Again Face Delay on Access to Birth Records," *Oregonian*, April 6, 2000, B6.

50. Bill Graves, "Another Court Delay Thwarts Adoptees," *Oregonian*, April 11, 2000, A1.

51. *Or. Admin R.* 9.07(3).

52. *Jane Does 1, 2, 4, 5, 6, and 7 v. The State of Oregon and the Intervenors*, "Petition for Reconsideraton," May 2, 2000 (State Court Administrator's Office, Salem, Ore., 2000), 1–38, quotation on 37.

53. About.com, "Alabama Opens the Records," May 15, 2000, <http://adoptionou . . . ting/adoption/library/blalopen.htm> (May 18, 2000).

54. Hunsaker, interview.

55. Hunsaker quoted in Tara Burghart, "Adoption Petition Denied by Oregon Court," May 16, 2000, <http://www.nandotimes.com/noframes . . . 50205002 84962-501531678-0,00.html> (May 17, 2000); Hunsaker quoted in Janie Har,

"Oregon High Court Again Rejects Adoption Law Plea," *Oregonian*, May 17, 2000, B1.

56. Hunsaker, interview.

57. Burghart, "Adoption Petition Denied by Oregon Court"; Har, "Oregon High Court Again Rejects Adoption Law Plea."

58. Janie Har, "Adoption Law May Face Further Delay," *Oregonian*, May 20, 2000, B2; Bill Graves and Janie Har, "Adoption Law Moves Forward," *Oregonian*, May 24, 2000, A1; Janie Har, "Supreme Court Asked to Delay Adoption Law," *Oregonian*, May 27, 2000, B3.

59. Hunsaker, interview; Donna Martz, "AP Oregon Article," May 23, 2000, <best@lakenet.org> (May 24, 2000).

60. Graves and Har, "Adoption Law Moves Forward."

61. *Jane Does 1, et al. v. Oregon, et al.*, Application No. 99A979, U.S. 2000 (LEXIS 4683); Janie Har and Bill Graves, "Adoption Law: In Effect Today," *Oregonian*, May 30, 2000, A1.

62. Hester, Wick, and McDermott quoted in Har and Graves, "Adoption Law: In Effect Today"; Hill quoted in Bill Graves, "Court Hands Adoptees a Big Victory," *Oregonian*, May 31, 2000, A1; Nast quoted in Kim Cobb, "Oregon Releases Birth Certificates for Adoptees," *Houston Chronicle*, May 30, 2000, A1.

63. Karen Ofenham-Brioso, letter to the editor, *Oregonian*, June 15, 2000, D12. Stonum and McDermott quoted in Kate Taylor, "Adoption Rights Leader Stumbled on the Secret of Her Own Adoption," *Oregonian*, June 1, 2000, A1.

64. Hunsaker quoted in Har and Graves, "Adoption Law: In Effect Today."

65. Graves, "Court Hands Adoptees a Big Victory"; McDermott quoted in Randall Sullivan, "The Bastard Chronicles, Part Two: The Birth Mother's Story," *Rolling Stone*, March 1, 2001, 48.

66. Charles E. Beggs, "Full Supreme Court Denies Adoption Law Stay," *AP*, June 12, 2000, <http://www.oregonlive...-AdoptionLa&news&newsflash-oregon> (June 12, 2000). Hunsaker had one more option. He could have filed for a writ of certiorari before mid-August and asked the U.S. Supreme Court for an emergency stay. But one of the grounds for doing so is that the petitioner has to believe that the motion will prevail. Hunsaker realized that after the Court had rebuffed him twice—first by Justice O'Connor and then by the full Court—it was unlikely to entertain a third motion to issue a stay. Thus, he let the mid-August deadline for petitioning the Court for certiorari pass. Hunsaker, interview.

67. McDermott quoted in Janie Har, "Fight against Oregon's Adoption Law Appears Over," *Oregonian*, June 13, 2000, B1.

68. "Teller: Oregon Law Will Not Discourage Adoption," *CNN Today*, <http://www.cnn.comTRANSCRIPTS/0005/31/tod.06.html> (May 31, 2000); "Should Adoptees Have Access to Their Birth Records," *TalkBack Live*, <http://www.cnn.comTRANSCRIPTS/0005/31/tl.00.html> (May 31, 2000); "Do

Adopted Kids Have a Right to Learn about Their Roots," *Crossfire,* <http://www.cnn.com/TRANSCRIPTS/0005/31/cf.00.html> (May 31, 2000).

Conclusion

1. Kate Taylor, "Nearly 2,400 Adoptees Have Filed for Records," *Oregonian,* June 1, 2000, A8. For the 3,655 figure, see Kate Taylor, "Birth Certificate Speeds Reunion," *Oregonian,* June 27, 2000, B7; Bill Graves, "Fewer Adoptee Requests Made," *Oregonian,* Nov. 6, 2000, E1. Graves noted that the number of requests had slowed from thirty to forty a week to less than twenty. He also stated that 4,773 birth records had been issued and 325 contact preference forms received. Of the latter, 214 birth mothers wanted direct contact, 21 wanted contact through an intermediary, and 77 wanted no contact. Ibid. As this book goes to press, 7,606 original birth certificates have been requested and 7,422 have been issued; and 466 contact preference forms have been filed, with 357 wanting direct contact, 28 contact through an intermediary, and 81 no contact. Carol Sanders, telephone conversation with the author, Aug. 7, 2003.

2. Serdy and Widerburg quoted in Taylor, "Nearly 2,400 Adoptees." For other adoptees' reasons for requesting birth certificates, see Sue Bernert, letter to the editor, *Oregonian,* June 5, 2000, E10; Bree Kilbourne, letter to the editor, *Oregonian,* June 8, 2000, C10.

3. Janie Har, "Detective Work Eased for Adoptees," *Oregonian,* June 2, 2000, A1. For a more fatalistic look at reunions, see the comments in the AP story "Oregon Law Gives Woman Hope She'll Finally Find Her Birth Mom," *Oregonian,* July 1, 2000, D2. The advice on how to contact birth mothers continued through July. See Kate Taylor, "Much Rests on First Call to Birth Parents," *Oregonian,* July 30, 2000, L7.

4. Bill Graves, "Adoptees' Rush Is On for Birth Records," *Oregonian,* June 3, 2000, B1. For a long op-ed piece that the *Oregonian* published asking for understanding and compassion for birth mothers, see I. Franklin Hunsaker, "Respect, Please Don't Confront, Birth Mothers," *Oregonian,* June 12, 2000, E11.

5. Abby quoted in AP story, "La Grande Man Tracks Down Birth Mother," *Oregonian,* June 26, 2000, E2. A week earlier, on June 21, Gina Stonum had had a successful reunion with her birth mother, but the story did not appear publicly until Sept. 4, 2000, in *People Magazine,* 103–104.

6. Taylor, "Birth Certificate Speeds Reunion." Ironically, Kim requested that her full name not be used in the story "to protect her privacy." Ibid.

7. Ibid.

8. See, for example, Kate Taylor, "Reunion Sends Oregon Adoptee and Her Birth Mother through the Looking Glass," *Oregonian,* July 8, 2000, D1. Kate Taylor's article "Closing the Family Circle" appeared on the front page of the Sunday *Oregonian,* Oct. 2000, A1, A8–A9.

9. McDermott, Hill, and Hunsaker quoted in Taylor, "Birth Certificate Speeds Reunion."

10. Maryanne Cohen, "BEST: Fwd: Oregon Update :-)," June 28, 2000, <best@lakenet.org> (Dec. 22, 2001). So few problems emerged over the issue of birth mothers' privacy rights that the *Oregonian* ran a story on the emotional strain that search and reunion placed on *adoptees*. Bill Graves, "Revealing Adoption Secrets Carries a Price," *Oregonian,* July 17, 2000, A1.

11. Cynthia Bertrand Holub, "Re: BEST: Bastards: All Things to All People? (minor vent)," June 2, 1998, <best@lakenet.org> (Nov. 6, 1998).

12. David S. Broder, *Democracy Derailed: Initiative Campaigns and the Power of Money* (New York: Harcourt, 2000), 78.

13. Ansardi reply to Albert Wei, "Re: BEST: Baltimore Sun Editorial and Preview of a Rebuttal," July 3, 2000, <best@lakenet.org> (Dec. 22, 2001).

14. Steven J. Drahozal, "Re: BEST: Baltimore Sun Editorial and Preview of a Rebuttal," June 29, 2000, <best@lakenet.org> (Dec. 22, 2001).

15. Cynthia Bertrand Holub, "BEST: Membership Boosterism—RAH! RAH! RAH!" June 30, 2000, <best@lakenet.org> (Dec. 22, 2001).

16. Albert Wei, "Re: BEST: Baltimore Sun Editorial and Preview of a Rebuttal," July 3, 2000, <best@lakenet.org> (Dec. 22, 2001).

17. Cynthia Bertrand Holub, "BEST: Membership Boosterism."

18. Bastard Nation, "The WHO'S NEXT? Adoptee Rights Fund," Aug. 8, 2000, <http://www.plumsite.com/whosnext/> (Aug. 8, 2000).

19. "Legislative Watch," *Bastard Nation* 5:2 (2001): 22–23.

20. Wayne L . Francis, *The Legislative Committee Game: A Comparative Analysis of Fifty States* (Columbus: Ohio State University Press, 1989).

BIBLIOGRAPHY

Manuscript and Archival Collections

Child Welfare League of America. Child Welfare League of America Records. Social Welfare History Archives, University of Minnesota, Minneapolis, Minn.

Papers of Jean Paton (in possession of the author).

U.S. Department of Labor. Records of the U.S. Children's Bureau. National Archives, Washington, D.C.

Interviews

All interviews were conducted and tape recorded by the author.

Michael H. Balter, Portland, Ore., March 29, 2001

Paul J. De Muniz, Salem, Ore., March 21, 2001

Warren Deras, Portland, Ore., Jan. 17, 2001

Lauren Greenbaum, Beaverton, Ore., March 10, 2001

Fredrick F. Greenman, Jr., New York, N.Y., Oct. 13, 2000

Donna Harris, Portland, Ore., Dec. 12, 2000

Helen Hill, Nehalem, Ore., Dec. 13, 2000, and Aug. 28, 2001

I. Franklin Hunsaker, Portland, Ore., Sept. 5, 2000

Paula Lang and Douglas S. Alles, Portland, Ore., April 20, 2001

Paul J. Lipscomb, Salem, Ore., Dec. 4, 2001

Thomas E. McDermott, Portland, Ore., Sept. 5, 2000

Nancy P. Simpson, Portland, Ore., Feb. 23, 2001

Delores Teller, Beaverton, Ore., Nov. 27, 2000

James R. Wheeler, West Linn, Ore., Sept. 27, 2001

Government Documents

Oregon State Archives, Salem, Ore.

State of Oregon. *1998 General Election Voters' Pamphlet*. Salem: State of Oregon, 1998.

———. *1998 State Initiative and Referendum Manual*. Salem: Elections Division, 1998.

———. Office of the Secretary of State. "Signature Verification Results Announced for Second Sampling of Initiative Petition #46." News release, June 19, 1998.

U.S. Department of Labor. Children's Bureau. *The Confidential Nature of Birth Records*, Pub. 332. Washington, D.C.: Government Printing Office, 1949.
U.S. State Department. "Immigrant Visas Issued to Orphans Coming to the U.S. 2002." <http://travel.state.gov/orphan_numbers.html> (April 24, 2003).

Legal Cases

ALMA Soc'y, Inc. v. Mellon, 601 F.2d 1225 (2d Cir.), *cert. denied*, 100 S. Ct. 531 (1979).
Application of Maples, 563 S.W.2d 760 (Mo. 1978).
Bradey v. Children's Bureau, 274 S.E.2d 418, 422 (S.C. 1981).
Chattman v. Bennett, 57 A.D.2d 618, 393 N.Y.2d 768 (1977).
Doe v. Sundquist, 2 S.W.3d 919, 927 (Tenn. 1999).
Eckles v. State of Oregon, 306 Or. 380, 390, 760 P.2d 846 (1988), *appeal dismissed* 490 U.S. 1032 (1989).
Griswold v. Connecticut, 381 U.S. 479 (1965).
Hughes v. State of Oregon, 314 Or. 1, 13, 838 P.2d 1018 (1992).
In re Anonymous, 92 Misc. 2d 224, 399 N.Y.S.2d 857 (Sur. Ct. Queens County 1977).
In re Application of George, 625 S.W.2d 151 (Mo. App. 1981).
In re C.A.B., 384 A.2d 679 (D.C. Ct. App. 1978).
In re Carol S., 172 N.Y.L.J. 31 (Sup. Ct.).
In re Linda F.M., 148 N.J. Super., 310, 372, A.2d at 650 (1977).
In re Maxtone-Graham, 92 Misc. 2d 224, 399 N.Y.S.2d 857 (Sur. Ct. 1977).
In re Roger B., 84 Ill.2d 323, 418 N.E.2d 751 (1981).
In re Sage, 21 Wash. App. 803, 586 P.2d 1201 (1979).
In re Spinks, 32 N.C. App. 422, 232 S.E.2d 479 (1977).
Jane Does 1, 2, 3, 4, 5, 6, and 7 v. STATE, 993 P.2d 822 (Or. App. 1999).
Meyer v. Grant, 486 U.S. 414 (1988).
Mills v. Atlantic City Department of Vital Statistics, 148 N.J. Super. 302, 372 A.2d 646 (1977).
Olmstead v. United States, 277 U.S. 438, 278 (1928).
Roe v. Wade, 410 U.S. 113, 152 (1973).
Spillman v. Parker, 332 So. 2d 573, 576 (La. App. 1976).

Unpublished Materials

Bastard Nation. "Birth of a Bastard Nation Conference." Program for Chicago Conference [n.p., 1997].
Ecumenical Ministries of Oregon. *Voters' Guide Pamphlet.* "58 Requires Issuing Copy of Original Birth Certificate to Adoptees" [n.p., n.d.].

Hill, Helen. "Adoptee Rights Initiative Speeds to Ballot." Press release, July 9, 1998.

Jane Does 1–7 v. State of Oregon. Oregon Court of Appeals Oral Argument. Nov. 22, 1999. State Court Administrator's Office, Salem, Ore.

Jane Does 1, 2, 4, 5, 6, and 7 v. The State of Oregon. Plaintiff's Memorandum in Support of Motion for Summary Judgment Challenging the Constitutionality of Ballot Measure No. 58. Marion County, Oregon Circuit Court, Salem, Ore.

Jane Does 1, 2, 4, 5, 6, and 7 v. The State of Oregon and Intervenors (Case No. 98C20424). Appellants' Abstract of Record. August 1999. Marion County, Oregon Circuit Court, Salem, Ore.

Jane Does 1, 2, 4, 5, 6, and 7 v. The State of Oregon and Intervenors. Redacted Joint Respondents' Brief Pursuant to Court Order Sealing Depositon Testimony. Oct. 26, 1999. State Court Administrator's Office, Salem, Ore.

Jane Does 1, 2, 3, 4, 5, 6 and 7 v. The State of Oregon and Intervenors (Case No. 98C20424). Transcript of Proceedings. July 14, 1999. Marion County, Oregon Circuit Court, Salem, Ore.

National Committee for Adoption. "1980–81 Goals of the National Committee for Adoption, Inc." [n.p.].

O'Brien, Kathleen. "Access to the Past: Opening Oregon's Sealed Adoption Records." Manuscript.

Newspapers

Albany (Ore.) Democrat-Herald, Aug. 5, 1998–Sept. 20, 1998
Bend (Ore.) Bulletin, Sept. 20, 1998–Nov. 5, 1998
Boston Globe, Oct. 2, 1998–Nov. 5, 1998
Corvallis (Ore.) Gazette-Times, Oct. 13, 1998–Nov. 5, 1998
Eugene (Ore.) Register-Guard, Oct. 7, 1998–Nov. 5, 1998
Grant's Pass (Ore.) Daily Courier, Sept. 26, 1998–Nov. 5, 1998
Houston Chronicle, May 30, 2000–June 5, 2000
Los Angeles Times, Oct. 12, 1975
Medford (Ore.) Mail Tribune, Oct. 4, 1998–Nov. 5, 1998
New York Times, July 25, 1972–Oct. 25, 2000
Oregonian, Sept. 23, 1998–July 17, 2000
Salem (Ore.) Statesman Journal, May 22, 1998–Nov. 5, 1998
Seattle Times, Oct. 25, 1998–Nov. 5, 1998
Tillamook (Ore.) Headlight-Herald, Oct. 20, 1998
Tillamook (Ore.) Preview, Oct. 15, 1998
USA Today, Jan. 10, 2000
Washington Post, Nov. 26, 1998
Washington Times, Nov. 12, 1998
Willamette Week, Dec. 10, 1997–July 21, 1999

Other Primary Sources

ACLU of Oregon. *Voters Guide to Ballot Measures.* Oct. 8, 1998. <http://www. aclu-or.org/voters.htm#Measure58> (Sept. 25, 2000).

Bastard Nation. "Introduction: What Is Bastard Nation." *The Basic Bastard.* (Des Moines, Wash.: Bastard Nation [n.d.]).

Child Welfare League of America. *Standards for Adoption Service.* New York: Child Welfare League of America, 1958.

———. *Standards of Excellence: CWLA Standards of Excellence for Adoption Services.* Rev. ed. Washington, D.C.: Child Welfare League of America, 2000.

Evan B. Donaldson Adoption Institute. *Benchmark Adoption Survey: Report on the Findings.* New York: Evan B. Donaldson Institute, 1997.

National Conference of Commissioners on Uniform State Laws. *Uniform Adoption Act 1994.* Chicago: National Conference of Commissioners on Uniform State Laws, 1994.

Pierce, William L. Meet the Fellows. <http://www.discovery.org/fellows/Bill Pierce/index.html>.

Town Hall. Channel 2, KATU-TV, Portland, Ore. Oct. 4, 1998. Videocassette recording.

UNICEF. Convention on the Rights of the Child. Nov. 20, 1989. <http://www. unicef.org/crc/>.

Secondary Sources

Adam, Tom. *Grass Roots: How Ordinary People Are Changing America.* New York: Carol Publishing Group, 1991.

Aigner, Hal. *Faint Trails: A Guide to Adult Adoptee–Birth Parent Reunification Searches.* Greenbrae, Calif.: Paradigm Press, 1987.

Allan, Leslie. "Confirming the Constitutionality of Sealing Adoption Records." *Brooklyn Law Review* 46 (1980): 717–745.

Arndt, Melissa. "Severed Roots: The Sealed Adoption Records Controversy." *Northern Illinois University Law Review* 6:1 (1986): 103–127.

Baran, Annette, and Reuben Pannor. "It's Time for Sweeping Change." *Decree* (Summer 1990): 5.

———. "Open Adoption." In David M. Brodzinsky and Marshall D. Schechter, eds., *The Psychology of Adoption.* New York: Oxford University Press, 1990.

Baran, Annette, Reuben Pannor, and Arthur D. Sorosky. "Adoptive Parents and the Sealed Record Controversy." *Social Casework* 55 (November 1974) 531–536.

———. "Open Adoption." *Social Work* 21 (March 1976): 97–100.

Baran, Annette, Arthur D. Sorosky, and Reuben Pannor. "The Dilemma of Our Adoptees." *Psychology Today* 9 (1975): 38, 42, 96, 98.

Bastard Nation. "Mission Statement." *Bastard Quarterly* 1:2 (1997): [back page].

Bernard, Viola W. "Application of Psychoanalytic Concepts to Adoption Agency Practice." In Marcel Heiman and M. Ralph Kaufman, eds., *Psychoanalysis and Social Work*. New York: International Universities Press, 1953.

Boggs, Dana. "Adoptee Humor." *Bastard Quarterly* 1:1 (1997): 5.

Broder, David S. *Democracy Derailed: Initiative Campaigns and the Power of Money*. New York: Harcourt, 2000.

Burke, Kate. "The Case for Open Adoption Records." *Decree* 13:1 (1996): 1.

Burns, Stewart. *Social Movements of the 1960s: Searching for Democracy*. Boston: Twayne, 1990.

Caher, John. "Rediscovered Father Seeks Adoption Reform." *New York Law Journal*, Aug. 15, 2000.

Cahn, Naomi, and Jana Singer. "Adoption, Identity, and the Constitution: The Case for Opening Closed Records." *University of Pennsylvania Journal of Constitutional Law* 2 (1999): 150–194.

Carp, E. Wayne. "Adoption, Blood Kinship, Stigma, and the Adoption Reform Movement: A Historical Perspective." *Law & Society Review* 36:1 (October 2002): 433–459.

———. *Family Matters: Secrecy and Disclosure in the History of Adoption*. Cambridge, Mass.: Harvard University Press, 1998.

Chalmers, David. *And the Crooked Places Made Straight: The Struggle for Social Change in the 1960s*. Baltimore: Johns Hopkins University Press, 1991.

Charen, Mona. "What 'Measure 58' Would Do." *Jewish World Review*, Oct. 28, 1998.

Child Welfare League of Adoption. "Regarding America." *Special Bulletin* (March 1937): 3–7.

Childs, Robert. "The Orphaned Element of the Adoptive Experience." *Adoption Therapist* 4 (Spring 1993): 1–4.

Chumney, Carol. "Tennessee's New Adoption Contact Veto Is Cold Comfort to Birth Parents." *University of Memphis Law Review* 27 (1997): 843–884.

Clanton, Gene. *Populism: The Humane Preference in America, 1890–1900*. Boston: Twayne, 1991.

Clothier, Florence. "Some Aspects of the Problem of Adoption." *American Journal of Orthopsychiatry* 9 (1939): 598–615.

———. "The Psychology of the Adopted Child." *Mental Hygiene* 27 (April 1943): 223–230.

Cohen, Mary Ann. "Annual Conference Offers Something for Everyone," *Decree* 13:2 (1995): 14.

———. "Join Your Partners." *Decree"* 13:3 (1996): 15–16.

Collmeyer, Patricia M. "From 'Operation Brown Baby' to 'Opportunity': The Placement of Children of Color at the Boys and Girls Aid Society of Oregon." *Child Welfare* 74:1 (January–February 1995): 242–263.

Crane, Anne. "Unsealing Adoption Records: The Right to Know versus the Right to Privacy." *1986 Annual Survey of American Law* (1986): 645–666.

Cronin, Thomas. *Direct Democracy: The Politics of Initiative, Referendum, and Recall.* Cambridge, Mass.: Harvard University Press, 1989.

Crozier, Michael J., Samuel P. Huntington, and Joji Watanuki. *The Crisis of Democracy: Report on the Governability of Democracies to the Trilateral Commission.* New York: New York University Press, 1975.

Curtis, Patrick A. "The Dialectics of Open versus Closed Adoptions of Infants." *Child Welfare* 65 (September–October 1986): 437–445.

Davis, Richard. *The Web of Politics: The Internet's Impact on the American Political System.* New York: Oxford University Press, 1999.

Dubious, Philip L., and Floyd Fennel. *Lawmaking by Initiative: Issues, Options, and Comparisons.* New York: Agathon Press, 1998.

Eaton, Allen H. *The Oregon System: The Story of Direct Legislation in Oregon.* Chicago: A. C. McClurg & Co., 1912.

Ellis, Richard J. *Democratic Delusions: The Initiative Process in America.* Lawrence: University Press of Kansas, 2002.

Farber, David. *The Age of Great Dreams: America in the 1960s.* New York: Hill and Wang, 1994.

Fisher, Florence. "Our Time Is Now!!" *Alma Searchlight* (1976): 2.

———. *The Search for Anna Fisher.* New York: Fawcett Crest, 1973.

Francis, Wayne L. *The Legislative Committee Game: A Comparative Analysis of Fifty States.* Columbus: Ohio State University Press, 1989.

Gafke, Roger, and David Leuthod. "The Effect on Voters of Misleading, Confusing, and Difficult Ballot Titles." *Public Opinion Quarterly* 43:3 (1979): 394–401.

Gallay, Alan. *The Indian Slave Trade: The Rise of the English Empire in the American South, 1670–1717.* New Haven: Yale University Press, 2002.

Gamble, Barbara S. "Putting Civil Rights to a Popular Vote." *American Journal of Political Science* 41:1 (1997): 245–269.

Giddings, Kathryn J. "The Current Status of the Right of Adult Adoptees to Know the Identity of Their Natural Parents." *Washington University Law Quarterly* 58:3 (1980): 677–702.

Gloor, Carol. "Breaking the Seal: Constitutional and Statutory Approaches to Adult Adoptees' Right to Identity." *Northwestern University Law Review* 75:2 (1980): 316–344.

Greiner, Marley Elizabeth. "Letter from the Executive Chair." *Bastard Quarterly* 1:2 (1997): 4.

Griffin, Marcie A. "The Adult Adoptee: The Biological Alien." *Adoption Therapist* 2 (fall 1991): 8–9.

Grimm, Shea. "Why Contact Vetoes Are Not an Acceptable Compromise." *Bastard Quarterly* 1:1 (1997): 2–3.

Hauben, Michael, and Ronda Hauben. *Netizens: On the History and Impact of Usenet and the Internet.* Los Alamos, Calif.: IEEE Computer Society Press, 1997.

Hill, Helen. "Bastard Recipes." *Bastard Quarterly* 1:2 (1997): 6.

———. "Secrets of the Universe." *Bastard Quarterly* 1:3 (1997): 12–13.

Hollinger, Joan H., ed. "Aftermath of Adoption: Legal and Social Consequences." *Adoption Law and Practice.* 2000 Supplement, vol. 2. New York: Matthew Bender, 2000.

Horvat, Robert. "The Oregon Initiative Process: A Critical Appraisal." *Oregon Law Review* 65:1 (1986): 169–184.

Howard, Sheldon L., and Henry B. Hemenway. "Birth Records of Illegitimates and of Adopted Children." *American Journal of Public Health* 21 (June 1931): 641–647.

Huffman, Helen C. "The Importance of Birth Records." In *National Conference of Social Work, Proceedings.* New York: Columbia University Press, 1949.

Hunsaker, I. Franklin. "Oregon's Ballot Measure 58: A Grossly Unfair and State-Sanctioned Betrayal of Birth Mothers." *Family Court Review* 39:1 (2001): 75–84.

Kadushin, Alfred, and Judith A. Martin. *Child Welfare Services.* 4th ed. New York: Macmillan, 1988.

Kiester, Edwin, Jr. "Should We Unlock the Adoption Files?" *Today's Health* 52 (August 1974): 59.

Kirschner, David. "The Adopted Child Syndrome: Considerations for Psychotherapy." *Psychotherapy in Private Practice* 8:3 (1990): 93–100.

———. " 'Son of Sam' and the Adopted Child Syndrome." *Adelphi University Society for Psychoanalysis and Psychotherapy Newsletter* (June 1978): 7–9.

———. "Understanding Adoptees Who Kill: Dissociation, Patricide, and the Psychodynamics of Adoption." *International Journal of Offender Therapy and Comparative Criminology* 36 (1992): 323–333.

Kittson, Ruthena Hill [Jean Paton]. *Orphan Voyage.* New York: Vantage Press, 1968.

Klibanoff, Elton B. "Genealogical Information in Adoption: The Adoptee's Quest and the Law." *Family Law Quarterly* 11:2 (1977): 185–198.

Kreider, Rose M. *Adopted Children and Stepchildren: 2000 Census.* 2000 Special Reports. CENSR-6. Washington, D.C.: U.S. Census Bureau, 2003.

Kuhns, Jason. "The Sealed Adoption Records Controversy: Breaking Down the Walls of Secrecy." *Golden Gate University Law Review* 24:1 (Spring 1994): 259–297.

Lapalombara, Joseph G. *The Initiative and Referendum in Oregon, 1938–1948.* Corvallis: Oregon State College Press, 1950.

Lapalombara, Joseph G., and Charles B. Hagan. "Direct Legislation: An Appraisal and a Suggestion." *American Political Science Review* 45:2 (1951): 400–421.

Leavy, Morton L. *Law of Adoption Simplified.* New York: Oceana, 1948.

Levin, Marshall A. "The Adoption Trilemma: The Adult Adoptee's Emerging Search for His Ancestral Identity." *University of Baltimore Law Review* 8:3 (1979): 497–518.

Lifton, Betty Jean. *Journey of the Adopted Self: A Quest for Wholeness.* New York: Basic Books, 1994.

———. "The Search." *New York Times Magazine,* Jan. 25, 1976, 15–19.

———. *Twice Born: Memoirs of an Adopted Daughter.* New York: McGraw Hill, 1975.

Lifton, Robert Jay. "Foreword." In Mary Kathleen Benet, *The Politics of Adoption.* New York: Free Press, 1976.

Linde, Hans A. "When Initiative Lawmaking Is Not 'Republican Government': The Campaign against Homosexuality." *Oregon Law Review* 72 (1993): 36–48.

Lupack, Patricia Gallagher. "Sealed Records in Adoptions: The Need for Legislative Reform." *Catholic Lawyer* 21 (Summer 1975): 211–228.

Magleby, David B. *Direct Legislation: Voting on Ballot Propositions in the United States.* Baltimore: Johns Hopkins University Press, 1984.

Mech, Edmund V. "Adoption: A Policy Perspective." In Bettye M. Caldwell and Henry N. Ricciuti, eds., *Review of Child Development Research,* vol. 3 Chicago: University of Chicago Press, 1973.

Miller, Douglas T. *On Our Own: America in the Sixties.* Lexington, Mass.: D. C. Heath, 1996.

Modell, Judith, "Natural Bonds, Legal Boundaries: Modes of Persuasion in Adoption Rhetoric." In Marianne Novy, ed., *Imagining Adoption: Essays on Literature and Culture.* Ann Arbor: University of Michigan Press, 2001.

Morgan, Edward P. *The Sixties Experience: Hard Lessons about Modern America.* Philadelphia: Temple University Press, 1991.

Morgan, Ron. "BN Hits the Oscars." *Bastard Quarterly* 1:3 (1997): 4–5, 8–10.

National Council for Adoption. *Adoption Factbook 3.* Waite Park, Minn.: National Council for Adoption, 1999.

Oakley, Lisa, and Thomas H. Neale. *Citizen Initiative Proposals Appearing on State Ballots, 1976–1992.* Washington, D.C.: Congressional Research Service, Library of Congress, 1995.

Pannor, Reuben, Arthur D. Sorosky, and Annette Baran. "Opening the Sealed Record in Adoption—The Human Need for Continuity." *Journal of Jewish Communal Service* 51 (1974): 188–196.

Patterson, James T. *Grand Expectations: The United States, 1945–1974.* New York: Oxford University Press, 1996.

Person, Gavi. "Bastard Cheers." *Bastard Quarterly* 1:2 (1997): 12.

Pertman, Adam. *Adoption Nation: How the Adoption Revolution Is Transforming America.* New York: Basic Books, 2000.

Pierce, Charles. "Signing for Fun and Profit: The Business of Gathering Petition Signatures." *California Journal* (November 1992): 545–548.

Placek, Paul J. "National Adoption Data." In National Council for Adoption, *Adoption Factbook 3.* Waite Park, Minn.: Park Press, 1999.

Plum, Damsel. "The Psychology of Self-Defeatism in Adoption Reform." *Bastard Quarterly* 1:2 (1997): 1, 13.

Poulin, Debra D. "The Open Adoption Records Movement: Constitutional Cases and Legislative Compromise." *Journal of Family Law* 26 (1987–1988): 395–418.

"Report Card to the Membership." *Decree* 13:1 (1996): 21.

Rovella, David E. "Two Dads, Two Responses." *National Law Journal,* March 13, 2000, A1, A10–A11.

Rueff, M. Christina. "A Comparison of Tennessee's Open Records Law with Relevant Laws in Other English-Speaking Countries." *Brandeis Law Journal* 37:3 (1998–1999): 453–468.

Samuels, Elizabeth J. "The Idea of Adoption: An Inquiry into the History of Adult Adoptee Access to Birth Records." *Rutgers Law Review* 53 (Winter 2001): 367–436.

Schmidt, David D. *Ballot Initiatives: History, Research, and Analysis of Recent Initiative and Referendum Campaigns.* Washington, D.C.: Initiative News Service, 1983.

———. *Citizen Lawmakers: The Ballot Initiative Revolution.* Philadelphia: Temple University Press, 1989.

Schwartz, Deb. "Bastard Nation Organizes Nationwide Open Records Events for *Secrets and Lies.*" *Bastard Quarterly* 1:1 (1997): 6–7.

Shaw, Randy. *The Activist's Handbook: A Primer for the 1990s and Beyond.* Berkeley: University of California Press, 1996.

———. *Reclaiming America: Nike, Clean Air, and the New National Activism.* Berkeley: University of California Press, 1999.

Smith, Gregory R. "In Re the Application of Annetta Louise Maples: The Adoptee's Right to Know." *Saint Louis University Law Journal* 23:4 (1979): 731–746.

Smith, Janna Malamud. *Private Matters: In Defense of the Personal Life.* Reading, Mass.: Addison-Wesley, 1997.

Sorosky, Arthur D., Annette Baran, and Reuben Pannor. "Adoption and the Adolescent: An Overview." In Sherman C. Feinstein and Peter L. Giovacchini, eds., *Adolescent Psychiatry,* vol. 5: *Annals of the American Society for Adolescent Psychiatry.* New York: Jason Aronson, 1977.

———. *The Adoption Triangle: The Effects of the Sealed Record on Adoptees, Birth Parents, and Adoptive Parents.* New York: Anchor Press/Doubleday, 1978.

———. "Identity Conflicts in Adoptees." *American Journal of Orthopsychiatry* 45 (1975): 18–27.

———. "The Reunion of Adoptees and Birth Relatives." *Journal of Youth and Adolescence* 3 (1974): 195–206.

Steigerwald, David. *The Sixties and the End of Modern America.* New York: St. Martin's Press, 1995.

Sullivan, Randall. "The Bastard Chronicles, Part One: Helen Hill's Crusade." *Rolling Stone,* Feb. 15, 2001, 53–62.

———. "The Bastard Chronicles, Part Two: The Birth Mother's Story." *Rolling Stone,* March 1, 2001, 41–48, 61.

Teller, Delores. "Open Records: The People Decide." *Adoptive Families* 31:5 (September–October 1998): 26–27.

Tolbert, Caroline J., Daniel H. Lowenstein, and Todd Donovan. "Election Law and Rules for Using Initiatives." In Caroline J. Tolbert, Daniel H. Lowenstein, and Todd Donovan, eds., *Citizens as Legislators: Direct Democracy in the United States*. Columbus: Ohio State University Press, 1998.

Tribe, Lawrence. *American Constitutional Law*. 2d ed. New York: Foundation Press, 1988.

Verrier, Nancy Newton. *The Primal Wound: Understanding the Adopted Child*. Baltimore, Md.: Gateway Press, 1993.

Wegar, Katarina. *Adoption, Identity, and Kinship: The Debate over Sealed Birth Records*. New Haven: Yale University Press: 1997.

Zimmerman, Joseph F. *The Initiative: Citizen Law-Making*. Westport, Conn.: Praeger, 1989.

Zisk, Betty H. *Money, Media, and the Grassroots: State Ballot Issues and the Electoral Process*. Newbury Park, Calif.: Sage, 1987.

INDEX